GOD
HAS A PLAN AND A PURPOSE
FOR
YOUR LIFE

Oliver E. Summers

XULON PRESS

CONTENTS

INTRODUCTION

"God has made everything beautiful in its time. He has also set eternity in the hearts of men; yet they cannot fathom what God has done from beginning to end."

Ecclesiastes 3:11 (NIV)

All men who will be honest with themselves are conscious of the belief that there is more to life than our time on earth. The purpose and goal of this book is to help you understand that before this earth and man were created, God already had a plan and purpose for your life. During this lifetime on earth, He is preparing you for that plan and purpose He has for your life.

Picture in your mind the human spinal cord that starts at the brain, then runs through the whole body with nerve endings reaching the toes of the feet. This book is an attempt to explain the plan and purpose of God for your life as a continuous cord beginning in eternity before creation of the earth and man, then running through man's time on earth and then returning back into eternity.

Also picture eternity as a never ending circle and time as a straight line that begins and ends in eternity. Genesis 1 tells us that God created this present world in seven days as a prophetic picture of man's time on earth. The Bible states in a number of places such as 2 Peter 3:8: " But, beloved, be not ignorant of this one thing, that one day is with the LORD as a thousand years, and a thousand years as one day."

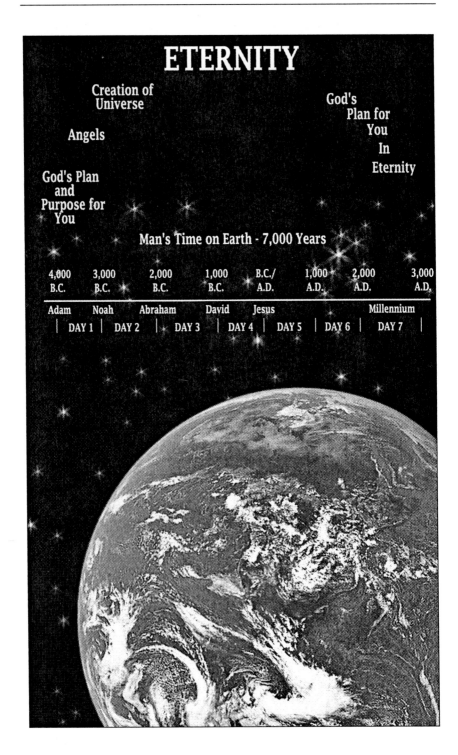

ETERNITY

Creation of Universe

Angels

God's Plan for You In Eternity

God's Plan and Purpose for You

Man's Time on Earth - 7,000 Years

4,000 B.C.	3,000 B.C.	2,000 B.C.	1,000 B.C.	B.C./ A.D.	1,000 A.D.	2,000 A.D.	3,000 A.D.
Adam	Noah	Abraham	David	Jesus		Millennium	
DAY 1	DAY 2	DAY 3	DAY 4	DAY 5	DAY 6	DAY 7	

A thought provoking verse in the Bible is, "For the living know they will die . . . never again will they have a part in anything that happens under the sun" (Eccles 9:5-6 NIV). This verse tells us that our life on earth is the arena of opportunity for us to prepare for the plan and purpose God has for us in eternity.

SPECIAL NOTE: All quotations from the Bible in this book are from King James Version unless otherwise noted. Old English words like "thou" are updated to current usage as "you" and all pronouns referring to God or Jesus Christ are capitalized.

In the Hebrew manuscripts of the Old Testament, the name of God was written as YHWH and probably originally pronounced "Yahweh." Eventually the Jews gave up pronouncing it, considering the name too holy for human lips. Instead they said "Adonay" or "LORD." This led to the substitution of the word LORD in all capital letters by later Hebrews and by the translators of the King James version and other English versions, to use LORD where ever the name "Yahweh" appeared in the Hebrew text. In this book, in order to be consistent, an effort has been made to use LORD whenever it refers to God the Father or God the Son. This would include using LORD where ever the Hebrew text used "Yahweh" and the New Testament Greek text used "kurios."

In writing there are a number of different ways or methods to emphasize certain words, thoughts or points that the writer may wish to make. A word or thought may be put in *italics*, **bold print**, "quotation marks", or IN ALL CAPITAL LETTERS. The author has chosen to put many words and thoughts or points in "quotation marks" in order to emphasize them. To make a very important thought or statement, THE WORD OR THOUGHT HAS BEEN PUT IN ALL CAPITAL LETTERS.

Also the author has chosen to reverence certain places or entities as a proper name such as the Temple, Tabernacle, Ark of the Covenant, Church, Kingdom of God when used to refer to a "certain place or entity."

BIBLE QUOTATIONS:

- *The King James Study Bible*, Thomas Nelson Publishers, 1988.

- *Holy Bible: New International Version*, Zondervan Bible Publishers, 1984.

- *The Living Bible*, Tyndale House Publishers, 1971.

OUTLINE
GOD HAS A PLAN AND A PURPOSE
FOR YOUR LIFE

CHARTS AND ILLUSTRATIONS

CHAPTER ONE

THIS PLAN MADE BEFORE THE EARTH WAS CREATED

God has a definite plan and purpose for your life. However, most of us keep asking what is it and searching for it. The apostle Paul writes to his young son in the Lord, "For God has not given us the spirit of fear; but of power, and of love, and of a sound mind. . . Who has saved us, and called us with an holy calling, not according to our works, but according to His own purpose and grace, which was given us in Christ Jesus before the world began" (2 Tim. 1:7-9).

Here the Bible clearly and plainly declares that God's plan and purpose for your life was given before this present earth or world began, but what is this plan and purpose for your life? The way you and I treat God's plan and purpose for our lives reminds me of an incident that took place in Calcutta, India a number of years ago. At that time the city was noted for its abysmal poverty, filthiness, degradation and masses of people. One of its greatest problems was the vast number of orphans and street children who lived on the sidewalks and streets of the city.

On this particular day, a taxicab came careening around the corner. Before all the children could get out of the way, the taxicab hit a little boy and tossed his body like a dirty old rag into the gutter of the street. As the taxicab stopped, out of the back seat stepped a dignified man dressed in a white suit, who rushed over to the injured boy and picked him up. With the blood of the little boy running down all over his white suit, he rushed the little boy to the hospital. There the doctors and nurses began to set the broken bones, stitch the cuts and do everything possible to help the little boy recover from his injuries.

Every day this man and his wife would come to the hospital bed of the little boy to see how he was healing and to insure that he was being given the proper care. Many days passed as the little boy began to heal and the time was coming for him to be released from the hospital. This man was a high-ranking government official and very wealthy. He said to his wife, "Mother, all of our children are grown and I have come to love this little boy very much, why don't we take him home with us and adopt him as our own son." The wife agreed and so the little boy went to a large beautiful home, where he would be given all the advantages of earthly life. A loving family, good home, the finest education and the opportunity to be a wealthy, professional gentleman such as a government official, medical doctor or attorney.

After coming to his new home, the little boy would go every day to the doctors who continued to take care of his medical needs. After a number of weeks, his new mother said, "Son you are doing so well that today you may walk to the doctor's office by yourself. She pressed some money into his hand to pay for the office visit for that day. As the little boy walked down the sidewalk, suddenly he stopped, opened his hand and his eyes grew wide and big as he looked at the money in his hand. He had never seen so much money in his life. He closed his fist over the money and began to run down the street thinking he was rich. As he was running down the street away from home, thinking he had it all, he was actually running away from the love of a family, the advantages of a wealthy family, home, education, position and wealth all for a paltry sum of money in his hand.

This is a picture of you and me when we go after the things of this life and turn away from the plan and purpose that God has for our lives. God has created you and given you an earthly life. Jesus died on the cross to pay the price for you to have a special place and purpose in eternity that He purposed for your life before the creation of this world. Like the little boy, you have a decision to make.

The apostle Paul writes to the Church at Ephesus that he continually prays that God will give to each member of that Church an understanding of what that great plan and purpose that God has for their life.

"I cease not to give thanks for you, making mention of you in my prayers; That the God of our LORD Jesus Christ, the Father of glory, may give unto you the spirit of wisdom and revelation in the knowledge of Him: The eyes of your understanding being enlightened; that you may know what is the hope of His calling, and what the riches of the glory of His inheritance in the saints, And what is the exceeding greatness of His power to us-ward who believe, according to the working of His mighty power, which He wrought in Christ, when He raised Him from the dead, and set Him at His own right hand in heavenly places, Far above all principality, and power, and might, and dominion, and every name that is named, not only in this world, but also in that which is to come: And has put all things under His feet, and gave Him to be the head over all things to the church, which is His body. . . .And has raised us up together, and made us sit together in heavenly places in Christ Jesus: That in the ages to come He might show the exceeding riches of His grace in His kindness towards us through Christ Jesus" (Eph. 1:16-2:7).

One of the great saints of the Old Testament was King David. He realized that God's plan and purpose for his life was far above and greater than being the King of Israel with all of its wealth, power and prestige. Listen to what King David declares in Psalms 8:3-8: "When I consider Your heavens, the works of Your fingers, the moon and the stars, which You have ordained: What is man, that You are mindful of him? and the son of man, that You visit him? For You have made him a little lower than the angels." (The word "angels" does not appear in the original language of the Hebrew Bible. Instead, it is the Hebrew word "Elohim" which we translate as God.) What David is actually saying: "For You have made him a little lower than God, and have crowned him with glory and honor. You have made him to have dominion over the works of Your hands; You have put all things under his feet."

At this point, we need to stop and think what does all this mean? Let us start out with the very first verse in the Bible, Genesis 1:1, "In the beginning God created the heaven and the earth." In the Hebrew Bible, the original word is not just the heaven, but the plural form that means the entire universe. To understand God's plan and purpose for your life, you need to stretch your mind as much as is humanly possible to understand the awesome greatness of God.

During the time of King David, the ancients could only see about 5,119 stars with the naked eye. When the 100-inch telescope was made operational on Mt. Wilson in California, astronomers discovered that there were over 40 billion stars in the universe. When the 200-inch telescope was made operational on Mt. Palomar in California, astronomers discovered that in just the Milky Way galaxy (glow of which we can see with the eye) there were over 100 billion stars. But that was nothing, not even a drop in the bucket, because they could now see that there were at least another 100 billion galaxies, many of them larger than the Milky Way galaxy.

The December 2003 edition of the National Geographic states on page 54, "It just keeps getting better. NASA's Hubble Space Telescope with a new camera installed in March 2002, reveals the cosmos (universe) more clearly than ever before. . . EYE ON INFINITY." The February 2003 issue of the National Geographic states on page 26- 27, "Today we know that the Milky Way contains more that 100 billion stars and that there are some 100 billion galaxies in the universe." If you multiply 100 billion galaxies with over 100 billion stars each, you have at least 10 septillion stars. That is the number 10 with 21 zeros following it. That is a number beyond our comprehension. I don't know if there are enough blades of grass on the planet earth to represent that number.

Another way of stretching our minds would be to take the thickness of this page, which is 1/300 of an inch, and let us suppose that the thickness of this paper represents the distance from the earth to the sun, which is 93 million miles. It takes a ray of sun light eight minutes to travel to earth at a speed of 186, 000 miles per second. The distance from the nearest star to earth takes light 4 1/3 years to travel the distance. If we use the thickness of this paper as the distance between the earth and sun, it would take a stack of papers 71 feet high to represent the distance from the earth to the nearest star. The diameter of our Milky Way galaxy would take light 100,000 years to travel the distance. If we use the thickness of this paper as the distance between the earth and the sun, it would take a stack of papers 310 miles high to represent the distance of 100,000 light-years.

The distance to the edge of the universe as far as our telescopes can see would take light ten billion light-years to travel the distance. If we use the thickness of this paper as the distance between the earth and the sun, it would take a stack of papers 31 million miles high or about one-third of the distance from the earth to the sun to represent this distance.

However, stop and think. Right now, scientists have no idea where or how far the edge of the universe is from earth. Yet Genesis 1:1 says, "In the beginning God created the heaven (universe) and the earth." This same God not only created all this, but He also had an individual plan and purpose with your name on it for your life. Not for just this life, but for the ETERNAL LIFE!

The reason God created this earth was to bring you into existence and develop you to be able to fulfill the individual plan and purpose He has for your life. After God created the universe and earth, His next step was to develop the earth as a habitation for man to be trained and developed for the eternal plans and purpose that He had for man.

According to Genesis 1, God took seven days for this process. The apostle Peter writes in 2 Peter 3:8, "But, beloved, be not ignorant of this one thing, that one day is with the LORD as a thousand years, and a thousand years as one day." This was a prophetic picture that men's time on the earth would be seven thousand years. The Bible shows from the genealogies listed that man or Adam was created about 4004 B.C. Today we are beyond two thousand A.D. This prophesies that six days are about completed and that one day or one thousand years are left until God creates a new heaven and earth. The apostle John wrote in Revelation 21:1, "And I saw a new heaven and a new earth: for the first heaven and the first earth were passed away; and there was no more sea."

On the first day of this prophetic picture, God spoke and said let there be light. On the second day God spoke and said let there be a firmament (the earthly atmosphere). On day three God said let there be oceans and dry land and that the land bring forth vegetation. On day four God said let the lights in the heaven divide day and night and let them be for signs, seasons, days and years. On day five God spoke and life in the water came forth and winged fowl or birds came forth. Day six was the most important day when God spoke for animals and living creatures to come forth upon the land.

In the middle of day six, however, God stopped speaking and called for a conference. In all that had been accomplished, God did not find rest or as we might say, He had not accomplished the goal that He was after. In Genesis 1:26, a conference of the Godhead was called: "And God said, Let us make man in our image, after our likeness: and let them have dominion." All the rest of creation came into existence at the spoken word of God, but creating man was not so simple. This required a conference among the Godhead.

When God said, "Let us make man in our image, after our likeness" to whom was He talking? In Hebrew the word for God is "Elohim." This is the plural form for the word God, which in the singular form is "El." The Bible is very clear that there is God the Father, God the Son and God the Holy Spirit. How are we to understand all this? The New Testament Church spent hundreds of years trying to understand it. The Bible declares there is only one God yet there is God the Father, God the Son and God the Holy Spirit. The early Church adopted the doctrine of the Trinity, which simply says there is only one God with one essence, yet three different persons and all are co-equal. In its last analysis, the doctrine of the Trinity is a deep mystery that cannot be fathomed by the finite human mind. However there can be no reasonable doubt that it is taught in the Scripture. It is a doctrine to be believed even though it may not be thoroughly understood.

In the desire to create man, God says there are three goals:
1. Let us make man in our image
2. After our likeness
3. Let them have dominion

As Jesus was talking with the woman at the well of Jacob in Sychar, Samaria, Jesus very clearly tells us what the image of God is, "God is a Spirit; and they that worship Him must worship Him in spirit and in truth" (John 4:24). Man would have to be made a spirit in order to be in the image of God. To be made "after our likeness" would mean that as the Godhead was a TRINITY as Father, Son and Holy Spirit, man also would have to be made a trinity.

Therefore in Genesis 2:7, "And the LORD God formed man of the dust of the ground, (man's body was made out of elements from the earth) and breathed into his nostrils the breath of life (God does not breath air as our physical bodies do, but God is a spirit and imparted spirit into man's being) and man became a living soul." AS A RESULT, MAN BECAME A TRINITY: SPIRIT, SOUL AND BODY.

Man was made a living "spirit" like God is a SPIRIT. With our spirit we are able to continually be conscious of God's Spirit and to be able to fellowship and commune with His Spirit, to know and be aware of God's presence or Spirit. Our soul is the natural man with our intellect, emotions, personality, talents, ego, minds, etc. And we all understand the physical body of man.

Below is an attempt to illustrate the relationship between God and man.

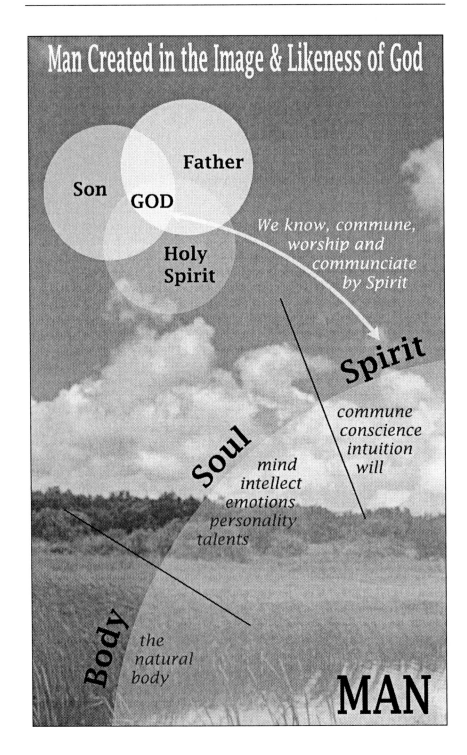

Man Created in the Image & Likeness of God

Father

Son GOD

Holy Spirit

We know, commune, worship and communciate by Spirit

Spirit

commune conscience intuition will

Soul

mind intellect emotions personality talents

Body

the natural body

MAN

In the three goals that God had for man according to Genesis 1:20, "And God said, Let us make man in our image, after our likeness; and let them have dominion." Goals one and two were accomplished. The third goal of dominion was to be learned and developed in this life and fulfilled in eternity. I will explain this as we progress.

Man was not an accident or an afterthought in God's plan. God clearly outlined man's position on the great blueprint for the universe. God's eternal purpose is bound up with man. Not only was man to be made in God's image (spirit) and after God's likeness (a trinity), but also man was to have DOMINION. Man was not only to be a being who would fellowship with God, but would also have the ability TO DO, TO CREATE and TO RULE. God intended man to wield power, to reign and rule, to control other created things. Note that the special sphere of this is ALL THE EARTH.

Although salvation is the central theme of the Bible, that was not God's original design or plan for man. He never intended for man to sin and still less for man to perish or be eternally separated from Him. The record of Adam and Eve in the third chapter of Genesis eating of the Tree of Knowledge of Good and Evil represents man's history. This was NOT God's purpose for man.

Picture in your mind, a father and his son building a new home. While putting on the roof, the son falls off the roof during construction and is seriously injured. The father never intended the son to fall off the roof and injure himself. However, in order to complete the job, the father has to help the son get over his injuries and get him back on the roof.

MAN WAS CREATED FOR DOMINION. Genesis 1:26-28 notes the area of man's dominion: "and let them have dominion over the fish of the sea, and over the fowl of the air, and over the cattle, and over all the earth, and over every creeping thing that crawls on the earth. So God created man. . . male and female. . . And God blessed them, and God said unto them, Be fruitful, and multiply, and replenish the earth, and subdue it."

Our first parents, Adam and Eve have often been pictured as adult-sized children wandering among the flowers and trees, looking curiously at the birds and butterflies. Somehow, we fail to see them as they really were:

- Mature adults
- Possessing wisdom and intelligent judgment

For a moment picture the lordly Adam, as God brings every animal and fowl of the air to Adam to see what he would name them. In majestic dignity as all the animals of the earth pass in review, Adam assigns them their names. Man was made for magnificence, capable of unlimited development and above all enjoying face-to-face fellowship with his Creator (Gen. 2:19-20). Adam was God's appointed business manager of this earth.

During the first six days of earth's creation, God created the light, the earth's atmosphere, the land, sea and vegetation, set the lights in the heaven (sun, moon, stars) to divide day and night, for signs, seasons, days and years. God brought forth life in the waters and winged fowl in the atmosphere and on the sixth day animals and living creatures.

But in these God did not find rest. His ultimate goal and purpose for earth's creation had not been accomplished. After man was created, Genesis 2:1-3 tells us that God rested from all His work. All preparations before man were preparatory. All God's expectations were focused upon man. When God gained a man, He was satisfied and rested. If we see that God rests in a certain thing, then we know that is something He was originally after. God's rest reveals to us that God accomplished His heart's desire. He did something, which made Him rejoice, and therefore, He could rest.

God had a purpose, and this purpose was to gain man. Who would be created in His own image and likeness to rule and reign with Him and to forever fellowship with Him. Only the realization of this purpose could satisfy God's heart.

"To him that overcomes will I grant to sit with Me in My throne, even as I also overcame, and am set down with My Father in His throne" (Rev. 3:21). "And has raised us up together, and made us sit together in heavenly places in Christ Jesus: That in the ages to come He might show the exceeding riches of His grace and

His kindness toward us through Christ Jesus" (Eph. 2:6-7). "Eye has not seen, nor ear heard, neither have entered into the heart of man, the things which God has prepared for them that love Him" (1 Cor. 2:9). On the night before His crucifixion, Jesus prayed, "And the glory which You have given Me I have given them; that they may be one even as We are one" (John 17:22).

Now we come to the most important aspect of man's creation by God. Not only did God want a being that was created in His image (spirit) and likeness (trinity – body, soul, spirit), but most important would be that man would be a free moral agent. Man would not be a robot, but in God's likeness with the capacity and ability to choose what he wanted. To love God or not to love God. To obey God or to do his own thing or desire. To have what we in theology term as "free will."

The Bible teaches that all of God's present angels serve Him because they choose to serve Him. There was a point in eternity that a third of angels, led by the archangel Lucifer (also called Satan) rebelled against God and were cast out of the third heaven or God's throne. Their final destination will be the everlasting lake of fire that was God's creation to separate them from His presence forever.

After God had created Adam and Eve and saw that everything He created was good, He planted a garden eastward in Eden and put man there to oversee the garden and to begin to learn to rule and take dominion. However, He also made provision for man's free will. In the garden were many trees including the Tree of Life. "Of every tree of the garden you may freely eat: But of the Tree of Knowledge of Good and Evil, you shall not eat of it; for in the day that you eat thereof you shall surely die" (Gen. 2:16-17).

God wanted a being with a FREE WILL who would be as family, who would love Him, who would fellowship with Him, and would choose to do so because that would be what he wanted to do. Therefore, the Tree of Knowledge of Good and Evil was planted there in the Garden of Eden. Men would have a choice. To confront men with this choice, Lucifer (Satan) was allowed to enter the Garden of Eden. Satan came in the form of a serpent and endeavored to get man to question God's command. The weapons that Satan is allowed to use against man are: 1) deception – to question,

2) accusation, 3) condemnation, and 4) fear. I will have more to say about this later on in the book. Here in the Garden of Eden, Satan's first strategy was to get man to question what God had said. "And he said unto the woman, Yes, has God said, you shall not eat of every tree in the garden?" (Gen. 3:1).

Once Satan was able to get Eve to question what God has said, he then was able to plant deception in her mind by saying, "God knows that in the day you eat of that tree, your eyes will be opened and you shall be as gods, knowing good and evil." So far Satan was telling the truth, but now come the lies or deception, "You shall not surely die." Eve and Adam were deceived and ate the fruit of the Tree of Knowledge of Good and Evil. Sure enough, their eyes were opened and they saw that they were naked and began to know good and evil. They sought to clothe themselves with fig leaves and to hide themselves from God in the garden.

Throughout the Bible, we are told that God cannot fellowship with sin, but that He must separate Himself from sin, just as He had to separate Himself from Satan and the angels that rebelled against Him in heaven. God had plainly told Adam and Eve, the day that they eat of the Tree of Knowledge of Good and Evil they would surely die. This did not just mean a physical death of the body, but eternal separation of man's spirit and soul from God forever. So what was God suppose to do with man that He loved?

The first step was that man would be put out of the Garden of Eden and his body would begin to grow old and eventually die. But what about man's spirit and soul that was created in the image and likeness of God? God's Word proclaimed that sin could only be paid for by death. By man dying physically and his spirit and soul being forever separated from God would pay for his sin. But then God's purpose for creating man would also be gone and His plans and purpose for man defeated. The good news of the Bible is: "For God so loved the world, that He gave His only begotten Son, that whosoever believes in Him should not perish, but have everlasting life" (John 3:16).

As the apostle John writes in the Gospel of John: "In the beginning was the Word (Jesus), and the Word (Jesus) was with God, and the Word (Jesus) was God. . . . All things were made by Him

(Jesus); and without Him was not anything made that was made. . . And the Word (Jesus) was made flesh, and dwelt among us, (and we beheld His glory, the glory as of the only begotten of the Father,) full of grace and truth" (John 1:1,3,14).

In simple terms, God the Son said to God the Father, "I will be born as man, live an earthly life without sin, and then I will give My earthly life in death on the cross to die for each man's sins, so that each man's sins will be paid for by death, My death as Jesus Christ on the cross. All that men will have to do is believe on Me, ask forgiveness of his sins and accept My death on the cross in substitution for the penalty of death for his own sins."

As the apostle Paul so beautifully writes in Philippians 2:5-11, "Let this mind be in you, which was also in Christ Jesus: Who, being in the form of God, thought it not robbery to be equal with God: But made Himself of no reputation, and took upon Him the form of a servant and was made in the likeness of men; And being found in fashion as a man, He humbled Himself, and became obedient unto death, even the death of the cross. . . And that every tongue should confess that Jesus Christ is LORD, to the glory of God the Father."

Back on that day in the Garden of Eden, God said to Satan, "And I will put enmity between you and the woman, and between your seed and her seed; it shall bruise your head, and you shall bruise his heel" (Gen. 3:15).

Here God the Father was giving the promise that God the Son would be born of the Virgin Mary. Although Satan, as the serpent, would cause Jesus to be crucified on the cross (you shall bruise His heel. . . would cause physical pain and suffering, but would not defeat Him) Jesus shall bruise your head or would totally defeat Satan.

God in His love promises to send his Son into this world in the fullness of TIME. Jesus would go to the cross and die for man's sins and pay the penalty that all of us owe for sin. All that man would have to do is repent of his sins, accept Jesus Christ and believe that He paid the penalty for his sins and then receive the gift of everlasting life.

In order to give man time to repent, God inserted this incredible thing we call TIME into the fabric of eternity. By this amazing device of creating TIME and inserting it between the pronouncement of doom upon sin and the carrying out of the sentence, God gave Adam and all men room in which to repent. Earth's time might also be compared to an hourglass. Man only sees the bottom half. God sees both the top half and the bottom half. Therefore, God sees the end from the beginning and seeing the end from the beginning, God sent Christ in the fullness of time. Remember that one day with the LORD is a thousand years and a thousand years as one day. Not because God feels time differently from us, but because He is outside of time, He is using it for His eternal purposes and to His glory.

It is absolutely important that we understand that what takes place in eternity is fixed and final forever. Only in a temporal environment can we put things behind us, change directions and turn as the Bible so often exhorts us to do. There is no hint in the Bible that Satan can repent. Why? Because his rebellion occurred in eternity and its results are eternally binding. "God spared not the angels that sinned, but cast them down to hell, and delivered them into chains of darkness, to be reserved unto judgment" (2 Pet. 2:4). When man enters into eternity, all things are final. There is no more turning, changing or repenting. It is as the prophet Jeremiah said, "The harvest is past, the summer is ended, and we are not saved" (Jer. 8:20).

God showed His love to man by creating this earth in six days and resting on the seventh day. In other words He created time and put man in it to prepare man for the eternal purpose and plan that He had for man. That way if man failed, rebelled or sinned, he would still be in time and could repent and return. Satan's sin occurred in eternity and therefore, there could be no repenting or turning.

God in His mercy quickly banned Adam and Eve from the Garden of Eden to keep them from eating of the Tree of Life. Why? As we read in Genesis 3:22, "Lest he put forth his hand and take also of the Tree of Life, and eat and live forever." If they ate of the Tree of Life, Adam and Eve would have immediately become a part of eternity as sinners and could never repent and return. Once we leave time, we become a part of eternity and all is fixed and final forever. "It is appointed unto men once to die, but after this the judgment" (Heb. 9:27). When we die we enter into eternity and there we will face the Judge of all the universe, the Almighty God. This will be a time of sentencing. To those who have believed and received Christ, the sentence will be: "Well done, you good and faithful servant: you have been faithful over a few things, I will make you ruler over many things: enter into the joy of your LORD" (Matt. 25:21). To all others it will be: "Depart from me, you cursed, into everlasting fire, prepared for the devil and his angels" (Matt. 25:41).

As Adam and Eve were escorted out of the Garden of Eden, the rest of the Bible covers basically two themes. The first theme is how God was going to accomplish the redemption of man. The second theme is how man is being prepared for the plan and purpose that God has for man's life, that of dominion and rulership in eternity.

God has in the very simplest of terms told us what His plan and purpose is for your life in the parable of the sower as it recorded in the Gospels of Matthew, Mark and Luke. There are three basic truths set forth in this parable:

1. THE SEED - The life God has given you.
2. THE FIELD - The world or field where the seed develops.
3. THE HARVEST - The fruit or the fulfillment of God's plan and purpose for the seed or life that was sown.

Parables were a common method of teaching in the Near East, used to convey spiritual truth through a series of earthly comparisons. Let us take an in depth look at God's plan and purpose for your life as illustrated in this parable.

A sower went forth to sow seed in the field. Some seed fell by the wayside and the fowls or the birds came and devoured the seed. Some seed fell on rocky ground and although it began to grow, its roots were shallow and when the sun came up, it was scorched and withered away. Some seed fell among thorns and when the seed began to grow, so did the thorns and they choked out the growth from the seed. However, other seed fell on good ground and the seed produced a harvest, some thirty fold, some sixty fold and some a hundred fold.

Jesus told His disciples to hear the meaning of the parable. The seed that fell by the wayside are those who hear the word but Satan comes and takes it away. The seed that fell on rocky ground are those who received the word with joy, but when tribulation and persecution came, they immediately withered or fell away. The seed that fell among the thorns were those who heard the word, but the cares of the world, the delight of riches and the desire for other things entered in and choked the word so the seed never produced any fruit. The seed that fell on the good ground refers to those who heard the word, accepted the word and held fast to the word with an honest and good heart, and brought forth fruit with patience. (See Matthew 13:1-23; Mark 4:2-20; Luke 8:4-15.)

CHAPTER TWO

HOW GOD PLANNED TO ACCOMPLISH THE REDEMPTION OF MAN

What a sad time as God had to lead Adam and Eve out of the Garden of Eden and place angels with flaming swords at the entrance to keep man from coming back in to eat of the Tree of Life. For if man now eats of the Tree of Life, he would live forever as a sinner and be eternally separated from God. However, the apostle John writes in Revelation 21:1 and 22:1-4, "And I saw a new heaven and a new earth: for the first heaven and the first earth were passed away; and there was no more sea. . . . And he showed me a pure river of water, clear as crystal, proceeding out of the throne of God. . . . and on either side of the river, was there the Tree of Life. . . . And there shall be no more curse: but the throne of God and the Lamb shall be in it: and His servants shall serve Him; And they shall see His face; and His name shall be in their foreheads."

As soon as man was placed outside the Garden of Eden, God in His love and mercy begins His plan to accomplish the redemption of man. In Galatians 4:4, the apostle Paul tells us that when the FULLNESS OF THE TIME was come, God would send his Son to redeem man that we might receive the adoption of sons.

As it was pointed out in chapter one, God's Word proclaims that sin could only be paid for by man dying physically and his spirit and soul being forever separated from God. The only other way acceptable to God would be another human being, without sin, dying in your place. Since all men have sinned and come short of the glory of God, the only other sacrifice that would be acceptable to God would be for His Son to come into this world as a man and live without ever committing a sin, and to die in our place. The Bible tells us over and over that the life of the body is in the blood.

Why? It is the blood that brings oxygen and nutrition to the body and cleanses the body from wastes. Blood would have to be shed. The soul and spirit would have to be separated from God.

Therefore, Jesus would come into this world as a baby and become fully man. He would live as a man without ever sinning. He would die by having His blood shed on the cross and experience having His soul and spirit separated from God. As Jesus died upon the cross, the greatest and most terrible part of His death was to suddenly realize that His soul and spirit had been separated from God. That is why Jesus cried out with a loud voice, "My God, My God, why has thou forsaken Me?"

Now we turn to see how God would accomplish this plan. As the apostle Paul writes in Ephesians 1:10-11, "That in the dispensation of the fullness of times He might gather together in one all things in Christ, both which are in heaven, and which are on earth; even in Him: In whom also we have obtained an inheritance, being predestinated according to the purpose of Him who works all things after the counsel of His own will." Or as we quoted the apostle Paul earlier in Galatians 4:4, "When the fullness of the time was come, God sent forth His Son, made of a woman."

There are three phases to the preparation of the fullness of time. Most of the Bible is devoted to phase one. Phases two and three are carried out in the latter part of the Bible. The three phases are:

1. PHASE ONE – Preparation of a people through whom Jesus would come and who would begin the preaching of the Gospel. This is Israel and the apostles.
2. PHASE TWO – The development of a common language and culture that would facilitate the spread of the Gospel. This was the Greek language and culture.
3. PHASE THREE – Preparation of a political climate and government that would facilitate the spread of the Gospel. This is Rome.

Let us begin with PHASE ONE - The preparation of a people. The first child of Adam and Eve was a son named Cain. The recorded second child was Abel. As the children grew into adulthood and began to serve God, Cain brought offerings of what he wanted to give God while Abel brought offerings of what God intended to be brought. As a result, Abel's offerings were accepted by God while the offerings of Cain were not. Cain became very angry. God spoke to Cain saying that if he would bring offerings that were what God had instructed, his would also be accepted. Cain continued to do his own thing and sin began to rule over him. In a fit of anger he slew his brother Abel. Cain then went out on his own and became the patriarch of an ungodly line of descendents that over the next 1,500 plus years developed into an ungodly and wicked generation.

Adam and Eve had a third son name Seth, from whom a more godly line of descendents were born. Two of the most outstanding descendents of Seth were Enoch and Noah. God took Enoch home. "And Enoch walked with God: and he was not; for God took him" (Gen. 5:24). But more than 1,500 years from Adam, the ungodly line of Cain so intermingled with the godly line of Seth that God said in Genesis 6:5-8, "And God saw that the wickedness of man was great in the earth, and that every imagination of the thought of his heart was only evil continually. And it repented the LORD that He had made man on the earth, and it grieved Him at His heart. And the LORD said, I will destroy man whom I have created from the face of the earth. . . . But Noah found grace in the eyes of the LORD."

Noah was a just man and perfect in his generation. Noah and his three sons, Shem, Ham and Japheth walked with God and served God. But the rest of mankind was corrupt and filled with violence. And God spoke to Noah, "The end of all flesh is come before Me; for the earth is filled with violence through them; and behold, I will destroy them with the earth" (Gen. 6:13).

So God instructed Noah to build an ark large enough for Noah, his wife, his three sons and their wives, plus room for a male and female of every living thing, including not only animals, but fowl and every creeping thing. In addition Noah was told to gather a store of food to sustain life while God would bring a flood of water to cover the earth to destroy every living being (everything in which there is the breath of life).

After entering the ark, mighty torrents of rain came down and subterranean waters burst forth upon the earth for forty days until the waters covered all the earth and all the high mountains. It was one year later before the earth was dry enough for Noah and the occupants of the ark were able to leave the ark and begin life anew on the earth. "And God blessed Noah and his sons, and said unto them, Be fruitful, and multiply and replenish the earth" (Gen. 9:1). Noah lived 350 years after the flood. It is believed that Noah and his sons served God. However, it is evident that many of their descendents did not.

In Genesis 11, we are told that when they came to a plain called Shinar, which is the area of present day Iraq, they started to build the Tower of Babel to make a name for themselves. In Genesis 11:5, we are told that God came down and confounded their language so that they could not understand one another's speech and scattered them abroad on the face of the earth.

According to the genealogies in Genesis, there are 1,656 years from Adam to the flood. Noah lived 350 years after the flood and died two years before the birth of Abraham. This amounts to 2008 (1656 + 350 + 2) years, or according to God's prophetic time clock described in chapter one, two days (a day with the Lord is as a thousand years and a thousand years as a day). It was definitely time for God to begin PHASE ONE of the fullness of time, the preparation of a people through whom Jesus would come – Israel. God would spend two days or two thousand years preparing Israel for the coming of His Son Jesus Christ and the cross. The entire Old Testament and the Gospels give us the story of this preparation of phase one. Now two thousand years after the creation and fall of man, God called Abraham to become the founder of a movement having as its objective the reclamation and redemption of mankind.

Abraham was born in Ur of the Chaldees. This would now be in the southern part of Iraq and not too far from where the attempt was made to build the Tower of Babel. Abraham's father was Terah and his lineage goes back ten generations to Shem, the son of Noah. Abraham's great ancestor Shem was still alive when Abraham was born and did not die until Abraham was 75 years old. We can assume Abraham was well acquainted with his ancestor Shem who undoubtedly told him all about the flood and Noah and those who preceded him.

Genesis 14 tells us that Abraham knew another interesting person, Melchizedek, King of Salem (ancient Jerusalem) to whom Abraham paid tithes. Melchizedek was the priest of the Most High who prayed and blessed Abraham as told in Genesis 14:17-20. The Bible does not give a record of Melchizedek's ancestors, but if he was an aged man, it is possible that Abraham knew him when Abraham was a young man back in Ur of the Chaldees. Hebrew tradition holds that Melchizedek was Shem, a son of Noah and survivor of the pre-flood world. Melchizedek had already come out of Babylonia to take possession of this particular spot (Jerusalem) in the name of God. For further details see *Halley's Bible Handbook*, page 38 (See Endnote 1). However, at this time, there is no proof that this is a fact. But it does give us the idea that there were other godly men in Abraham's time.

In God's plan to accomplish the redemption of man, God chose Abraham to fulfill a vital part. In PHASE ONE, Abraham was the beginning of the preparation of a people through whom Jesus would come – Israel. Undoubtedly, Abraham is the greatest man in the Bible. When God described Himself to Moses in the burning bush, He said, "I am the God of your father, the God of Abraham, the God of Isaac, and the God of Jacob. And Moses hid his face; for he was afraid to look upon God" (Exod. 3:6).

Of all the Old Testament characters, the name of Abraham was most frequently on the lips of Jesus. One day while teaching in the temple at Jerusalem, Jesus told the religious leaders: "Your father Abraham rejoiced to see My day: and he saw it, and was glad. Then said the Jews unto Him, You are not yet fifty years old, and have you seen Abraham? Jesus said unto them, Verily, verily, I say unto you, Before Abraham was, I Am" (John 8: 56-58).

God made a BLOOD COVENANT with Abraham that fore-shadowed the EVERLASTING BLOOD COVENANT that Jesus would make on the cross for all mankind. As Jesus told Nicodemus, a ruler of the Jews: "For God so loved the world, that He gave His only begotten Son, that whosoever believes in Him should not perish, but have everlasting life" (John 3:16).

Our Bible is divided into two sections: The Old Testament and The New Testament. In the original languages of the Bible, Hebrew and Greek, the word translated as "testament" actually was "covenant," a covenant made by blood. Remember at the Last Supper, Jesus took the cup and gave it to them saying, "Drink you all of it; For this is My blood of the new testament (covenant), which is shed for many for the remission of sins" (Matt. 26:27-28).

In our present generations, we use legal contracts and written agreements. Ancient civilizations had something far more binding – blood covenants. As far back as human history goes, peoples have practiced the blood covenant in some form. It was practiced by Europeans, tribes in Africa, the Americans Indians and the Arabs to mention a few. In some places it had degenerated into a very grotesque rite, but nevertheless, it was a blood covenant.

The reasons for making a blood covenant may vary. Protection was one reason. If a strong tribe lives by the side of a weaker tribe, and there is danger of the weaker tribe being destroyed, the weaker tribe will seek to cut a blood covenant with the stronger tribe that they may be preserved. Two business men entering into a partnership might cut a blood covenant to insure that neither would take advantage of the other. If two men become fast friends, such as we read in the Bible about David and Jonathan, they would enter into a blood covenant to protect each other and their families.

The method of cutting the covenant was generally the same although some degradation entered into the practice of various cultures. Two men who wished to cut the covenant would come together with their friends and a priest. If it were two tribes or two groups of people, each tribe would select a representative.

First they exchanged gifts. By this exchange of gifts they indicated that all that one has the other owns, if necessary. Then a cup of wine was brought and a cut was made in the arm of each man. Drops of blood from each man were dropped into the same cup. The contents of the cup were stirred and mixed. Afterwards each man would drink from the cup. Often times, they then would put their cuts together so that their bloods mingled. The result was that they were now "blood brothers."

Several of the early missionaries to Africa, such as David Livingstone and Henry Stanley, said they never knew this covenant to be broken in Africa, no matter what the provocation. The covenant was so sacred that the children of the blood brothers would honor it and keep it until the third and fourth generations.

A story is told when Henry Stanley was seeking David Livingstone in Africa and came in contact with a powerful native tribe that was very war-like. At this time, Stanley was very ill, weak and in no condition to fight them. Finally, his interpreter asked him why he didn't make a blood covenant with the tribe. Stanley asked him what was involved and the idea revolted Stanley. However, Stanley's condition grew worse and the young black man encouraged him once again to cut the covenant with the chieftain of the tribe. Stanley asked what the results of such a covenant would be, and the interpreter answered, "Everything the chieftain has will be yours if you need it."

This appealed to Stanley and he investigated. After several days a decision was made to enter into a blood covenant with the native tribe. The chieftain questioned Stanley as to his motives and his ability to keep the covenant.

The first step was the exchanging of gifts. The old chieftain wanted Stanley's new white goat. At this time, Stanley was in such poor health and goat's milk was about all he could take for nourishment. This was hard for Stanley to give up, but the chieftain seemed to want nothing else. In exchange for the goat, the old chieftain handed him his seven-foot copper-wound spear. Stanley thought he had been taken by the old chieftain, but later Stanley came to realize that wherever he went in Africa with that spear, everybody bowed to him and submitted to him.

The second step was that the old chieftain selected one of his princes to represent him and the tribe and Stanley selected one of his men from England. Then a priest came forward with a cup of wine, made an incision in the young black's wrist, and let the blood drip into the cup of wine. Then he cut a like incision in the wrist of the Englishman, and let his blood also drip into the cup of wine. Then the wine was stirred, mixing the blood. The priest then handed the cup to the Englishman who drank part of it and then the cup was handed to the black man who drank the rest of it.

Next, they rubbed their wrists together so that their bloods mingled. Although these two men were only substitutes, they had bound Stanley and the chieftain, and Stanley's men and the chieftain's tribe into a blood brotherhood that was indissoluble.

The final step in this ceremony was the planting of trees that were known for their long life. When the planting of the trees was completed, then the chieftain stepped forward and shouted, "Come, buy and sell with Stanley, for he is our blood brother."

A few hours before, Stanley's men had to stand on guard about their bales of cotton cloth and trinkets. Now they could open the bales and leave them on the trail and nothing was disturbed. For anyone to steal from their blood brother Stanley it would be a death penalty. The old chieftain couldn't do enough for his new found brother (See Endnote 2).

Genesis 12 records God calling Abraham out of the home and land of his father Terah to go into the land that would become the land of Abraham and Israel. It would be here in this land that God would complete the preparation of phase one, the preparation of a people through whom Jesus would come and who would begin the preaching of the Gospel.

Abraham obeyed and left all his past at the age of 75. After he had been in the new land for a number of years, the LORD said to Abraham, "Lift up now your eyes, and look from the place where you are northward, and southward, and eastward, and westward: For all the land which you see, to you will I give it, and to your seed forever. And I will make your seed as the dust of the earth: so that if a man can number the dust of the earth, then shall your seed also be numbered. Arise, walk through the land in the length of it and in the breadth of it; for I will give it unto you" (Gen. 13:14-17).

In Genesis 15-17, we read about the blood covenant that God makes with Abraham. Remember, the first step in making a blood covenant is exchanging gifts. Abraham was a wealthy man with many herds and servants but he and Sarah never had any children. For many years Abraham and Sarah had desired children. So God offers two gifts to Abraham. In Genesis 15:4-6, God told Abraham that not only would he have a son that would come out of his own bowels (or body), but God also took him outside on a dark night. He told him to look up in the heaven and tell God how many stars are there, if he was able to number them. Then God told Abraham,

"So shall your seed be." God said as a part of this covenant, "I have given this land, from the river of Egypt unto the great river, the river Euphrates" (Gen. 15:18).

God told Abraham in Genesis 15: 9-18 to take for His part of cutting a blood covenant, a heifer of three years old, a she goat of three years, a ram of three years, a turtledove and a young pigeon. Then Abraham was to cut them apart down the middle, and separate the halves. That evening as the sun was going down, a deep sleep fell upon Abraham, and a deep and awesome darkness fell upon him. As the sun went down and it was dark, Abraham saw a smoking fire-pot and a flaming torch that passed between the halves of the carcasses. Genesis 15:18 declares, "In the same day the LORD made a covenant with Abraham."

That day God made a blood covenant with Abraham, giving him the gifts of (1) a promised seed, (2) Promised Land, (3) promised life and (4) to be his protector and friend. In Genesis 15:6 we read, "And he (Abraham) believed in the LORD; and He counted it to him for righteousness."

Two thousand years later Jesus would do this for all mankind. The Gospel of John records the new blood covenant that Jesus entered into for all mankind, "For God so loved the world, that He gave His only begotten Son, that whosoever believes in Him should not perish, but have everlasting life" (John 3:16).

Now let us look at Abraham's part of this blood covenant. In Genesis 17:1 we read, "The LORD appeared to Abraham and said unto him, I am the Almighty God, walk before Me, and be you perfect." The only gift that God wanted from man for this blood covenant was to "walk before Me, and be you perfect." Just simply give your life to Me and serve Me. As for man's part in cutting a covenant, God told Abraham in Genesis 17:10-11, "This is My covenant, which you shall keep, between Me and you and your seed after you; Every man and child among you shall be circumcised. And you shall circumcise the flesh of your foreskin; and it shall be a token of the covenant between Me and you."

Now in a blood covenant relationship, it means for both parties to the covenant, that all you have is for me if I need it and all that I have is for you if you need it. Now there are many things that God has that man may think he needs. But let us ask the question: "What do I have that God would ever need?" Abraham could ask many things from God. But what could Abraham ever give God that God would need?

In Genesis 22, we read that God did put Abraham to the test. "And it came to pass after these things, that God did tempt (put Abraham to the test) Abraham, and said unto him, Abraham: and he said, Behold here I am. And He said, Take now your son, your only son Isaac, whom you love, and get you into the land of Moriah; and offer him there for a burnt offering upon one of the mountains which I will tell you of" (Gen. 22: 1-2).

Abraham rose up early the next morning and took his young son along with wood for the fire and went to the place where God told him to offer his son as a burnt offering unto God. Abraham reached the place, built the altar, laid the wood upon the altar, bound up his son Isaac and placed him upon the altar. As Abraham raised his knife to slay his son, the LORD called unto Abraham saying, "Lay not your hand upon the lad, neither do you anything unto him: for now I know that you fearest God, seeing you have not withheld your son, your only son from Me" (Gen. 22:12). As Abraham looked up, he saw a ram caught in a thicket by his horns, and Abraham took the ram and offered it up instead of his son.

And the LORD called unto Abraham out of heaven the second time and said; "By Myself have I sworn, says the LORD, for because you have done this thing, and have not withheld your son, your only son; That in blessing, I will bless you, and in multiplying I will multiply your seed as the stars of the heaven, and as the sand which is upon the sea shore. . . and in your seed shall all the nations of the earth be blessed; because you have obeyed My voice" (Gen. 22:16-18).

God was in the process of preparing a people through whom Jesus would come to make the perfect and eternal blood covenant between God and man. The next step would be the establishment of the nation Israel. The young son of Abraham, Isaac, was a miracle child in that he was born when his mother was ninety years old and his father was one hundred years old. Isaac served the God of his father Abraham faithfully all of the days of his life. However, it would be through Isaac's son Jacob that the nation Israel would come into being.

During his childhood years, Jacob loved God and wanted the promises and blessings of God. However, it is believed that it took 97 years of Jacob's life for God to prepare Jacob for the plan and purpose that God had for his life. In the next chapter we will spend sometime on the life of Jacob for some very valuable lessons. The big change that occurred in Jacob's life took place when he was about 97 years of age (See Endnote 3), while returning from Haran with his four wives and eleven of his sons to meet again with his brother Esau and his father Isaac.

In Genesis 32, Jacob had returned to the land that would be named after him and was at the brook named Peniel. The next day he was to meet his brother Esau whom he had not seen for over 20 years and whom he had cheated out of his birth right. Jacob spent the whole night in prayer and wrestled with the angel of the LORD all night until the breaking of day. The angel of the LORD said, "Let me go, for day breaks." And Jacob said, "I will not let you go, except you bless me." Then the angel of the LORD said, "Your name shall be called no more Jacob, but Israel: for as a prince have you power with God and with man, and have prevailed" (Gen. 32:28). And there the angel of the LORD blessed him and Jacob called the name of the place Peniel saying, "For I have seen God face to face, and my life is preserved" (Gen. 32:30).

The name Isra (prince) el (God), became Jacob's name and that next morning it was a "prince of God" that crossed the brook and that went to meet his brother Esau. His twelfth son Benjamin was born shortly after entering the Promised Land. His new name would be the name for the new nation called Israel and his twelve sons the names for the twelve tribes of Israel.

The next step in God's preparation of a people through whom Jesus would come and who would begin the preaching of the Gospel, was to take Israel (Jacob) and his twelve sons and develop and nurture them into a special nation of people. In a series of events as we will discuss in chapter three, Joseph (the favorite son of Jacob) was brought to Egypt and became the second ruler of the land of Egypt under Pharaoh. We will see that this was God's way of taking this family of a father (Jacob) and his twelve sons into a fertile area of their world, under the care of the rulers of Egypt, to nurture and protect this small family into a nation of several million people. When God made the blood covenant with their grandfather Abraham, God told Abraham, "Know of a surety that your seed shall be a stranger in a land that is not theirs, and shall serve them; and they shall afflict them four hundred years; And also that nation, whom they shall serve, will I judge: and afterward shall they come out with great substance" (Gen. 15:13-14).

Most all of us are well acquainted with the story of Moses and the Ten Commandments. At the time of the birth of Moses, the children of Israel were growing so rapidly, the Egyptians were fearful that they might become more mighty than the Egyptians. As a new Pharaoh took the throne of Egypt who did not know Joseph, he made the children of Israel slaves, treated them harshly and gave orders that any male child born to the children of Israel was to be put to death at birth.

However, God, who "makes all things work together for good to them that love God, to them who are called according to His purpose" (Rom. 8:28), used this to bring about Moses and his calling upon Moses. When Moses was born, his mother hid the newborn baby for three months. When she could no longer hide the baby, she made a small basket of papyrus reeds, water proofed it, put the baby in the basket and laid it among the reeds along the river's edge. The baby's sister watched from a distance to see what would happen to the baby.

As God would have it, one of Pharaoh's daughters came down to bathe in the river. As she and her maids were walking along the river bank, she spied the little boat among the reeds and sent one of the maids to bring it to her. When she opened it, there was a baby! And he was crying. This touched her heart. "He must be one of the Hebrew children!" she said.

Then the baby's sister approached the princess and asked her, "Shall I go and find one of the Hebrew woman to nurse the baby for you?"

"Yes, do!" the princess replied. So the little girl rushed home and called her mother. As she returned with her mother, the princess instructed the baby's mother, "Take this child home and nurse him for me and I will pay you well."

Later, when Moses was older, she brought him back to the princess and he became her son. She named him Moses, meaning "to draw out", because she had drawn him out of the water. (See Exodus 2:1-10 TLB).

God prepared Moses for the earthly plan and purpose that he had for Moses in three stages. As a baby he was with his mother long enough to have God implanted in his heart and life. As a child and young man, he was adopted as the son of Pharaoh's daughter and the grandson of the Pharaoh. In this position of privilege, he was taught and trained in all the wisdom and skill of the Egyptian and became a mighty prince and orator. (See Acts 7:21-22.)

The writer of the book of Hebrews tells us that when Moses came to maturity at forty years of age, he refused to be treated as the grandson of the king. He chose to suffer affliction with the people of God rather than enjoy the pleasures of sin for a season. He thought that it was better to suffer for the promised Christ than to own all the treasures of Egypt, for he was looking forward to the great reward that God would give him. By faith he left the land of Egypt and wasn't afraid of the Pharaoh's anger. Moses kept right on going. It seemed as though he could see God there with him. (See Hebrews 11:24-27.)

The third stage of Moses' life was when he spent forty years on the back side of the desert as a shepherd taking care of sheep for his wife's father. That must have been a very difficult forty years when it seemed that every step he took seemed to say: "Failure, failure, failure!"

One day he saw a burning bush that did not burn up. He turned to investigate this strange happening when all of the sudden he heard the voice of God calling: "Moses! Moses!" When Moses answered the voice, God said, "Take off your shoes, for you are standing on holy ground. I am the God of your fathers, the God of Abraham, of Isaac, and of Jacob." Moses hid his face for he was afraid to look upon God. God instructed Moses that His plan and purpose for Moses was to go tell Pharaoh to let the children of Israel go out of Egypt and to lead them back into the land that He had promised to give to Abraham, Isaac and Jacob. Moses exclaimed, "But I'm not the person for a job like that!" Then God told him, "I will certainly be with you. . . and I know that Pharaoh will not let you go except under heavy pressure. So I will give him all the pressure he needs! I will destroy Egypt with My miracles, and then at last he will let you go. And I will see to it that the Egyptians load you down with gifts when you leave, so that you will by no means go out empty-handed! Every woman will ask for jewels, silver, gold, and the finest of clothes from her Egyptian master's wife and neighbors. You will clothe your sons and daughters with the best of Egypt." (See Exodus 3:4-22 TLB.)

Sure enough Pharaoh at first refused to let the children of Israel go until ten plagues had been sent by God upon the Egyptians. At the end of the tenth plague, which was the death of the first born male of each family, Pharaoh finally let the children of Israel depart out of Egypt. But no sooner had the children of Israel departed, Pharaoh changed his mind and pursued them with the Egyptian army. When the Egyptian army caught up with them, they were at the Red Sea.

In the natural, the situation looked like certain doom. However, as the children of Israel cried out to the LORD, the LORD put a cloud of darkness between them and the Egyptians that night. Moses was instructed to stretch out his shepherd's staff over the Red Sea and the waters of the sea were parted. In the morning, all the Israelites passed over on dry ground. The Egyptians decided to follow them. When they were about half-way across, the LORD caused the waters of the Red Sea to return together again, drowning Pharaoh and his army.

When the children of Israel first came to Egypt, there was Israel, his sons and their wives and children. All together it added up to seventy persons. When they came out of Egypt about 400 years later, there was a census taken one year after leaving Egypt. It showed that there were 603,550 males above the age of 20, in addition to 22,300 males of the tribe of Levi and no count of the women and children. However, many scholars estimate the population was approximately three million.

The next step of God in preparing a people through whom Jesus would come and who would begin the preaching of the Gospel was to develop them into a nation. As this group of people came out of Egypt into the desert wilderness, the LORD was going to take them to the next step in His plans and purpose. When they came to Mt. Sinai, Moses went up into the mount and God told him to give this message to the children of Israel.

> You have seen what I did unto the Egyptians, and how I bare you on eagles' wings, and brought you unto Myself. Now therefore, if you will obey My voice indeed, and keep My covenant, then you shall be a peculiar (special) treasure unto Me above all people: for all the earth is Mine: And you shall be unto Me a kingdom of priests, and a holy nation. These are the words which you shall speak unto the children of Israel. (Exodus 19:4-6).

This next step for the children of Israel was not only extremely important for Israel, but would also be a graphic, prophetic picture of God's plan and purpose for all mankind. Israel was already in a "Blood Covenant" relationship with God as they continued to practice circumcision. The next two steps were extremely important. God was going to give them a body of laws that would include the Ten Commandments, the Tabernacle along with the offerings and sacrifices and the way to worship and serve Him. In Hebrews 8:5, the Bible says these things served as a model or shadow of heavenly things. Moses was given this command, "See, says He (God), that you make all things according to the pattern shown to you in the mount."

The Tabernacle was a likeness of something, a copy and shadow of heavenly things. It had special meaning to the nation of Israel, yet it was also a "pattern of things to come." The Tabernacle and then the Temple, which was built after the pattern of the Tabernacle, became the center of national life for Israel.

The second step was the most important one. Moses was to make the Ark of the Covenant. It would be made of acacia wood with dimensions of 3 ¾ feet long, 2 ¼ feet wide and 2 ¼ feet high. It was overlaid inside and outside with pure gold. Inside would be placed the Ten Commandments engraved on tablets of stone. Then a lid of pure gold with two angels at each end of the lid facing each other would be installed on the Ark. The space between the two angels was to be called the mercy seat. Then God said to Moses, "And there I will meet with you, and I will commune with you from above the mercy seat, from between the two cherubim which are upon the Ark of the Testimony" (Exod. 25:22).

This Ark of the Covenant was to be placed in the Tabernacle in an inner room that would be called the Holy of Holies. Only the chief high priest of Israel could go in once a year to sprinkle the blood of a sin offering (sacrifice of a lamb) upon the mercy seat and make atonement for the sins of the people.

God instructed Moses to speak to Aaron, Israel's first high priest and the brother of Moses, "that he come not at all times into the holy place within the veil before the mercy seat, which is upon the Ark; that he die not: for I will appear in the cloud upon the mercy seat" (Lev. 16:2). The Jews described this as a bright cloud of light that they called the "shekinah glory." Several scriptural references would be, "Out of Zion, the perfection of beauty, God has shined" (Ps. 50:2). Also, "Give ear, O Shepherd of Israel, You that leadest Joseph like a flock; You that dwellest between the cherubim, shine forth" (Ps. 80:1).

Here God was taking the step for a physical manifestation of His presence to continually dwell with man. It was a prophetic picture of how God the Son would come into this world and physically dwell with man. As the apostle John writes in the Gospel of John, "In the beginning was the Word, and the Word was with God, and the Word was God. The same was in the beginning with God. All things were made by Him; and without Him was not anything made that was made. In Him was life; and the life was the light of man. And the light shines in the darkness. . . . And the Word was made flesh, and dwelt among us, and we beheld His glory, the glory as of the only begotten of the Father, full of grace and truth" (John 1:1-14).

Let us take a moment to summarize the steps that God had taken to prepare a people through whom Jesus would come and who would begin the preaching of the Gospel.

1. God had chosen Abraham and entered into a blood covenant with him.

2. This Blood Covenant continued to his son Isaac and to his grandson Jacob, whose name was changed to Israel, "a prince with God."

3. Israel had twelve sons who were the start of the nation of Israel.

4. For over four hundred years, Israel and his sons lived in Egypt until they became a company of about three million souls.

5. God raised up Moses and prepared him to lead the children of Israel out of the land of Egypt.

6. Through mighty signs and wonders, the children of Israel were brought out of the land of Egypt by God into the wilderness under Mt. Sinai.

7. At Mt. Sinai, God developed the children of Israel into the nation of Israel. The Blood Covenant was continued. The Ten Commandments, the Law with the offerings and sacrifices and the Tabernacle were given to them. The most important step was that God's presence came to dwell with them above the mercy seat of the Ark of the Covenant.

All the above was a prophetic picture of how in the fullness of time God the Son would come and bring man back into the plan and purpose that He has for man, and for you personally, before He created this world. It would be approximately another 1,400 years before the fullness of time. Next, we will take a brief look at the rest of the preparation of the people (Israel).

Within a period of less than two years, Israel could have departed from Egypt, received all that God had for them at Mt. Sinai, and entered into the Promised Land. However, at the edge of the Promised Land, they sent twelve spies to spy out the land. Ten of the spies returned and gave an evil report that there were giants in the land, the cities had high walls around them. They believed that God had brought them out into the wilderness to die. They wanted to go back to Egypt. Two of the spies, Joshua and Caleb, along with Moses endeavored to encourage the people to believe God and enter into the land. But the people would not listen to them and were ready to stone Moses, Joshua and Caleb. Suddenly the glory of the LORD appeared in the Tabernacle and the LORD said, "How long will this people provoke Me? and how long will it be before they believe Me, for all the signs which I have shown among them?" (Num. 14:11).

Then God told Moses to say unto the people, "As you have spoken in My ears, so will I do to you: Your carcasses shall fall in the wilderness; and all that are twenty years old and upward, which have murmured against Me. . .shall not come into the land. . . . But your little ones, which you said should be a prey, them will I bring in, and they shall know the land which you have despised" (Num. 14:28-31).

For the next forty years the children of Israel wandered around in the wilderness until all those twenty years and older had died. Then Joshua and Caleb led all the children under twenty years of age, who had now matured and had children of their own, into the Promised Land that God had originally promised to Abraham and Israel. The LORD delivered all the land into their possession with mighty miracles and victories.

During the first 350 years that Israel was in the Promised Land, the children of Israel were led by Joshua and after him by judges that God raised up to lead the people. They had no king, for God considered Himself to be their King. When Samuel, the last judge, became old the people came to him and said, "Behold, you are old, and your sons walk not in your ways: now make us a king to judge us like all the nations. But the thing displeased Samuel, when they said, Give us a king to judge us. And Samuel prayed unto the LORD. And the LORD said unto Samuel, Harken unto the voice of the people in all that they say unto you: for they have not rejected you, but they have rejected Me, that I should not reign over them" (1 Sam. 8:5-7).

Then God said something that is very surprising, "Since the day that I brought them up and out of Egypt even unto this day, they continue to forsake Me and serve other gods at various times" (1 Sam. 8:8 paraphrased). The people as a whole had not come to understand that there are no other gods except the LORD. To them there was the LORD, but there were also other gods.

At the direction of the LORD, Samuel anointed Saul, the son of Kish, as Israel's first human king. Saul was tall, handsome and every inch of him looked like a king. However, Israel's first king was a failure because he would not obey the LORD. Then the LORD told Samuel to anoint David, the son of Jesse, as the next king. King David became a man after God's own heart and was a magnificent success. The apostle Paul gives the following testimony about David, "God raised up unto them David to be their king; to whom also He gave testimony and said, I have found David the son of Jesse, a man after Mine own heart, which shall fulfill all My will" (Acts 13:22).

So after becoming king over all Israel, David made Jerusalem his capital. Then he took an insignificant nation, and within a few years built it into a mighty kingdom completely subduing all neighboring nations from the brook of Egypt to almost the Euphrates River. This goes back to the covenant that God made with Abraham in Genesis 15:18, "In the same day the LORD made a covenant with Abraham, saying, Unto your seed have I given this land, from the river of Egypt unto the great river, the river Euphrates." David took an insignificant nation, and within a few years, built it into a mighty kingdom. Although it did not become a world empire, it did become one of the most powerful kingdoms on earth at the time.

David took the Ark of the Covenant that Moses made for the Tabernacle in the wilderness and brought it from its present place in Kirjath-Jearim in Judah into Jerusalem. He placed it in a Tabernacle on Mt. Zion in Jerusalem. He drew up the plans for the Temple that would be built in Jerusalem by his son Solomon in which the Ark of the Covenant would come to rest.

In my opinion, David's greatest accomplishments were the choirs, orchestras and the priesthood that he organized for the continual worshipping of God in the Tabernacle of David on Mt. Zion, as well as later on in the Temple built by Solomon. Many of the Psalms were also written by David.

God made this promise to David in 2 Samuel 7:16, "And your kingdom shall be established forever before you; your throne shall be established forever." Then we read in the Gospel of Luke 1:30-33 when the angel Gabriel came to Mary saying, "Fear not, Mary: for you have found favor with God. And, behold, you shall conceive in your womb, and bring forth a Son, and shall call His name Jesus. He shall be great, and shall be called the Son of the Highest: and the LORD God shall give unto Him the throne of His father David. And He shall reign over the house of Jacob forever; and of His kingdom there shall be no end."

King David is a prophetic picture of Jesus Christ who will reign on this earth for a thousand years in the Millennium. (This will be described in chapter six.) However, the greatest event was when God "raised Him (Jesus) from the dead, and set Him at His own right hand in heavenly places, Far above all principality, and power, and might, and dominion, and every name that is named, not only in this world, but also in that which is to come: And has put all things under His feet, and gave Him to be the head over all things (for the benefit of the church)" (Eph. 1:20-22).

It does not end there! Ephesians 2:6-7 says, "And has raised us up together, and made us sit together in heavenly places in Christ Jesus: That in the ages to come He might show the exceeding riches of His grace in His kindness towards us through Christ Jesus." As Jesus told the apostle John in Revelation 3:21, "To him that over-comes, will I grant to sit with Me on My throne, even as I also over-came, and am set down with My Father on His throne." THIS IS GOD'S ULTIMATE PLAN AND PURPOSE FOR YOUR LIFE, as I will describe in chapter seven.

King David was followed on the throne of Israel by his son Solomon, who built the Temple and continued the worship of God instituted by his father at the Tabernacle of David on Mt. Zion. This era of David and Solomon was the Golden Age of Israel's history. David was a warrior. Solomon was a builder. David made the kingdom. Solomon built the Temple. In the outside world, this was the age of Homer, the beginning of Greek history. At the time Egypt, Assyria and Babylon were weak. Israel was the most powerful kingdom in the world. Jerusalem was the most magnificent city and the Temple the most splendid building on earth. People came from the ends of the earth to hear Solomon's wisdom and see his glory.

The famous Queen of Sheba exclaimed, "The half was not told me."

Solomon's glorious reign was clouded by a grand mistake: his marriages to idolatrous women. He had seven hundred wives and three hundred concubines which, in itself, was a crime, both against himself and his wives. Dr. Henry H. Halley writes: "This wise man of the ages, in this respect at least, we think, was just a plain common fool. Many of these women were 'idolaters,' daughters of heathen kings, wedded for the sake of political alliance. For them, he, who had built God's Temple, built alongside of it heathen altars. Thus, idolatry, which David had been so zealous to suppress, was re-established in the palace. This brought to a close the glorious era ushered in by David and started the nation on its road to ruin. The apostasy of Solomon's old age is one of the saddest accounts in the Bible. Perhaps the account of it was intended of God to be an example of what luxury and ceaseless rounds of pleasure will do to even the best of men." (See Endnote 4.)

After the death of Solomon, the Kingdom of Israel was divided into two kingdoms. The northern kingdom consisted of ten tribes and was called Israel. It lasted a little over two hundred years and was destroyed by Assyria in 721 B.C. In all it had 19 different kings, many of whom worshipped other gods. Not one of these kings attempted to bring the people back to God.

The southern kingdom, which included the tribes of Judah and Benjamin, was called Judah. It had twenty different kings and lasted a little over three hundred years before it was defeated and then taken over by Babylon in 606 B.C. Jerusalem and the Temple were destroyed in 586 B.C. Of these kings, there were about eight who could be described as good kings. Time after time, God sent prophets to warn the people to turn from their own ways unto Him and to serve only Him. For brief periods, they would serve God. But as God said to the prophet Samuel when he was told to anoint Saul as Israel's first king, "Since the day I brought them up out of Egypt even unto this day, they continue to forsake Me and serve other gods at various times" (1 Sam. 8:8 paraphrased). The people as a whole still had not come to understand that there are no other gods except the LORD. To them there was the LORD, but many also believed that there were other gods also.

In a final effort to prepare a people through whom Jesus would come and who would begin the preaching of the Gospel, God allowed the Babylonians to carry off thousands of the Israelites into captivity in Babylon for over 70 years. After being in captivity in Babylon for many years, the Israelites finally came to the place where they knew there were no other gods except the LORD their God. In 536 B.C. 49,897 Israelites were allowed to return from Babylon to Jerusalem under the leadership of Zerubbabel to rebuild the temple and begin the worship of the only one and true God. From 457 B.C. to 432 B.C., Nehemiah as governor and Ezra as high priest rebuilt the walls and restored Jerusalem as a fortified city.

From that time on, the nation of Israel believed there was only one God, and no other gods existed. They were zealous in following the blood covenant made with Abraham and practiced circumcisions and did their best to follow the ten commandments and the Law of Moses along with observing the offerings, sacrifices and festivals that God gave to Moses and Israel at Mt. Sinai. They began to look for and long for the coming of the Messiah who would free them from foreign domination and who would be their king and rule over Israel and the rest of the world.

Finally, God had a prepared people through whom Jesus would come. Now there remained only two more phases of preparation before Jesus would come: PHASE TWO - The development of a common language and culture that would facilitate the spread of the Gospel. And PHASE THREE - The preparation of a political climate and government that would facilitate the spread of the Gospel.

PHASE TWO began with the rising power of Greece which parallels the rise of the Kingdom of Israel. The brilliant era of Pericles, 465-429 B.C., and the era of Socrates, 469-399 B.C., were contemporaneous with Ezra and Nehemiah and the times of the Old Testament prophet Malachi, 450-400 B.C. There is a period of 400 years of silence in the Bible between the Old Testament and the New Testament. However, during these 400 years of silence, we turn to history to see what was happening.

Alexander the Great, 336 B.C., at the age of 20, assumed command of the Greek army, and like a meteor, swept eastward over the lands that had been under the dominion of Egypt, Assyria, Babylon and Persia. By 331 B.C. the whole civilized world lay at his feet. On his invasion of the land of Israel in 332 B.C., he showed great consideration to the Jews, spared Jerusalem and offered immunities to the Jews to settle in Alexandria, Egypt. He established Greek cities all over his conquered domains and Greek culture and the Greek language became the common language and culture.

In His providence God was making the nations ready. Greece united the civilizations of Asia, Europe and Africa, and established one universal language. The language that the original New Testament books of the Bible would be written in was Greek.

PHASE THREE began with the rise of the Roman Empire. Rome first subdued Italy, 343-272 B.C., Greece and Asia Minor, 215-146 B.C., and Spain, Gaul, Britain, Teutons, 133-31 B.C. The Roman Empire reached the Zenith of its power from 46 B.C.-180 A.D. The Roman Empire extended from the Atlantic Ocean to the Euphrates River and from the North Sea to the African desert. Rome made one empire of the whole civilized world, and Roman roads made all parts of it accessible. Rome ruled its empire with a rod of iron so that there was real law and order with peace throughout the Empire.

As a result of this, there was a dispersion of Israelites through out the Empire with their synagogues and the Old Testament scriptures written in both Hebrew as well as in Greek called "The Septuagint." In Alexandria, Egypt, there were many Greek speaking Israelites and tradition tells us that one of the Greek rulers (Ptolemy Philadelphus) had 70 skillful Jewish linguists translate the Old Testament from Hebrew into Greek. Remember that Greek was the language of the world at that time. This version of the Old Testament was in common use in the days of Christ. And since the New Testament was written in Greek, many of its quotations from the Old Testament are from the "Septuagint" or Greek version of the Hebrew Old Testament.

So at the time of the birth of Jesus Christ, about 3 or 4 B.C., we can understand what the apostle Paul meant when he wrote: "When THE FULLNESS OF THE TIME was come, God sent forth his Son, made of a woman" (Gal. 4:4).

1. God had prepared a people through whom Jesus would come. A people who knew God and had been praying for the coming of the Messiah or Jesus, a people who would be able to go immediately into all the world and preach the Gospel.

2. God had prepared a world where there was a common culture and language (Greek) and all the Old Testament Scripture had been translated into Greek.

3. God had prepared a world with one government that provided law, order and peace and with roads that made all the civilized world accessible.

Within a normal lifetime of 70 to 80 years from the time of Jesus' birth, look at what happened. Not only was Jesus Christ born in Bethlehem, preached the Gospel, died on the cross to pay for our sins, established the new blood covenant (New Testament), arose from the grave and ascended into heaven, but also sent His disciples out unto the world to preach the Gospel.

Jesus Christ was thirty-three years old when He died on the cross. Yet within 40 years, the apostle Peter and the apostle Paul went to the west to Rome. According to tradition Paul went west as far as Spain. Tradition says that the apostle Thomas went to the east as far as India. Others went north and others south. The common language, culture, peace, law and order, along with Jews or Israelites that had scattered among the nations, paved the way for the propagation of the Gospel of Christ in their synagogues and their scriptures.

By 313 A.D. less than three hundred years after the birth of Jesus, "Christians numbered about one-half the population of the Roman Empire."(See Endnote 5.) In 313 A.D., the Roman Emperor Constantine issued an "Edict of Toleration" granting Christians full liberty to follow their religion. In 325 A.D., Constantine issued a general exhortation to all his subjects to embrace Christianity and made Christianity the religion of his court.

Today in 2005 A.D., there are missionaries to every country of the world. As the apostle John saw in a vision almost two thousand years ago, "And I saw another angel fly in the midst of heaven, having the everlasting Gospel to preach unto them that dwell on the earth, and to every nation, and kindred, and tongue, and people" (Rev. 14:6). Today we are witness to the fact that many, many television stations around the world are broadcasting the Gospel 24 hours a day, seven days a week. An example is Trinity Broadcasting Network that started with one station in Santa Ana, California 31 years ago. Now there are 6,525 stations world wide with broadcasts fed by 47 satellites circling the globe broadcasting the Gospel in many different languages. There are many mass crusades with evangelists such as Benny Hinn and Reinhardt Bonnke who are preaching the Gospel face to face in Gospel crusades with more than one million people in attendance. Now we can understand what Paul meant "In the fullness of time."

Prepare you the way of the LORD is how Mark begins the Gospel of Mark. For the first time in 400 years of prophetic silence, the prophet John the Baptist in the wilderness east of Jerusalem breaks the silence proclaiming the coming of the long awaited God the Son. Using the prophetic words given by the prophet Isaiah some seven hundred years earlier, John the Baptist tells the multitudes of people who came out into the wilderness to hear him preach to be baptized by him, "Prepare you the way of the LORD, make His paths straight." The writers of the Gospels tell us that all the land of Judea, and they of Jerusalem went out unto him and were baptized by him in the river of Jordan, confessing their sins.

During those days, Jesus Christ walked through the multitudes of people to John the Baptist. Upon seeing Jesus, John the Baptist proclaims to all, "BEHOLD THE LAMB OF GOD, WHICH TAKETH AWAY THE SIN OF THE WORLD" (John 1:29). Just as the high priest of Israel would take the blood of a sacrificial lamb into the Holy of Holies in the Temple once a year to make atonement for the sins of the people, Jesus would be the High Priest of all mankind who would take His own blood into the Holy of Holies in Heaven to make atonement once and for all for the sins of the world.

John the Baptist witnessed to the people that God the Father had told him that he would see God the Holy Spirit descending from heaven like a dove and abiding upon one who would be God the

Son come in human flesh. This would be the Son of God who has always existed and would baptize believers with the Holy Spirit. This happened while John the Baptist was baptizing Jesus and John bore record that Jesus is the Son of God.

The next day, John the Baptist was standing with two of his disciples, John and Andrew, and again told them, "Behold the Lamb of God!" Both John and Andrew understood what John the Baptist was saying and immediately began following Jesus. Andrew then finds his brother Simon Peter telling him, "We have found the Messiah, which is, being interpreted, the Christ" (John 1:40-41). In the next few days Jesus began calling together twelve men who would be His disciples and whom He would prepare for the next three years to be apostles to preach and spread the Gospel. They all believed He was the Son of God and the promised Messiah. They were expecting Jesus to overthrow the Romans who ruled over the land of Israel and were focused on His kingship. At first they did not understand that He had come first and primarily to be the High Priest that would make atonement for their sins and the sins of the world so that they could dwell with Him forever and God the Father and God the Holy Spirit.

When the angels announced the birth of Jesus to Mary and then Joseph, they both believed that He was the Messiah. When Joseph and Mary took the newborn child who was 40 days old to present him to the LORD at the Temple, they were met by an old prophet named Simeon and also an old prophetess named Anna. They told Joseph and Mary who this baby was and what He would be and do. The Bible tells us that Mary and Joseph pondered these things in their hearts trying to fit all the information together.

The apostle Paul so beautifully describes this whole process in Philippians 2:5-11, "Let this mind be in you, which was also in Christ Jesus: Who, being in the form of God, thought it not robbery to be equal with God: But made Himself of no reputation, and took upon Him the form of a servant, and was made in the likeness of man: And being found in fashion as a man, He humbled Himself, and became obedient unto death, even the death of the cross. Wherefore, God also has highly exalted Him, and given Him a name which is above every name: That at the name of Jesus every knee should bow, of things in heaven, and things in earth, and things under the earth; and that every tongue should confess that Jesus Christ is LORD, to the glory of God the Father."

The Bible tells us very little about the childhood and maturing years of Jesus. The only incident was when He was 12 years old sharing with the elders of the Temple in Jerusalem asking and answering questions. "And all that heard Him were astonished at His understanding and answers" (Luke 2:46-47).

Luke 3:23 tells Jesus began His ministry at about 30 years of age. This was the age that a priest of the tribe of Levi would begin his ministry in the Tabernacle or Temple and serve until about 50 years of age.

The public ministry of Jesus was about three-and-one-half years. The Bible tells us the common people gladly heard Him and paid attention to His words and miracles. Many really believed that He was the Messiah and were looking for Him to begin His reign over Israel and send the Romans on their way. However, the leaders of Israel were afraid that He would upset the Romans and that they would lose their positions of wealth and place in Jewish society. For a number of years the Jewish leaders were unable to find a way to stop Jesus.

However, it turned out that three-and-one-half years was enough time to present the Gospel, inaugurate the message of the Kingdom of God (as will be shared in chapter five: The Kingdom of God) and prepare His disciples to take the Gospel to the ends of the earth.

Now it was the FULLNESS OF TIME for Him to be the sacrificial Lamb of God and our High Priest to make atonement for all the sins of mankind and to bring about the PLAN AND PURPOSE GOD HAS FOR YOUR LIFE. That Jesus would make a NEW BLOOD COVENANT between man and God that would supersede the OLD BLOOD COVENANT made with Abraham and Israel.

Actually all that happened with Abraham when the old Blood Covenant was established, what happened to Israel as they and Moses came to Mt. Sinai in the wilderness receiving the Ten Commandments, the Law with the sacrifices and offerings, the Tabernacle and above all the Ark of the Covenant, all of these were a prophetic picture of what God the Son, Jesus Christ would accomplish at Jerusalem.

When Moses brought the Ark of the Covenant into the Holy of Holies in the Tabernacle, and King David brought the Ark of the Covenant to Jerusalem and when the Temple was built, the Ark of the Covenant was brought into the Holy of Holies in the Temple, God's actual presence filled both the Tabernacle and later on the Temple. As was pointed out earlier, the Israelites called it the Shekinah Glory (a glowing cloud of God's presence).

On the first Palm Sunday when Jesus came into Jerusalem riding on a donkey, the crowds welcomed Him by laying down their garments and palm branches before Him and shouting, "Hosanna to the Son of David: Blessed is He that cometh in the name of the LORD; Hosanna in the highest" (Matt. 21:9). All the city of Jerusalem was moved as Jesus went into the Temple and the chief priests and scribes saw the wonderful things that He did and the people rejoicing and praising God. Now it was more than the shekinah glory. It was God the Son who had physically come to fill the Temple with His actual physical presence.

Now no longer would the Ark of the Covenant be needed, because God the Son had physically come. For the next several days Jesus spent the days teaching, ministering, blessing and performing miracles in the Temple. As the apostle John wrote in his Gospel, "And the Word was made flesh, and dwelt among us, (and we beheld His glory, the glory as of the only begotten of the Father,) full of grace and truth." (John 1:14).

On the following Thursday evening, Jesus celebrated the feast of the Passover with His disciples in an upper room. The first Passover took place the day before Israel was led out of Egypt by Moses. Remember, God had instructed Moses to have each family in Israel prepare a lamb for a sacrifice, and to take the blood of the lamb and put it on the door posts and lintel of their house. That night, God sent a death angel to all the families in the land of Egypt. If the blood was not on the door post the death angel took the life of the first born in the family, whether it was an Egyptian family or a family of Israel. If the blood was on the door post, the angel of death would "pass over" the family. God said, "And the blood shall be to you for a token upon the houses where you are: and when I see the blood, I will pass over you, and the plague shall not be upon you to destroy you, when I smite the land of Egypt" (Exod. 12:13). The next morning all the Egyptian families had death in them and they begged the children of Israel to leave the land that day.

Jesus had come as the Lamb of God, to have His blood shed as the final sacrifice for the sins of mankind, to make atonement for our sins so that we would be able to come back into eternal fellowship with God.

That evening as Jesus celebrated the feast of the Passover with His disciples, He took a cup of wine and gave thanks, and gave it to them saying, "Drink you all of it; For this is My blood of the new testament (covenant), which is shed for many for the remission of sins" (Matt. 26:27-28). For years I wondered why the disciples were silent until I began to understand that the very silence of the disciples indicated they understood what He meant. They knew He was making a new blood covenant between man and God that would supersede the blood covenant made with Abraham.

This time the blood would actually be the blood of Jesus for man and for Christ the Son of God, establishing an everlasting, eternal blood covenant between man and God. Just as the golden text of the Bible says, "For God so loved the world, that He gave His only begotten Son, that whosoever believes in Him should not perish, but have everlasting life" (John 3:16).

That same evening, Jesus and His disciples left the upper room and went to the Garden of Gethsemane to pray. While there, Jesus was betrayed by Judas, one of His disciples, who led a band of soldiers and some officers of the chief priests to arrest Him. That night Jesus was tried by the religious authorities and then in the morning they tried Jesus before the Roman civil authorities asking for the death penalty of crucifixion. The Roman governor gave into the demands of the religious authorities and released Jesus to be crucified on the cross after having the soldiers scourge Him.

On Friday morning, the Roman soldiers led Jesus outside of the city of Jerusalem to crucify Him along with two other criminals. At about noon time, a great darkness covered the whole land. As you look, you can see three men hanging on three crosses. Two of them are struggling in agony, but the one in the middle is still in death. Take a good look at the one on the middle cross, he hardly looks human.

Hanging there limp in death, head bent low, and held only by the nails in his hands, his arms stretching upward from his hanging body. A rough crown of thorns clings to the head as it hangs down. His hair is matted with sweat and blood from the wounds by the thorns.

The Roman soldiers had used the whipping scourge well. His back, face and shoulders bear the deep gashes the pieces of metal of the whipping scourge had torn into his flesh. His body is covered by crimson blood oozing from the wounds. How truly did the prophet Isaiah describe Him hundreds of years before:

> "His visage was so marred more than any man, and
> His form more than the sons of men."
>
> Isaiah 52:14

> "He has no form nor comeliness and when we shall
> see Him, there is no beauty that we should desire
> Him. He is despised and rejected of men. . . and we
> hid as it were our faces from Him."
>
> Isaiah 53:2-3

From noon until 3:00 p.m., darkness covered the land and the crowd was now awe struck and silent. During these three hours Jesus had not uttered a word. Then suddenly like a sharp clap of thunder, a cry renders the heavens:

"MY GOD, MY GOD, WHY HAVE YOU FORSAKEN ME?"

Had God forsaken Him? When Jesus took upon Himself the sins of all mankind, God's holiness demanded that He separate Himself from His beloved Son. I believe that as Jesus went to the cross, He knew God would have to forsake Him for a time, that He would have to suffer the pains and penalty of sin. Jesus hung on the cross for six hours with it being dark during the last three hours, WHICH PICTURES SEPARATION FROM GOD. To Jesus the separation seemed to be a permanent desertion. The fear gripped Him that He Himself would be lost throughout eternity. In despair and desperation He cries out:

"MY GOD, MY GOD, WHY HAVE YOU FORSAKEN ME?"

The death of Christ is a picture of the death of a sinner. When those who have not accepted Christ as their Savior die in their sins, they go out into the black night of eternity without God. It will only be moments before they realize that all hope is gone and they are a lost, undying spirit facing the black night of eternity without God. "The harvest is past, the summer is ended, and we are not saved" (Jer. 8:20). They will experience that same terrible loneliness that Jesus did – being completely forsaken by God.

That evening was the beginning of the Sabbath day and the Jews did not want to leave bodies hanging on the crosses, so the soldiers came to break the legs of those crucified in order to hasten death. When they came to Jesus, they were utterly amazed that Jesus was already dead. One of the soldiers took his spear and thrust it into the side of Jesus and blood and water poured out. The prophet Zechariah had prophesied over 400 years ago concerning this: "They shall look upon Me whom they have pierced" (Zech. 12:10).

As it was pointed out in the first of this Second Chapter, God's Word proclaims that sin could only be paid for by death. By man dying physically and his spirit and soul being forever separated from God. The only other way or alternative acceptable to God would be another human being without "sin" dying in your place. Since all men have sinned and come short of the glory of God, the only other sacrifice that would be acceptable to God would be for His Son to come into their world as a man and live without ever committing a sin, and to die in our place. The Bible tells us over and over that the life of the body is in the blood. Why? It is the blood that brings oxygen, nutrition, etc. to the body and cleanses the body from wastes. Therefore, blood would have to be shed. The soul and spirit would have to be separated from God.

Therefore, Jesus would come into this world as a baby and become fully man. Live as a man without ever sinning. Then He would die by having His blood shed on the cross and experience having His soul and spirit separated from God. As Jesus died upon the cross, the greatest and most terrible part of His death was when as a sinner dies and goes out into eternity, to all of a sudden realize that his soul and spirit have been separated from God. That is why Jesus cried out with a loud voice, "MY GOD, MY GOD, WHY HAVE YOU FORSAKEN ME?"

As was also pointed out earlier in this chapter, when John the Baptist saw Jesus walking towards him through the multitudes of people he proclaimed to all, "BEHOLD THE LAMB OF GOD, WHICH TAKETH AWAY THE SIN OF THE WORLD." (John 1:29). Just as the High Priest of Israel would take the blood of a sacrificial lamb - once a year into the Holy of Holies in the Temple to make atonement for the sins of the people, Jesus would be the High Priest of all mankind who would take His own blood into the Holy of Holies in Heaven to make atonement once and for all for the sins of the world.

The writer of the book of Hebrews tells us that "Though He were a Son, yet learned He obedience by the things which He suffered; And being made perfect, He became the author of eternal salvation unto all them that obey Him; called of God a high priest after the order of Melchizedek" (Heb. 5:8-10).

The writer of Hebrews goes on to declare: "Seeing then that we have a great high priest, that is passed into the heavens, Jesus the Son of God, let us hold fast our profession" (Heb. 4:14).

This part I love: "Now of the things which we have spoken this is the sum: We have such a high priest, who is set on the right hand of the throne of the Majesty in the heavens; A minister of the sanctuary, and of the true Tabernacle, which the LORD pitched, and not man" (Heb. 8:1-2). Then we read in Hebrews 9:24, "For Christ is not entered into the holy places made with hands, which are the figures of the true; but into Heaven itself, now to appear in the presence of God for us."

With these declarations by the writer of Hebrews in mind, let us go back to Hebrews 9:11-12, "But Christ being come a high priest of good things to come, by a greater and more perfect Tabernacle, not made with hands, that is to say, not of this building: Neither by the blood of goats and calves, but by His own blood He entered in once into the holy place, having obtained eternal redemption for us."

The writer of Hebrews is able to declare, "And for this cause He is the mediator of the new testament (the new blood covenant), that by means of death, for the redemption of the transgressions that were under the first testament (the old blood covenant with Abraham), they which are called might receive the promise of eternal inheritance" (Heb. 9:15). This agrees with what the writer of Hebrews declares earlier: "By so much was Jesus made a surety of a better testament (covenant)" (Heb.7:22). Because of all these things, the writer of Hebrews encourages all of us as follows:

> "Seeing then that we have a great high priest, that is passed into the heavens, Jesus the Son of God, let us hold fast our profession. For we have not a high priest which cannot be touched with the feelings of our infirmities; but was in all points tempted like as we are, yet without sin. Let us therefore come boldly unto the throne of grace, that we may obtain mercy, and find grace to help in time of need." (Heb. 4:14-16)

The last words that Jesus spoke on the cross were this declaration: "IT IS FINISHED" (John 19:30). The body of Jesus was taken down from the cross, wrapped in linen cloths with spices and placed in a rock-hewn tomb in a nearby garden. A great rock stone rolled in front of the entrance which was sealed and a guard of soldiers placed in front of it.

On the third day early in the morning, there was a great earthquake as an angel of the LORD descended from heaven and rolled back the stone and then sat upon it. Tremendous fear fell on the guards, who trembled and became like dead men. When enough of their strength had returned to them, the guards went into the city and told the chief priests.

At that same time some of the women came with additional spices to finish the burial process. They were startled to see the stone rolled away. As they looked into the tomb, they saw the angel sitting on the right side dressed in a white robe. The angel told them not to be afraid and said to them, "Why do you seek the living among the dead? He is not here, but is risen: remember how He told you, when He was still in Galilee, Saying, The Son of man must be delivered into the hands of sinful men, and be crucified, and the third day rise again. And they remembered His words" (Luke 24:5-8). Then the angel told them to go quickly and tell his disciples.

That evening the disciples gathered together in a room with the doors shut for fear of the Jews, when suddenly Jesus stood in the midst of them. They were startled and frightened, and supposed that they saw a spirit. Then Jesus said, "Peace be unto you." As He said this, He showed them His hands and His side. Then the disciples were glad when they saw the LORD.

The apostle Luke tells us in the first chapter of the book of Acts that Jesus was seen by His disciples for the next 40 days. He was instructing them that they would receive the power of the Holy Spirit in Jerusalem in the next few days and then they were to take the Gospel not only to Jerusalem, Judea and Samaria, but unto the ends of the earth. Then they saw Him ascended up into the sky and a cloud received Him out of their sight. As they were seeing this, suddenly two angels in white appeared, stood by them and gave them this promise: "This same Jesus, which is taken up from you into heaven, shall so come in like manner as you have seen Him go into heaven" (Acts 1:11).

There were two other great events that occurred at this time. Before the CROSS, when the righteous died, they could not go into heaven until Jesus had made the final atonement for sin on the cross. The Bible describes that there was an abode for the dead called Sheol or Hades. It was divided into two separate compartments, one for the righteous and one for the sinful. As Jesus told the story of Lazarus and the rich man, Lazarus loved and served the LORD whereas the rich man lived only for self. When Lazarus died, he was carried by the angels into Abraham's bosom or as the Bible describes as paradise. The rich man also died and was buried, but he was not carried by the angels into Abraham's bosom. The next thing he knew he was in hell. When he lifted up his eyes, being in torment, he sees Abraham afar off and Lazarus with him.

The Bible says the rich man cried to Abraham saying, "Father Abraham have mercy on me, and send Lazarus, that he may dip the tip of his finger in water, and cool my tongue; for I am tormented in this flame. But Abraham said, Son, remember that you in your lifetime received your good things, and likewise Lazarus evil things: but now he is comforted, and you are tormented. And besides all this, between us and you there is a great gulf fixed: so that they which would pass from here to you cannot; neither can they pass to us, that would come from there" (Luke 16:24-26).

Then the lost rich man pleaded for Abraham to send Lazarus back to earthly life to warn his five brothers so that they would not come to this place of torment. Abraham told him that during this earthly life each one of us has to make his own decision. This goes back to what was explained in chapter one, that God has made each one of us with a free will. Each one has to make his own choice.

Remember that there were two thieves crucified with Christ. One mocked Jesus, but the other asked Jesus saying, "LORD, remember me when you come into Your kingdom. And Jesus said unto him, Verily I say unto you, Today shall you be with Me in paradise" (Luke 23:42-43).

You may wonder why Jesus did not go to heaven first, but instead went to paradise. All those who chose to serve God from Adam's time until that moment could not enter heaven until Jesus had made the final atonement for the sins of mankind. But at that moment in time, when the final atonement for sin had been made, He came to lead all these in Abraham's bosom (paradise) into the eternal presence of God the Father in heaven. Here is the apostle Paul's description, "Wherefore He says, When He ascended up on high, He led captivity captive, and gave gifts unto men. Now that He ascended, what is it but that He also descended first into the lower parts of the earth? He that descended is the same also that ascended up far above all heavens, that He might fill all things (Eph. 4:8-10).

The apostle Paul also declares that when God the Father raised Jesus Christ from the dead, that He set Jesus at His own right hand in heavenly places. "Far above all principality, and power, and might, and dominion, and every name that is named, not only in this world, but also in that which is to come: And has put all things under His feet and gave Him to be the head over all things to the church, Which is His body" (Eph. 1:21-23).

The apostle Paul made it definitely clear to the New Testament church that to be absent from the body is to be present with the LORD. (See 2 Corinthians 5:6-8.) All those who die in the LORD now go directly into Heaven to be with Jesus because the final atonement has been made for our sins.

However, Jesus gave us all an even greater promise and destiny. When Jesus appeared to the apostle John while he was banished to the island of Patmos, He told John, "Behold, I stand at the door, and knock: if any man hear My voice, and open the door, I will come into him, and will sup (live) with him, and he with Me. TO HIM THAT OVERCOMETH WILL I GRANT TO SIT WITH ME IN MY THRONE, EVEN AS I ALSO OVERCAME, AND AM SET DOWN WITH MY FATHER IN HIS THRONE" (Rev. 3:20 - 21).

WOW! WHAT A PURPOSE! WHAT A DESTINY! WHAT A PLAN!

In the next chapter, we will learn how God is preparing you for the plan and purpose for your life.

Endnotes:

[1] Henry H. Halley, *Halley's Bible Handbook,* (Zondervan Publishing House, 1965) p. 38.

[2] E.W. Kenyon, The Blood Covenant (Kenyon's Gospel Publishing Society, 1949) pp. 11-13.

[3] Henry S. Gehman, Editor *The New Westminster Dictionary Of The Bible*, (The Westminster Press, 1970) p. 439.

[4] Henry H. Halley, *Halley's Bible Handbook*, (Zondervan Publishing House, 1965) p. 192-193.

[5] Ibid, page 759

CHAPTER THREE

HOW GOD IS PREPARING YOU FOR THE PLAN AND PURPOSE FOR YOUR LIFE

Now we come to a very serious question. What is life's highest purpose? What is the one imperative thing – above all other things – most needful in life? Take a minute before you answer this question. Your answer will reveal a great deal concerning you. Your answer will uncover the attitude of your heart towards life, towards God and your purpose for living.

The ordinary man on the street may answer, "For me, the one most needful thing is to find happiness and the fullest enjoyment of life."

The religious person may say, "Fear God, and keep His commandments: for this is the whole duty of man."

I think of the testimony of an elderly woman in church who had a limited conception of life's highest purpose: "My highest aim is to make heaven my home." The great majority of the congregation listening to her testimony nodded their heads in agreement that this also was their highest goal in life.

In our society we usually judge men by their ability to obtain wealth, fame or power. They are rated according to the distance they have climbed up the ladder of success. If you are at the bottom of the ladder, you are considered a failure. If you reach the top of the ladder, you are considered a success. Those in between the bottom and the top represent the majority of us who sweat and struggle from youth to old age.

A few give up the climb and slide to the bottom and become inhabitants of a skid row. Others just continue to subsist on hand outs until nature forecloses on them and death takes them away. A few make it to the top. However, many of those who make it to the top are seldom happy and content for very long. They are tormented by fears that they may slip back.

This mania to succeed is a good thing perverted. The desire to fulfill the purpose God created for you is good. Sin has twisted this impulse into a selfish lust for first place or for top honors. By this lust the whole world of mankind is driven as by a demon, and there is no escape. This brings to mind Adolph Hitler of Germany or Joseph Stalin of Russia. When we come to the real plan and purpose that God has for our life we enter into a very different world. Jesus Christ said:

> "Blessed are the poor in spirit: for theirs is the kingdom of heaven."   Matthew 5:3

> "Blessed are the meek: for they shall inherit the earth."   Matthew 5:5

> "The last shall be first, and the first last."
>   Matthew 20:16

> "Whosoever shall seek to save his life shall lose it; and whosoever shall lose his life shall preserve it."
>   Luke 17:35

By man's standards, Jesus died an apparent failure on the cross. He had been discredited by the religious leaders and forsaken by His friends. Pilate, the Roman governor who ordered His death on the cross, was the apparent successful statesman whose hand all the political hacks kissed. It took the resurrection to demonstrate how gloriously Jesus Christ had triumphed and how tragically the governor had failed.

Yet today many in the church seem to have learned nothing. We are still seeing as men see and judging after the manner of man's judgment. How many hours of prayer are wasted asking God to bless projects that are geared to the glorification of men? Success in the eyes of men does not make us dearer to God or more valuable to the total scheme of things.

Is the success we want the success that is measured by man's standards or by our own standards? Or is it the success measured by what God thinks of us? Read what God said about the three following men:

> Enoch –"By faith Enoch was translated that he should not see death; and was not found, because God had translated him: for before his translation he had this testimony, that he please God" (Heb. 11:5).
> Abraham – "And the scripture was fulfilled which says, Abraham believed God, and it was imputed unto him for righteousness: and he was called the friend of God" (James 2:23).
> David – "God raised up unto them David to be their king; to whom also He gave testimony, and said, I have found David the son of Jesse, a man after Mine own heart, which shall fulfill all My will" (Acts 13:22).

However, the apostle Paul's great prayer for the Church was that each one of us would come to understand that the plan and purpose for your life is far beyond what most of mankind even begins to think about. Once again listen to what Paul says in Ephesians 1:16-2:10. Paul tells us that he ceases not to pray that the God of our LORD Jesus Christ would open the eyes of your understanding to understand the hope of His calling and the riches of the glory of His inheritance in the saints. As Jesus tells us in Revelation 3:21, we have been called to sit with Him on His throne and reign with Him in eternity, and that we would share in the riches of the glory of His inheritance. What does it mean to reign with Him and what are these riches that we have been called to share? In chapter seven we endeavor to give you a glimpse of these things as we talk about fulfilling God's plan and purpose for your life in eternity.

Paul continues to pray in Ephesians 1:16-2:10 that we would know "the exceeding greatness of His (God's) power to us-ward." That same power that raised Jesus Christ from the dead and set Him at His own right hand in heavenly places. That same power will also raise us up to sit with Christ in heavenly places. What God has planned for Christ, He wants you and I to be a part of it. "That in the ages to come He might show the exceeding riches of His grace in His kindness toward us through Christ Jesus" (Eph. 2:7).

As was stated back in chapter one, the reason God created this earth was to bring you and I into existence and to train and develop us for the eternal plans and purposes that He has for us in eternity. During our time on earth, you will have a vocation or several vocations; however, this should not be considered as your calling. Your earthly vocation may be that of an educator, minister, scientist, mother, etc. Your calling is God's plan and purpose for you in eternity.

There are seven major steps in answering God's calling.

STEP ONE – To Answer Yes

As Jesus said in Revelation 3:20, "Behold, I stand at the door, and knock: if any man hear My voice, and open the door, I will come in to him, and will sup (dine or live) with him, and he with Me."

Each one of us is a free moral agent. Each one of us has a free will. We have to decide whether we want to answer God's call or go our own way.

STEP TWO – Love

Jesus said the first and great commandment is, "You shall love the LORD your God with all your heart, and with all your soul and with all your mind" (Matt. 22:37).

What did Jesus mean by the word love? In our everyday life there are different types of love. There is the love between sweethearts, which is different than the love between a father and his son. Then there is the love between friends, which is different from the love a man has for his dog.

Which of these loves does Jesus command us to have? The answer is none of them. Does this surprise you? The answer is found in the name of God which is "Yahweh" in the Hebrew language and in the English it is translated "Jehovah." When Moses saw the burning bush in the wilderness and turned to investigate the burning bush, God spoke to him from the bush and instructed him to go to Pharaoh of Egypt and to tell him let God's people (Israel) go. Moses asked God what to say if they asked him what is his God's name? "And God said unto Moses, 'I AM that I AM': and He said, This shall you say unto the children of Israel, I AM has sent me unto you" (Exod. 3:14).

I AM is the first person singular of the verb "be." In the Hebrew language, the noun form of this verb is "Yahweh." God's name describes Him as the "self-being" or "self-existing one," having no beginning or no end. Now a "self-being" can either be self-giving or self-seeking. The Bible declares that God's love is that of a self-giving being as we read in John 3:16, "For God so loved the world, that He gave His only begotten Son, that whosoever believes in Him should not perish, but have everlasting life." Or as the apostle Paul writes in Romans 5:7-8, "For scarcely for a righteous man will one die: yet peradventure for a good man some would even dare to die. But God commendeth His love towards us, in that, while we were yet sinners, Christ died for us."

Although we have only one word in the English language for the word love, in the Greek language of the New Testament there are a number words that we translate with only the word love. In the Greek language of the New Testament there is the word "agape" which describes self-giving love, a love that will love without being loved in return that gives value to the person being loved. A second word is "phileo" which describes the love between a father and son or family members. A third word commonly used in Greek literature was "eros" which is never found in the New Testament. It is a love that is self-seeking, that loves because it gets something out of it, a love that springs from sensual desire. Our English word "erotic" comes from this word.

In the New Testament the word used to describe God's love for us is "agape." When Jesus said, "You shall love the LORD your God with all your heart, and with all your soul, and with all your mind," the Greek word "agape" is used. God's love is that action of a person giving of himself. This is how you and I are to love God - to give of ourselves.

The opposite of real love is a person seeking for self. Listen to the description the Bible gives of Satan in Isaiah 14:12-14, "How are you fallen from heaven, O Lucifer, son of the morning! how are you cut down to the ground. . . . For you have said in your heart, I will ascend into heaven, I will exalt my throne above the stars of God: I will sit also upon the mount of the congregation in the side of the north. . . . I will be like the most High." He was entirely self-seeking.

When Adam and Eve ate of the Tree of Knowledge of Good and Evil, they did it out of selfishness. They saw a tree to be desired for food, to make one wise. Selfishness does not love. It thinks only of itself and seeks only for itself. In answering God's calling, His eternal plan and purpose for your life, is to respond with a love of giving yourself completely to God. Your only desire is to please Him and not for what you can get out of Him.

STEP THREE – Faith

The Bible declares, "But without faith it is impossible to please God" (Heb. 11:6). Before Enoch was translated, he had this testimony that he pleased God. Why? Because he had faith. Why was Abraham called the friend of God? Because he believed God, and God counted it unto him for righteousness and he was called the friend of God. (See James 2:23.)

The Bible does not scientifically prove there is a God. The Bible starts out in Genesis 1:1, "In the beginning God. . ." There can be no dealings with the invisible God unless there is an absolute faith in His existence. We believe in His reality, even though we cannot see Him. In Hebrews 11:1 we read, "Now faith is the substance of things hoped for, the evidence of things not seen."

So what is faith? Many people look for some kind of a feeling. In my teen years I believed that faith had something to do with feelings. For example, when I messed up some situation and asked God for forgiveness, I would peer inside of my self to see if I felt forgiven. If I could locate such feelings, then I was sure that God had heard my prayer and had forgiven me. Now I know that this was a false test of faith.

None of us would be so foolish to go to a railroad station and board the first car we saw, then sit down in it and try to feel whether or not this was the train that would take us where we wanted to go. Our feelings would obviously have no bearing on the facts. Yet, I know now that at times my actions in the spiritual realm have been just that foolish. If you do not know what train to board, you would ask the station manager or conductor for directions and then act on their word.

In the same sense, faith begins when you hear God's word and believe His word. Then faith grows when you not only believe God's word, but begin to obey His word. When God spoke to Noah that a flood was coming and that he should build the ark to save himself and his family, Noah believed God's word and built the ark. Noah did not see any rain at first. He did not see any threatening danger. However, he still believed God's word and obeyed. That is faith and it pleases God.

When Abraham was told to leave his homeland and journey to a distant land that God would show him, he did not know where he was going. But he believed God's word, obeyed and started traveling. Faith is simply believing, obeying and doing God's word. The Bible tells us that this pleases God.

God's word tells us that we are to work six days, and on the seventh day you are to rest and keep it as a day unto the LORD. Faith is simply believing God's word and obeying His word. God's word tells us to bring one-tenth of all your increase or income unto the house of the LORD and to prove Him. Faith is believing His word and obeying it by bringing one-tenth of your increase or income into His house. This is faith and it pleases God.

For years a lot of us have thought that faith was some complicated thing or mystical thing that brought about miracles. Faith is nothing more than just believing God's word and obeying it. God's word says in Revelation 3:20, "Behold, I stand at the door, and knock: if any man hear My voice, and open the door, I will come in to him, and will sup (dine or live) with him, and he with Me." The "knocking at the door" is simply when we hear the Gospel, to "open the door" and to simply believe what we are hearing and receive it. Then Jesus will literally come into your life.

The Bible declares in Romans 10:17, "So then faith comes by hearing, and hearing by the Word of God." Now catch these two words: FAITH COMES. When we hear God's word, receive and believe His word, FAITH COMES.

I want to make a distinction between the following:

SAVING FAITH - FRUIT OF FAITH - GIFT OF FAITH

In Ephesians 2:8 we read, "For by grace are you saved through faith; and that not of yourselves: it is the gift of God." When we hear Jesus knocking at the door of our heart or hear and believe the message of salvation, and ask Jesus to come into our life, not only does Jesus Christ come into our life, but the Bible promises: "The Spirit (Holy Spirit) itself bears witness with our spirit, that we are the Children of God" (Rom. 8:16). That "witness" is a special gift that God gives us to confirm our faith. This is what many of us like to call "saving faith".

Now that faith has been planted in our lives, God wants that faith to grow as a tree brings forth much fruit, that we continually hear and believe His word and obey it and let it bring forth much fruit in our lives.

There are times when the Holy Spirit will give you a "special word" from God. Many times it may be like a special word dropped into your heart and a "witness of the Holy Spirit" that this is God's special word. As you believe and obey that special word, miracles or supernatural things take place. This is what I would call a "gift of faith".

STEP FOUR – Obey

Now if we love God the Father, God the Son, God the Holy Spirit, and if we believe what God says unto us about having faith, then next step is to "obey". As Jesus said in the Sermon on the Mount in Matthew 7:21, "Not everyone that says unto Me, Lord, Lord, shall enter into the kingdom of heaven; but he that does the will of My Father which is in heaven."

As I pointed out in chapter one, God created man to have dominion. The other creatures of creation were put under man's authority. Adam and Eve were told that they could eat of the trees of the Garden of Eden with the one exception; the Tree of Knowledge of Good and Evil. The crux of this charge was more than the forbiddance to eat the fruit of a certain tree. It was that God was putting Adam and Eve under His authority so that Adam and Eve might learn obedience. If Adam and Eve had learned to be obedient, God would have entrusted them with more authority. But like Satan who rebelled in heaven, Adam did his own thing and thought he was able to distinguish good from evil and to judge what was right and what was wrong.

The greatest of God's demands on man is not for him to bear a cross, make offerings or even deny himself. The greatest demand is for him to simply "obey". In Genesis 12:1-4, when God told Abraham to leave his homeland, his father's family and relatives and go to a land that He would show him, what did Abraham do? He obeyed and started out for a land without knowing where he was going, but believed that God would direct him.

When God told Abraham in Genesis 22:2 to take his son Isaac and offer him as a burnt offering on Mount Moriah, (which is now the Temple Mount in Jerusalem) what did Abraham do? He obeyed. And because Abraham not only believed God, he obeyed God's direction and built an altar and placed Isaac on the altar. As Abraham raised the knife to slay Isaac as an offering, God stopped him. God said there was a ram caught in a thicket behind him that Abraham could use as the offering. Then God said this, "By Myself have I sworn, says the LORD, for because you have done this thing, and have not withheld your son, your only son: That in blessing I will bless you, and in multiplying I will multiply your seed as the stars of the heaven. . . . And in your seed shall all the nations of the earth be blessed; because you have obeyed My voice" (Gen. 22:16-18).

The first king of Israel was King Saul. He missed what God had planned for him. On one occasion as he was preparing for battle with the Philistines, the prophet Samuel instructed him before going to battle to wait at Gilgal for seven days until Samuel came to offer the burnt offerings and peace offerings to the LORD. When Samuel had not come ahead of time and the army was beginning to scatter, Saul took it upon himself to make the offerings. Just as he finished making the offerings, Samuel came. Samuel asked Saul what he had done. Saul replied the people were scattering and he forced himself to make the offerings rather than wait for Samuel. Then Samuel told Saul, "You have done foolishly: you have not kept the commandment of the LORD your God, which He commanded you: for now would the LORD have established your kingdom upon Israel. . . . But now your kingdom shall not continue" (1 Sam. 13:13-14).

Later on the LORD commanded King Saul to go into battle against the people of Amalek and utterly destroy all men, women, children and animals. The LORD gave King Saul and Israel a tremendous victory over the Amalekites, but King Saul spared Agag, the king of the Amalekites, and the best of the flocks and herds. When Samuel came to King Saul after the victory, he asked Saul why he had not obeyed the command of the LORD to utterly destroy all the people and animals. Saul blamed it on the people who said they wanted to offer the animals as an offering unto the LORD. Samuel's answer to Saul demonstrates how important it is to obey the LORD. I Samuel 15:22-23, "And Samuel said, 'Has the LORD as great delight in burnt offerings and sacrifices, as in obeying the voice of the LORD? Behold, to obey is better than sacrifice, and to hearken than the fat of rams. For rebellion is as the sin of witchcraft, and stubbornness is as iniquity and idolatry. Because you have rejected the word of the LORD, He has also rejected you from being king.' "

God chose David to become king of Israel in place of Saul. In the next chapter we will spend some time on how God prepared David for kingship. Even though David had some problems and committed some terrible sins, he finally came to the place where he became completely obedient to God. As the apostle Paul says in Acts 13:22, "And when He (God) had removed him (Saul), He raised up unto them David to be their king; to whom also He gave testimony, and said, I have found David the son of Jesse, a man after Mine own heart, which shall fulfill all My will."

The Bible teaches that when Jesus came into this world as flesh, as a child and as a man, He learned obedience. At the age of twelve He went to Jerusalem with Mary and Joseph at the time of the

Passover. He spent His whole time in the Temple hearing the teachers of the Law and asking them questions. When the family left to go back to Nazareth, Mary and Joseph assumed that Jesus was with the group of family and friends going back to Nazareth. After a day of traveling, Mary and Joseph looked for Jesus, but could not find Him. Going back to Jerusalem, on the third day they found Jesus sitting in the Temple listening and asking questions of the teachers of the Law. Mary and Joseph could not understand why Jesus would have stayed behind without telling them. Jesus replied, "did you not know that I must be about My Father's business?" (Luke 2:49). But Jesus obeyed them immediately and went back to Nazareth and was subject to them.

When Jesus went into the Garden of Gethsemane with His disciples on the night before His crucifixion, He separated Himself from them a small distance and fell on His face and prayed that He would not have to face the horrible ordeal of death on the cross and separation from His Father. The Bible says that His sweat became like great drops of blood falling down upon the ground. Many think this was due to the fear and dread of the crucifixion, but it goes back to 1 Samuel 15:22, "Behold, to obey is better than sacrifice, and to harken than the fat of rams." Jesus ended His time of praying saying, "Not My will but Your will be done" (Luke 22:42).

As the apostle Paul writes in Philippians 2:8, "And being found in fashion as a man, He humbled Himself, and became obedient unto death, even the death of the cross." Or as the Bible says in Hebrews 5:8-9, "Though He were a Son, yet learned He obedience by the things which He suffered, And being made perfect, He became the author of eternal salvation unto all them that obey Him."

Wouldn't it be wonderful if obedience could be imparted as a gift like salvation or eternal life? But God made obedience something to be learned. It does not come naturally, but is a learned accomplishment.

I well remember when in high school I took a typing class to learn how to type. Each one of us had a typewriter with a keyboard. However, the top of the keys had no letters of identification. My first reaction was, "That's the dumbest thing I ever saw." All the while I was poking the keys on that machine, it kept right on misspelling what I was trying to type. Many a time I would get so frustrated that I wanted to take my fist and punch it right into the middle of the keyboard. However, with strong trying and frustration, I persevered. Day by day I kept at it until suddenly that typewriter began to click, click, click. To my amazement, it started spelling. Every skill is acquired by repetition. God has ordained that we learn obedience this same way, day by day.

STEP FIVE – Overcome

Jesus Christ promised you and me in Revelation 3:21, "To him that overcomes will I grant to sit with Me in My throne, even as I also overcame, and am set down with My Father in His throne." Remember that Jesus said in the previous verse Revelation 3:20 that He stands at the door (man's will) and knocks and if any man will open the door, He will come in and live with him and that man will live with Him. Salvation and eternal life with Jesus is a free gift. If we accept Jesus into our lives, we will live with Him forever. However, there is another step that we can take that we will not only live with Him forever, but that we will be able to sit with Him on His throne and be with Him at the center of all that He is doing through all eternity. There is this requirement, "To him that overcomes will I grant to sit with Me." What does Jesus mean by "overcome"?

That evening before His crucifixion Jesus told His disciples, "These things I have spoken unto you, that in Me you might have peace. In the world you shall have tribulation: but be of good cheer; I have overcome the world" (John 16:33). Picture Jesus at that moment. The next morning He would be crucified and the next afternoon placed in a tomb. It looks like a picture of total defeat. Yet Jesus is saying, "I have conquered the world or overcome the world." Caesar and the Roman Empire have disappeared, but Jesus is still building His kingdom.

One of the most important things for you to see is that all the promises in the Bible are yours. And one of them is: "In the world you shall have tribulation." That means trials, tests, problems and troubles. You can't escape that, it is one of the promises. But Jesus also promised, "In Me you shall have peace, so cheer up, I have conquered the world." He wants you and I to learn to reign over life. He is preparing us to sit with Him on His throne and to reign with Him in eternity.

It is not whether you have problems, troubles or trials, but how you react or respond to them. God is preparing you to reign with Him in eternity. As the apostle Paul writes in Romans 5:3-5, ". . . but we glory in tribulations also: knowing that tribulation works patience; And patience, experience; and experience, hope: And hope makes not ashamed; because the love of God is shed abroad in our hearts by the Holy Spirit which is given unto us." Through the trials, tribulations and experiences in life we are learning to "overcome" them and God is building character in our lives in order to bring us to a level of maturity so that we will be able to reign with Him.

Picture these experiences as stair steps that lead us to full maturity or to become a true "overcomer".

Self-Control

Humility

Goodness

Love

Joy

Peace

Faith

Hope

Experience

Patience

Tribulation

Another picture of an "overcomer" is in the parable where Jesus said the Kingdom of God is as a man traveling into a far country, who called his own servants and delivered unto them his goods. And unto one he gave five talents, to another two and to another one. Then he left on his journey.

While the master was away on his long journey, the servant who received five talents went out and traded with them and gained five more talents. And likewise he who had received the two talents, he also gained two more talents. But the one who had received the one talent went and dug a hole in the ground and hid his master's money.

After a long time, the master returned and called all these servants to give an account. The man to whom he had entrusted five talents and who went out and made another five talents, brought back the ten talents to this master. The master praised him for his good work and said since he had been faithful over a few things, he would make him ruler over many things. Next came the man who had received two talents with the report, "Sir you gave me two talents to use and I have doubled it." "Good work," his master said. "You are a good and faithful servant. You have been faithful over this small amount, so now I will give you much more." Then he which had received the one talent came and said, "Sir, I knew you were a hard man, and I was afraid, so I hid your money in the earth and here it is." Instead of receiving any praise, the master condemned him and had him cast out. Two of these servants are a picture of an "overcomer" and the third is a picture of a "failure".

The apostle Paul was able to say at the end of his life, "I have fought a good fight, I have finished my course, I have kept the faith: Henceforth there is laid up for me a crown of righteousness, which the LORD, the righteous judge, shall give me at that day: and not to me only, but unto all them also that love His appearing" (2 Tim. 4:7-8).

In the Bible, an Old Testament prophet by the name of Zechariah saw in a vision the high priest named Joshua standing before the LORD on His throne. I believe the LORD was telling Joshua that if he would be an "overcomer" he would rule with the LORD in His house, have charge of His courts, access to His presence and places to walk among those who stand by the throne. "If you will walk in My ways, and if you will keep My charge, then you shall also judge My house, and shall also keep My courts, and I will give you places to walk among these that stand by" (Zech. 3:7).

One of the greatest examples of how God wants you and I to become "overcomers" is the account of the children of Israel being led by Moses through the wilderness after they came out of Egypt. This was a time of preparation for them before they could enter into the Promised Land.

Remember our lives are only a time of preparation for what God has planned for us in eternity. God has given us the promise of eternal life and the privilege of sitting with Him on His throne if we overcome. God has given us the principles that He wants us to follow to inherit or obtain these promises. We have already talked about four of them:

Step One – Yes
Step Two – Love
Step Three – Faith
Step Four – Obey

In step five God puts us to the test to prove us, like a test pilot takes up a new airplane into the sky to test and prove the flight ability of the airplane. If we pass the flight test, we are an overcomer. In the example of Israel we see these four principles explained in Deuteronomy Chapters 6 and 8.

Promise
Principles
Proving
Provision

Let us take a closer look at the four principles in becoming an overcomer.

PROMISE

- To give them the land promised to their fathers that flows with milk and honey (Deut. 6:3).
- To give you great and goodly cities, which you did not build (Deut. 6:10).
- To give you houses full of all good things, which you did not fill and wells you did not dig, vineyards and olive trees which you did not plant (Deut. 6:11).
- To give you the land which He sware unto your fathers (Deut. 6:23).

PRINCIPLES

Love – "You shall love the LORD your God with all your heart, and with all your soul, and with all your might" (Deut. 6:5).

Faith – "You shall fear the LORD your God, and serve Him, and shall swear by His name" (Deut. 6:13).

Obey –"You shall diligently keep the commandments of the LORD your God, and His testimonies, and His statutes, which He has commanded you" (Deut. 6:17).

PROVING

"And you shall remember all the way which the LORD your God led you these forty years in the wilderness, to humble you, and to prove you, to know what was in your heart, whether you would keep His commandments or not. And He humbled you, and suffered you to hunger, and fed you with manna, which you knew not, neither did your fathers know; that He might make you know that man does not live by bread only, but by every word that proceeds out of the mouth of the LORD does man live" (Deut. 8:2-3).

"Who fed you in the wilderness with manna, which your fathers knew not, that He might humble you, that He might prove you, to do you good at your later end" (Deut. 8:16).

PROVISION

Under the leadership of Joshua, Israel entered and conquered the Promised Land.

Now when Israel was going through the times of God's proving in the wilderness, they had the choice of three alternatives.

1. Take another lap. If they failed a time of proving, they

could take another "lap around the mountain," so to speak. This is illustrated by the number of times they failed to trust and believe God for water. When they first entered the wilderness, they came to Marah and the water was so bitter they could not drink of it. The people murmured and complained. Moses cried unto the LORD for help. The LORD instructed Moses how to make the waters sweet. However, the children of Israel did not learn the lesson of trusting the LORD. As they journeyed on in the desert wilderness to Rephidim, they came to a place where there was no water. Once again the people were ready to stone Moses. He cried out to the LORD for help. The LORD told Moses to stand before the rock in Horeb and smite it, which he did, and water came forth out of the rock.

Years later when the children of Israel came to Kadesh, there was no water. Once again they rebelled and accused Moses and the LORD of leading them into the wilderness to die. And once again Moses interceded with the LORD for them and water came out of the rock at Kadesh. For almost forty years the children of Israel wandered around in the wilderness <u>taking another lap</u> around the mountain.

2. <u>Bleached Bones</u>. Because of their unbelief, all the adults that left Egypt wandered in the desert wilderness up to forty years and died in the wilderness. They became <u>bleached bones</u>, so to speak. The only exceptions were Joshua, Caleb, Moses and all the children who were twenty years old or younger.

3. <u>Stand and Enter</u>. Joshua, Caleb and the younger generation believed God and obeyed by crossing the Jordan River and entered the Promised Land. They are examples of what an "overcomer" is.

We see this same principle in the earthly life of Jesus. As He was baptized by John the Baptist in water, the Holy Spirit descended upon Him like a dove and a voice from heaven said, "This is My beloved Son, in whom I am well pleased." Then Jesus was led by the Spirit into the wilderness to be tempted of the devil. Here we see the promise, "You are my beloved Son, in whom I am well pleased." Now the principle was would Jesus be tempted to doubt God's Word? The proving came as the devil tempted Him for forty days (as Jesus was fasting and praying) trying to get Him to question what God had said. "If you be the Son of God, command this stone that it be made bread" (Luke 4:3). Jesus answered the devil by quoting Deuteronomy 8:3, "man does not live by bread only, but by every word that proceeds out of the mouth of the LORD."

Then the devil took Jesus up into a high mountain and showed Him all the kingdoms of this world in a moment of time. And the devil said, "All this power will I give you, and the glory of them. . . . If you therefore will worship me, all shall be yours" (Luke 4:5-7). Jesus answered, "You shall worship the LORD your God, and Him only shall you serve" (Luke 4:8). (See also Deuteronomy 6:13.)

After this the devil took Jesus to a pinnacle of the Temple and said to Him, "If you be the Son of God, cast yourself down from here: For it is written, He shall give His angels charge over you, to keep you: and in their hands they shall bear you up, lest at any time you dash your foot against a stone" (Luke 4:9-11). Once again Jesus answered from Deuteronomy 6:16, "You shall not tempt the LORD your God."

After this time of proving, Jesus as an overcomer, returned in the power of the Spirit into Galilee and there went out a fame of him through all the region round about. If you and I are overcomers, we will also share with Jesus in His rulership. As He said in Revelation 3:21, "To him that overcomes will I grant to sit with Me in My throne, even as I also overcame, and am set down with My father in His throne."

When you and I enter eternity and stand before the Judgment Seat of Christ, He will examine our lives to see if we are "overcomers". The apostle Paul writes in 1 Corinthians 3:11-15 that all of us are building on the foundation of Jesus Christ.

> "For other foundation can no man lay than that is laid,
> which is Jesus Christ. Now if any man build upon

their foundation gold, silver, precious stones, wood, hay, stubble; Every man's work shall be made manifest: for the day shall declare it, because it shall be revealed by fire; and the fire shall try every man's work of what sort it is. If any man's work abide which he has built there upon, he shall receive a reward. If any man's work shall be burned, he shall suffer loss: but he himself shall be saved; yet so as by fire."

1 Corinthians 3:11-15

In Revelation 7:17 we read, "For the Lamb which is in the midst of the throne, shall feed them, and shall lead them unto living fountains of waters: and God shall wipe away all tears from their eyes." If they are already in Heaven, what are they crying about? In Revelation 21:4, the apostle John is describing the new heaven and the new earth as well as the new Jerusalem and that God Himself will be dwelling with us. Yet John goes on to say in Revelation 21:4, "And God shall wipe away all tears from their eyes; and there shall be no more death, neither sorrow, nor crying, neither shall there be any more pain: for the former things are passed away."

What do you think they are crying about? When they are in eternity, they will see what God's plan and purpose for their life was in eternity, but instead of being an overcomer, they will see that they traded it for a position, wealth, fame or something they thought was more important in their life on earth. They will be crying "Oh, LORD I didn't." But Jesus will have to say, "Yes you did! However in My love for you, you will be with Me forever and in My final act of grace, in order for you to enjoy eternity, I am washing away all your tears (I am going to remove this memory from you and the former things will come into your mind no more)."

STEP SIX – Prevailing in Prayer

When you and I stand before the Judgment Seat of Christ and we look back over our earthly life, the most amazing feature of that earthly life will be its prayerlessness. We shall be almost beside ourselves with astonishment that we spent so little time in real prayer and intercession. It is as the Bible tells us in Isaiah 59:16, "And He (God) saw that there was no man, and wondered that there was no intercessor." As Isaiah the prophet says, "And there is none that calls upon Your name, that stirs up himself to take hold of You" (Isa. 64:7). God has given man dominion over this world and only intervenes when we pray. When Jesus took His disciples with Him into the Garden of Gethsemane to pray on the night before His crucifixion, He asked them to pray with Him as He went a few steps away from them to pray Himself. A short time later, He came to the disciples and found them asleep. He asked, "What could you not watch with Me one hour?" (Matt. 26:40). Let us take a look at what happened when men did pray.

One day after Abraham entered the Promised Land, he was sitting in the door of his tent in the heat of the day. Suddenly three men appeared before him. One was the LORD and two were angels. He urged the three to stay there and have a meal with him, which they consented to do. After they finished eating, the LORD told Abraham that his wife Sarah, who was 89 years old, and Abraham, who was 99 years old, would have a son the next year according to the time of life. Sarah laughed, since both of them were well past the age of having children. However, the LORD reaffirmed that Sarah would have Isaac.

Then the LORD and the two angels arose and started toward Sodom. Abraham walked with them on the way. The LORD shared with Abraham why they were going to Sodom. The wickedness of the people, the homosexuality and their sins had come before Him and now the time of judgment was come. Abraham immediately thought of his nephew Lot and began to intercede in prevailing prayer for Lot and his family. Abraham drew near and said, "Will You also destroy the righteous with the wicked? Peradventure there be fifty righteous within the city, will You also destroy and not spare the place for the righteous that are there? That be far from You to do after this manner, to slay the righteous with the wicked: and that the righteous should be as the wicked, that be far from You: Shall not the Judge of all the earth do right?" (Gen. 18:23-25).

The LORD said He would spare the city if there were fifty righteous persons in the city. Then Abraham proceeded to prevail in prayer to the LORD that if there were only ten righteous persons in the city, would He spare it? As the two angels traveled to the city of Sodom, they did not even find ten righteous, but because Abraham had prevailed in prayer, they took Lot, his wife and two daughters by the arm and brought them outside the city before fire and brimstone were rained down upon the city and destroyed it. This type of praying (learning to prevail in prayer) was preparing Abraham for future rulership in eternity.

Now let us look at Abraham's grandson, Jacob. As a young man, Jacob wanted the things of God. However, his brother Esau was the first born and by rights, all the promises made to Abraham were to go to the first born. But Jacob schemed and cheated his brother Esau out of the birth rights and blessings. As a result, Esau planned to kill Jacob after the death of his father Isaac. Jacob fled to the ancestral homeland of his grandfather Abraham. Twenty years later the LORD told Jacob to return home to his father Isaac which also meant that he had to face his brother Esau.

When Esau learned that Jacob was returning home, he took a party of 400 men to meet Jacob on his return. In fear Jacob divided up the possessions that he had gained over the last 20 years in smaller groups and sent them ahead as presents to meet Esau, hoping to make the meeting friendly rather than a blood bath.

At the brook Peniel, Jacob sent all his possessions, wives and children before him across the brook while he remained that night and began to pray. The Bible tells us that Jacob was left alone and wrestled a man there all night. As day was breaking, the man saw that Jacob would not let him go, so He touched the hollow of Jacob's thigh and put his hip out of joint. He commanded Jacob to "Let me go, for day is breaking." But Jacob said, "I will not let you go, except you bless me." Jacob realized he was wrestling with the LORD and was determined not to let go. Then the LORD said to Jacob, "Your name shall be called no more Jacob (the heel-grabber or the supplanter), but Israel (a prince with God): for as a prince have you power with God and with men, and have prevailed" (Gen. 32:28). As the sun arose, Jacob called the brook "Peniel" which means "for I have seen God face to face, and my life is preserved"

(Gen. 32:30). As he crossed the brook, he was now a prince with God who had learned to prevail in prayer. Jacob took one of the most valuable steps that the LORD wants everyone of us to take in preparation for our future rulership with Christ in eternity.

Moses probably knew God better than any other man in the Old Testament and certainly had learned to prevail in prayer. Remember that Moses and Elijah appeared on that mountain in Galilee when Jesus was transfigured before Peter, James and John into His former glory. Both Moses and Elijah were speaking with Jesus concerning His coming crucifixion in Jerusalem. In the book of Exodus 31-32, we are told that when Moses was upon Mount Sinai receiving the Ten Commandments, the Law and instructions on the Tabernacle, that during his absence, Aaron and the children of Israel made an idol of a golden calf and began to worship it. In His anger God turned to Moses saying, "Now therefore let Me alone, that My wrath may wax hot against them, and I will make of you a great nation" (Exod. 32:10). Listen on how Moses prevailed in prayer for the children of Israel:

> "And Moses besought the LORD his God, and said, LORD, why does Your wrath wax hot against Your people, which You have brought forth out of the land of Egypt with great power, and with a mighty hand? Wherefore should the Egyptians speak and say, For mischief did He bring them out, to slay them in the mountains, and to consume them from the face of the earth? Turn from Your fierce wrath, and repent of this evil against Your people. Remember Abraham, Isaac and Israel, Your servants, to whom You swared by Your own self, and said to them, I will multiply your seed as the stars of heaven, and all the land that I have spoken of will I give unto your seed, and they shall inherit it for ever. And the LORD repented of the evil which He thought to do unto His people." Exodus 32:11-14

However, Moses did not stop there in praying for the people. When he went down from the mountain and saw for himself what the people had done, Moses' anger also waxed hot against the people. He threw down the tablets that God had written the Ten Commandments upon. The tablets were broken in pieces and then Moses took the golden calf idol they had made and ground it into powder and spread the powder on the drinking water and made the children of Israel drink the water. Then Moses went back to the LORD and continued to prevail in prayer.

> "Oh, what a great sin these people have committed! They have made themselves gods of gold. But now, please forgive their sin – but if not, then blot me out of the book You have written." The LORD replied to Moses, 'Whoever has sinned against Me I will blot out of My book. Now go, lead the people to the place I spoke of, and My angel will go before you.' "
>
> Exodus 32:31-34 NIV

Stop and think for a moment of the place Moses will have in ETERNITY. In responding to God's calling for God's plan and purpose for his life in eternity, Moses had learned to prevail in prayer.

The great prophet Elijah was also a man that knew how to prevail in prayer. When Israel had turned away from serving the LORD under King Ahab and Queen Jezebel, the prophet Elijah appeared one day before King Ahab and proclaimed, "As the LORD God of Israel lives, before whom I stand, there shall not be dew or rain these years, but according to my word" (1 Kings 17:1).

Three years later after there was no dew or rain and great famine in the land, Elijah presented himself to King Ahab with the challenge that all Israel and the prophets of Baal be gathered together at Mount Carmel. The prophets of Baal would take a bullock, cut it in pieces, lay it on wood and put no fire under it. Elijah would also do the same with another bullock. The challenge was that each group would call upon their god and the god that answered by fire, let him be God. The prophets of Baal went first and called upon their god Baal all day long and there was no answer. At the time of the evening sacrifice, Elijah had prepared his offering and had them pour twelve barrels of water on his sacrifice until the water ran around about the altar and also filled the trench around it with water. Then Elijah prayed a simple prayer and the fire of the LORD fell and consumed the sacrifice, the wood, the stone and licked up the water that was in the trench.

Then Elijah commanded the people to take all the false prophets of Baal (850 men) and Elijah brought them down to the brook Kishon and slew them there. After this Elijah told Ahab to get up, get something to eat and drink and prepare to get back to Jezreel (the palace) for a great rain storm was coming.

Elijah went up to the top of Mount Carmel and cast himself down upon the earth and put his face between his knees and began to pray for rain. After praying, Elijah sent his servant to go up and look toward the sea to see if any rain was coming. The servant went and came back and said there was no sign of rain. Instead of being discouraged, Elijah prayed and sent his servant again to go and look. The servant came back with the same report. However, Elijah learned how to prevail in prayer and sent the servant seven times. He was not giving up until the LORD answered.

The seventh time the servant came back and said, "Behold, there arises a little cloud out of the sea, like a man's hand" (1 Kings 18:44). Elijah told the servant to go up to King Ahab and tell him to prepare his chariot and get down to Jezreel before the rain would stop him. "And it came to pass in the meanwhile, that the heaven was black with clouds and wind, and there was a great rain. And Ahab rode, and went to Jezreel" (1 Kings 18:45). It is so important in our earthly sojourn, that we learn to prevail in prayer as we prepare for the plan and purpose that God has for us in eternity.

The great prophet Daniel knew what it was to fast and pray. Many of the prophecies that were revealed to him came as he prevailed in prayer. In Daniel 10, Daniel set his heart to prevail in prayer. As he fasted and prayed for 21 days, he finally prevailed in prayer as an angel appeared unto him. As Daniel was on his hands and knees trembling, the angel spoke to Daniel saying, "Fear not, Daniel; for from the first day that you did set your heart to understand, and to humble yourself before your God, your words were heard, and I am come for your words (in response to them). But the prince of the kingdom of Persia withstood me twenty-one days: but, lo, Michael, one of the chief princes, came to help me; and I remained there with the kings of Persia. Now I am come to make you understand what shall befall your people in the latter days: for yet the vision is for many days (a time yet to come)" (Dan. 10:12-14).

All of us have been called to rule and reign with Jesus Christ in eternity. However, a part of our preparation is learning to prevail in prayer. You may feel that you are a nobody and unimportant. Before Jesus was born in Bethlehem, there was an old man in Jerusalem by the name of Simeon who had prayed for years for the coming of the LORD's Christ. When the baby Jesus was brought to the Temple in Jerusalem for dedication, Mary and Joseph were met by Simeon. He took the Christ Child up in his arms and blessed God, the baby, Mary and Joseph. Simeon prophesied concerning the baby and what He would do. He had prevailed in prayer.

Also there was a widow by the name of Anna who was eighty-four years of age. She lived with her husband only seven years. Since his death, she did not depart from the Temple all those years, but fasted, prayed and served God night and day in prayers and fasting for the coming of the Christ. Although this man and woman were not important in the sight of man, they prevailed in prayer until the Messiah was born in Bethlehem. Their whole earthly life may not have been important in the sight of man. However, they were prepared for the plan and purpose God has for them in eternity. I truly believe that in eternity they will have a very important and blessed place as they rule and reign with Jesus Christ.

STEP SEVEN – The Development of the "spirit" that God Has Given Us to Worship, to Praise, to Take Authority and Dominion

A. Developing Our "spirit"

Have you ever stopped to think what God looks like? Do we look like Him? What kind of shape or form does He have? What do you expect to see when you get to heaven? Jesus gave us an answer to these questions when He was sitting at Jacob's well by the town of Sychar in Samaria. A woman of Samaria had come to draw water and Jesus asked her for a drink of water. The woman was surprised that Jesus, being a Jew, would ask her, a Samaritan, for a drink of water because the Jews would have no dealings with Samaritans. Then Jesus told her that if she knew who He was, she would ask Him for the living water. This surprised the woman because she knew Jesus had nothing to draw water with and the well was very deep. When Jesus began to tell the woman about her past, she said unto Him, "Sir, I perceive that you are a prophet."

She had some questions about God such as where was God worshipped, what was God like, and she wanted to know more about God. Jesus gave her a very direct answer, "God is a Spirit: and they that worship Him must worship Him in spirit and in truth" (John 4:24).

Now what did Jesus mean? Let us first see what is meant by "God is a Spirit." It is only natural for us to put God in human terms. If you are expecting God to have a physical form or body like ours, how would you explain the following scriptures?

> "No man has seen God at any time; the only begotten Son, which is in the bosom of the Father, He has declared him."   John 1:18

> "And the Father Himself, which has sent Me, has borne witness of Me. You have neither heard His voice at any time, nor seen His shape."   John 5:37

If the above scriptures are true, what did Moses see on Mount Sinai? What did Isaiah see in the Temple in Isaiah 6? What did the disciples hear on the Mount Transfiguration when they heard a voice from heaven saying, "This is My beloved Son, in whom I am well pleased" (Matt. 17:5). Does the Bible contradict itself? Look at the following three Bible verses:

> "Who is the image of the invisible God."
>   Colossians 1:15

"Now unto the King eternal, immortal, invisible, the only wise God, be honor and glory forever and ever."
1 Timothy 1:17

"Who only has immortality, dwelling in the light which no man can approach unto, whom no man has seen, nor can see."
1 Timothy 6:16

Here we read that Jesus, John and Paul declare no man has ever seen God. These Scriptures show that God has nothing of a material or bodily nature like ours. He is not to be seen with a material eye. He is not to be found in human terms or limitations. When King Solomon had built and dedicated the Temple in Jerusalem, he declared, "But will God indeed dwell on earth? behold, the heaven of heavens cannot contain You; how much less this house that I have builded?" (1 Kings 8:27).

It is a simple truth that graven images were not to be made unto God since no one knows what He looked like. "To whom then will you liken Me, or shall I be equal? says the Holy One. (Isa. 40:25).

This is why Jesus declared, "GOD IS A SPIRIT." When Jesus suddenly appeared to His disciples in a closed room on the evening of His resurrection, they all thought they were seeing a spirit and were terrified. He said unto them, "Why are you troubled? and why do thoughts arise in your hearts? Behold My hands and My feet, that it is I myself: handle Me, and see; for a spirit has not flesh and bones, as you see Me have" (Luke 24:38-39).

We have a very simple illustration of all this. When a person dies we put his body in the grave but believe that his spirit goes to heaven. But we cannot see the human spirit. You cannot see the real me or the inner man that dwells in my physical body. And when Jesus said, "God is a Spirit", He is also saying God is not to be thought of in anthropomorphic terms or physical terms. God is not to be apprehended by the five senses: sight, hearing, touch, smell or taste. But God is to be apprehended through our inner man or our spirit. That is why back in Genesis 1:26, "And God said, Let us make man in Our image." As God is a spirit, man is also a spirit dwelling in an earthly body.

Although God made our physical bodies out of the dust of the ground, He has uniquely designed man's inner-being as "spirit" after His own image or "Spirit." It is a whole new spiritual mechanism which operates on an entirely different frequency than the physical or natural. God has created man with a spirit which is designed to be able to continually be conscious of God's Spirit, to fellowship and commune with His Spirit and to know and be aware of His presence.

The trouble with most men is that they try to reach God through the natural or physical. But since God is a Spirit, He cannot be known through the physical. Whether man does it consciously or subconsciously, God can only be known through our spirit. The physical has not been designed by God for this special function of God-consciousness.

This is why Jesus told the Samaritan woman, "God is a Spirit" and they that worship Him must worship Him in spirit and truth. And all this takes us back to Genesis 1:26 when God had a conference among the Godhead concerning His plan and purpose for man at creation. "Let us make man in our image (God is a Spirit and man is a spirit) and likeness (God is a trinity and man is a trinity as pointed out in chapter one – body, soul, spirit) and let him have dominion. With our body we have contact with the physical realm. With our soul we have contact with our intellect, personality, talents, emotions, ego, mind and the natural realm. It is only with our spirit that we are able to continually be conscious of God's Spirit and to be able to fellowship and commune with Him.

The trouble with most men is that they try to reach God through the physical or mental realm. You cannot contact God with your mind. Your mind can only think about Him. You cannot contact God with your body. The physical has not been designed by God for this special function of God-consciousness. You can only contact God with your spirit. When God contacts you, it is through your spirit, unless He sends an angel or something in the natural realm.

When you hear the Word of God preached, at first you hear it with your physical ears. It then goes through your natural mind. But if it is to affect you, you must receive it in your spirit. Knowing that God contacts us through our spirit helps us to understand 1 Corinthians 2:14, "But the natural man receives not the things of the Spirit of God: for they are foolishness unto him: neither can he know them, because they are spiritually discerned."

You may have read certain portions of the Bible over many times, never understanding the meaning. Then one day as you read along, suddenly you see it. And you ask, "Why didn't I see that before?" It was just then that you understood it with your spirit. You must receive the revelation of God's Word in your spirit. It is spiritually understood and you have to understand it with your spirit. If you try to understand it with just the natural mind, many times it will remain as a mystery. As the Bible says in Proverbs 3:5, "Trust in the LORD with all your heart (spirit); and lean not unto your own understanding." Most of us practice this in reverse. We trust with all our understanding, and lean not to our own spirit (heart).

It is imperative that we as believers recognize a spirit exists within us. There is something extra to thought, knowledge, imagination and emotion. In Proverbs 20:27 we are told, "The spirit of man is the candle of the LORD, searching all the inward parts of the belly." Let the Holy Spirit light your candle. Let it shine. It is in our spirit that we can know God, fellowship with Him, sense His presence, hear His voice, know His will, sense other spirits and discern evil spirits. The apostle Paul encourages us in Romans 8:1, "walk not after the flesh, but after the Spirit."

We spend most of our earthly lives training and developing the body and the soul with its intellect, personality, talents and knowledge. However, the most important pursuit in our earthly lives should be to develop the spirit. The development of our spirit is what will be primary in God's plan and purpose for us in eternity. As we learn to develop the spirit that God has given us in learning how to worship, how to praise and how to take authority and dominion, only then will we be able to fulfill the plan and purpose God has for us in eternity.

When the apostle John was caught up into the third heaven and saw God's throne, the most important activity that he saw was the worship of the angels, the twenty-four elders and all the saints from all ages in worship before the throne. While here on our earthly journey, you and I can learn and develop the most important activity that we will be involved doing for eternity – WORSHIP.

Now we come to the most important part that I wish to share with you. Your spirit has to be trained, developed and exercised, just as you train your body through exercise; your mind by reading, listening, learning; just as you develop your personality by learning to share and communicate; just as you learn to control your emotions; just as you learn to exert your will. You and I need to not only recognize that we are a spirit, but learn to know it, train it, develop it and use it.

When Jesus called His twelve disciples, they were already developed in body, mind and personality. But then He discipled them for three years by enrolling them (as a manner of speaking) in the school of the Spirit in order to develop and train their spirits so that they would develop into the men of God that He was calling them to be and for the plans and purposes He had for them in eternity. In Matthew 19:27-28, Peter said unto Jesus, "Behold, we have forsaken all, and followed You; what shall we have therefore? And Jesus said unto them, Verily I say unto you, That you which have followed Me, in the regeneration when the Son of man shall sit in the throne of His glory, you also shall also sit upon twelve thrones, judging the twelve tribes of Israel."

In my own personal experience, I went through eight years of college in undergraduate studies and graduate studies. Yet I don't remember anyone ever telling me that I needed to train and develop my spirit. I was in the ministry a number of years when one Sunday evening, an evangelist came to visit in the evening service as a part of the congregation. After the service I had the privilege of meeting him for the first time and invited him to my home for an evening of fellowship.

As we sat there in the living room talking, he said he could tell me a number of things about various people in the congregation. I knew he had never met these people before, but as he described what the various people looked like, he began to tell me what was going on in their lives and what they were up to doing in the church. My first reaction was to think he had a spiritual gift of the Holy Spirit called the "word of knowledge," to which he replied, "No." He said, "Pastor you have never bothered to train your spirit. All that is happening is that my spirit is sensing what is in their spirits."

All of a sudden, I knew he was right. I had spent years developing the mind. Everything had to be logical, reasonable and acceptable to my mind. If I ever sensed anything with my spirit, I never paid any attention. I never knew I was to train and develop my spirit. I had spent a great deal of time developing my body, my mind and trying to win and influence people.

The apostle Paul spent a lot of time talking about new believers and comparing them to "babes in the LORD." When we first come to Jesus, we are like a new born baby spiritually. There is nothing wrong with being a baby as long as we do not remain a long time in this stage of development. We are to mature into a child and then into adulthood. Every adult begins as a child, but if we remain one too long, then we become a problem.

The apostle John tells us of a Jewish ruler named Nicodemus who came to Jesus by night. He realized Jesus was a teacher come from God and wanted to become a part of what Jesus was doing. Jesus told him, "I say unto you, Except a man be born again, he cannot see the Kingdom of God. Nicodemus said unto him, How can a man be born when he is old? can he enter the second time into his mother's womb, and be born? Jesus answered, Verily, verily, I say unto you, Except a man be born of water and of the Spirit, he cannot enter into the Kingdom of God. That which is born of the flesh is flesh; and that which is born of the Spirit is spirit" (John 3:3-6).

Up to this time, Nicodemus did not realize he had a spirit. But that evening, Nicodemus experienced his spirit being given a rebirth by God's Holy Spirit.

All of us need this rebirth of our own spirit by the Holy Spirit. God gave us a whole new spiritual mechanism which operates on an entirely different frequency than the soul and body. God has made us with a spirit which is designed to be able to be continually conscious of His Spirit and presence, to be able to fellowship and commune with Him.

The human spirit has a voice. We call that voice conscience. Sometimes we call it intuition or inner-voice. The world often calls it a hunch. But it is your spirit speaking to you. The Bible often refers to the "spirit of man," the "heart" or the "hidden man."

And as we previously said, the Bible compares a new believer to a baby in the LORD. The life in his spirit which has been born again is as a tiny and weak baby naturally born. There is nothing wrong with his being a baby as long as he does not remain too long a time at this stage. Each believer is to develop that spirit. When we ask Jesus to come into our life, there comes a time when we know that Jesus has come into our heart. As the apostle Paul writes in Romans 8:16, "The Spirit itself bears witness with our spirit, that we are the children of God."

There are a number of ways to develop our spirit. At this time I wish to point out seven steps. One of the most important steps to take is to ask Jesus for the baptism of the Holy Spirit. After Jesus arose from the dead and before He ascended back to heaven, He commanded His disciples not to depart from Jerusalem, but wait for the promise of the Father. "For John truly baptized with water; but you shall be baptized with the Holy Spirit not many days from now." And as a result, "you shall receive power, after that the Holy Spirit is come upon you: and you shall be witnesses unto Me in both Jerusalem, and in all Judea, and in Samaria, and into the ends of the earth." (Acts 1:4-8).

As Jesus finished speaking this to His disciples, He ascended into a cloud back to heaven. As they were watching this, two angels stood by in white apparel and told them as they saw Jesus ascend into heaven, so in like manner would they see Him return. The disciples obeyed and went back to Jerusalem into an upper room and there they fasted and prayed waiting for the Holy Spirit.

Ten days later on the day of Pentecost (the Feast Day that was a prophetic picture of the coming of the Holy Spirit, when the first of the grain harvest was dedicated to the LORD) these disciples were the first harvest of the church. As recorded in Acts 2:1-4, "And when the day of Pentecost was fully come. . . . suddenly there came a sound from heaven as of a rushing mighty wind, and it filled all the house where they were sitting. And there appeared unto them cloven tongues like as of fire, and it sat upon each of them. And they were all filled with the Holy Spirit, and began to speak with other tongues (or languages they did not know), as the Holy Spirit gave them utterance." There were about 120 disciples there. That same day, as Peter preached to the crowds that came to see what was going on, over three thousand people accepted Jesus as the Messiah and became a part of the Church. This was the first harvest of the Church represented by the Feast of Pentecost.

The languages or tongues that the disciples spoke under the power of the Holy Spirit did not come from their minds or languages that they knew. The Holy Spirit came upon their spirit and the language that they spoke came from their spirit. Their natural minds heard the words but did not understand the words. Others standing by who knew the language heard them speak. What amazed the bystanders was how these disciples, who were mostly from Galilee, could speak in these different languages. The important truth to see here is that the Holy Spirit was using their spirit to speak. As the apostle Paul says in 1 Corinthians 14:14-15, "For if I pray in an unknown tongue (language), my spirit prays, but my understanding (mind) is unfruitful. What is it then? I will pray with the spirit, and I will pray with the understanding also." But this process is learning to recognize and develop your spirit to fellowship, to communicate with the LORD and to be used by the LORD.

As you learn to recognize the Spirit of God communicating to you through your spirit, you need to listen and obey. How many times I have longed for the LORD to appear to me in a vision, dream or hear an audible voice. The keynote to every great life that is described in the Bible is they heard God speak and then did what God told them to do. Remember Jesus said in John 14:10, "The words that I speak unto you I speak not of Myself: but the Father that dwells in Me, He does the works." Here Jesus is saying that He was guided by an indwelling voice, not an external appearance. This saying of Christ is of great importance. For years I thought the men of the Bible always saw or heard an audible voice. But I have discovered that in the great majority of instances in Bible history, that they only heard an indwelling voice. We have no right to imagine an audible voice or visible appearance, unless it is distinctly stated to be such.

Before his conversion the apostle Paul was on the road to Damascus to arrest Christians and bring them back to Jerusalem. In order for God to get his attention, He had to knock him off his donkey. If you read the story, at high noon a bright light shined down from heaven and God had to speak audibly to him. Paul asked, "Who are you LORD?" (Acts 9:5). But from that time on, Paul learned that the Holy Spirit dwells within you, not in your head, but in your spirit, that God communicates with you through your spirit. God speaks to us with this inward voice to our spirit. As the apostle Paul says in Romans 8:14, "For as many as are led by the Spirit of God, they are the sons of God." God is going to lead you and guide you through your own spirit. You need to know that. "The spirit of man is the candle of the LORD." (Prov. 20:27). Too many believers miss it because they are not making full use of what belongs to them. It is like having a piano and only playing one key at a time.

A famous Chinese Christian leader, Watchman Nee, tells the story of some Chinese farmers in a remote area of China who accepted the LORD. There was no local church for them to be trained in and to learn the ways of the LORD. During the cold winters, the farmers liked their rice wine to keep warm. One day during the cold winter, the farmer said to his wife, "Resident Boss says for us not to drink the wine any more." He did not know how to put what he was experiencing in theological terms, but to him "Resident Boss" was the Holy Spirit speaking to his own personal spirit. When Watchman Nee came through their area a few months later, he asked Watchman Nee about the experience. Watchman Nee said, "Very good, very good brother, always obey what "Resident Boss" tells you to do." And then he went on to explain how the Holy Spirit speaks and works with our own spirit in the things of the LORD.

We need to realize that God is going to guide us through our own spirits. The Bible uses the terms "the heart" and "the spirit" interchangeably. As Hebrews 4:12 says, "For the word of God is quick, and powerful, and sharper than any two-edged sword, piercing even to the dividing asunder of soul and spirit, and of the joints and marrow, and is a discerner of the thoughts and intents of the heart." If our spirit or heart has been trained and developed in the Word of God and in the ways of God, our spirit becomes a safe guide. However, let me encourage you that just as you did not begin school in the first grade one week and graduate from the twelfth grade the next week, your spirit will not be educated or trained over night. You have to learn the difference between impressions that come from your emotions or mind, and those that come from the spirit. Remember emotional impressions come and go. The voice (impressions) of the Spirit are here today, tomorrow and next week.

The Holy Spirit always leads and guides as a shepherd does with sheep. If you feel pushed, hurried or pressured, remember the Holy Spirit is always gentle. Satan usually likes to push, pressure or make us feel hurried. For example, the Holy Spirit says, "Come and pray for awhile." Satan will say "Go pray". To illustrate this, go up to someone, push him and say "Go pray." That is how you usually feel when Satan is trying to lead you.

We have talked about two important ways to develop our spirit, the Baptism of the Holy Spirit and learning to recognize the indwelling voice of the Holy Spirit.

A third important step in developing our spirit is to let the peace of God rule our heart or spirit. As the apostle Paul writes in Colossians 3:15, "And let the peace of God rule in your hearts, to the which also you are called in one body; and be you thankful." The "peace of God" is another method the Holy Spirit uses to speak to our spirit. Many times I have received a telephone call and have been asked to do something or go someplace. Many times I would like to say, "Let me pray about it and I will call you back later." But the phone call required an immediate answer. All I could do was pause for a moment and see if I had the "peace of God" in my spirit. If the "peace of God" was there in my spirit, I could answer in the affirmative. But if there was no peace and only agitation, I would have to decline.

Many times I had the peace of God while going to a certain place or carrying out a request. Many times it was something I did not like personally, but I knew I was doing what God wanted because there was the peace of God in my spirit. However, if you are all upset, disturbed, troubled and maybe even irritated, that is not the peace of God. The indication in your spirit is that it is not God's will. When I first started listening to the prompting of the voice within, I often went the wrong direction.

I was relieved when I discovered that Peter, Paul and other disciples had this same problem. Remember one day when Jesus and the disciples were crossing the Sea of Galilee. Jesus said, "Beware of the leaven of the Pharisees" (Matt. 16:6). The disciples tried to reason what He meant. Is it that Jesus is telling us that we have forgotten to take the lunch? That had nothing to do with what Jesus was endeavoring to tell them. Their inability to perceive what Jesus was telling them is comforting to me in several ways. First it shows all good disciples at times are a little slow to understand. Secondly, it shows the Master is always rich in patience. Because of our slowness to understand, sometimes God is forced to use visions or dreams to guide us.

An example of this is found in Acts 16, Paul and Silas had gone throughout the region of Galatia. They wanted to go to Asia, but the Holy Spirit suffered them not. They could not sense the peace of God. Then they decided to go to Bithynia, but once again they did not have the peace of God. Then they stopped at Troas and knew they had to wait until the Spirit of God directed them. That night, the Master who is always rich in patience gave Paul a vision of a man standing in Macedonia and pleading with him, saying, "Come over into Macedonia and help us." Immediately, Paul and Silas and those with him sensed the peace of God and endeavored to go to Macedonia, concluding that God had called them to preach the Gospel in Macedonia. As a result a number of great New Testament churches were established in Macedonia and Greece.

When the peace of God is disturbed in your spirit, take care. When there is unrest, uncertainty, agitation or a pushing urgency, it could be from Satan or our own human nature. Remember, God leads, Satan pushes. You can be sure you are moving in the will of God when what you are doing is (1) in agreement with the written Word of God (The Bible), (2) you sense the Holy Spirit speaking to your spirit, and (3) you have the peace of God in your spirit.

A fourth step in developing our spirit is to learn to recognize various spirits by our own spirit. Throughout the Gospels we read about Jesus doing this. In Mark 2:8, "And immediately when Jesus perceived in His spirit that they so reasoned within themselves, He said unto them, Why reason you these things in your hearts?" In His spirit, Jesus perceived that the scribes sitting in a house where a man sick of palsy had been brought in were reasoning in their hearts (spirits) that Jesus was speaking blasphemies when He said to the sick man, "Son, your sins be forgiven you." Then He asked them directly, is it easier to say to the sick man, "Your sins be forgiven you; or to say, Arise, and take up your bed and walk?" (Mark 2:9). So Jesus commanded the man to take up his bed and walk. Jesus by His spirit sensed what they were thinking in their spirits.

With our own spirit we are able to recognize other spirits such as a person with a gentle spirit, proud spirit, contrite spirit, or evil spirit. Sometimes when your spirit is sensitive to other spirits, it is more than you can take when you are around many individuals that have a bad or evil spirit. So an important step in training and developing our spirit is to take time, relax and be sensitive to the spirits of other people around you.

I shared earlier in this chapter about the visiting evangelist that came to the Sunday evening service of a church that I was pastoring and afterwards in a time of fellowship in my home, he began to describe various people in the congregation that he had never met before and related what was going on in their lives and what they were doing in the church. As he described to me, it was not a gift of the Spirit, but that he had learned and developed his own spirit to be able to sense what kind of spirit other people had and what was happening in their lives. It would be somewhat like looking at another person with your eyes and taking note of the color of their eyes, their hair and other physical characteristics. Now, however, you would be focusing the attention of your spirit upon their spirit, taking note of what you sensed with your spirit. However, as a mature Christian, be careful not to get mystical and get carried away.

A fifth step in developing our spirit is learning "to obey" the inward voice of the Holy Spirit speaking to our spirit. As Jesus said in John 16:13, "Howbeit when He, the Spirit of truth, is come, He will guide you into all truth: for He shall not speak of Himself; but whatsoever He shall hear, that shall He speak: and He will show you things to come." Remember the Holy Spirit dwells within you, not in your head, but in your spirit. The Holy Spirit is going to communicate with you through your spirit because that is where He is. Your spirit gets its information and direction through Him, if you will listen. Many times we miss it because we try to get God to come over into the sense realm or physical realm. We want to put out a fleece or have a vision or something in the physical realm. But nowhere in the New Testament does it say: "As many as are led by a fleece, they are the sons of God." But the Bible does proclaim, "For as many as are led by the Spirit of God, they are the sons of God" (Rom. 8:14). God is going to lead you and guide you through your own spirit. Therefore, we need to learn to obey the voice of the Spirit speaking to our spirit.

A very important sixth step in developing our spirit in hearing the voice of the Holy Spirit is learning to be quiet before the LORD. A good example of this is when you may be working with a fish bowl and you get the sand and other particles in the water all stirred up. It is not possible to clearly see what is going on in the fish bowl. If the water is all stirred up, you have to stop and wait until all the sand and particles in the water settle down. Then you can clearly see and continue your project. In my experience, God has hardly ever spoken to me until I was quiet and relaxed in my spirit. In the Bible there are number of examples of this. The prophet Ezekiel in Ezekiel 44:15-16 says, "But the priests, the Levites, the sons of Zadok, that kept the charge of My sanctuary when the children of Israel went astray from Me, they shall come near to Me to minister unto Me, and they shall stand before Me to offer unto Me the fat and the blood, says the LORD God. They shall enter into My sanctuary, and they shall come near to My table, to minister unto Me, and they shall keep My charge."

They were only to come into the Holy Place by themselves, just the one priest in the presence of the LORD. Also they were only allowed to wear linen clothes and not wear any garment that would cause them to sweat. They were to be still, quiet, and at peace as they came before the LORD. It is as the psalmist says in Psalms 46:10, "Be still, and know that I am God." The writer of the Gospel of Luke tells us that Jesus needed to do this during His earthly ministry: "great multitudes came together to hear, and to be healed by Him of their infirmities. And He withdrew Himself into the wilderness, and prayed" (Luke 5:15-16). There is the old saying, "The bow that is always strung will soon lose its strength." You cannot be sensitive to the Spirit when all tense, tied up in programs and busy doing busy work.

Tradition tells us that when the apostle John was on the island Patmos and received the vision of Jesus and the visions recorded the Book of Revelation, he was relaxed and playing with a pet parrot.

The times in my own life when God's Spirit began speaking to my spirit was when I was quiet and relaxed. In 1962 I was walking down Spring Street in Los Angeles going to work and enjoying the morning. It was just as real as a person coming along and walking with me when the Holy Spirit began speaking that in a few weeks I would begin my first ministry as pastor of a church in Oregon. I remember standing across the street from an automobile dealer's showroom admiring a new 1967 Chrysler sedan. The Holy Spirit spoke and said that the LORD was going to give me that car. A few days later, one of the deacons in the church where I was pastor drove that same car into my driveway and said, "Here is your car."

I will never forget a time in the spring of 1969 when my ministry was in a time of transition. I had been fasting and praying and seeking the LORD. After a number of days I became discouraged because I had not heard from the LORD. I went home in frustration. I can remember sitting down in an easy chair, picked up the newspaper and was reading the comic strip. Suddenly I heard a voice speaking. I turned to my left to see where it was coming from. However, I realized it was not a physical voice, but the voice of the Holy Spirit, speaking to my spirit that in the coming summer season, I would be pastoring in the place the LORD wanted me to be. That summer I became pastor of a church that has been the most fruitful time of my ministry. I find that the LORD has never spoken to me when I have been all tensed-up and distracted.

A seventh step in developing our spirit is through prayer and fasting. In the Sermon on the Mount as recorded in Matthew 6:1-18, Jesus taught how the giving of alms, praying and fasting develops our spirit. Not only did He teach this, but demonstrated it by His own personal example. Immediately after being baptized in the Jordan River by John the Baptist, Jesus was led by the Holy Spirit to spend forty days praying and fasting in the wilderness. "And Jesus being full of the Holy Spirit returned from the Jordan, and was led by the Spirit into the wilderness. . . . And in those days He did eat nothing" (Luke 4:1-2).

When Jesus went into the wilderness, He was already full of the Holy Spirit, for the Bible distinctly tells us the Holy Spirit descended in a bodily shape like a dove upon Him (Luke 3:22). But after the praying and fasting in the wilderness, the Bible tells us: "Jesus returned in the power of the Spirit into Galilee: and there went out a fame of Him through all the region round about" (Luke 4:14).

In Psalms 35:13, King David said, "I humbled my soul with fasting." The apostle Paul says in 1 Corinthians 9:27, "But I keep under my body, and bring it into subjection: lest that by any means, when I have preached to others, I myself should be a castaway." Through prayer and fasting, the body and soul are brought under subjection to the spirit which allows the spirit to be more fully developed under the Holy Spirit. Our body and soul make wonderful servants of our innermost self, the spirit. But if not kept under the control of the spirit, they can become terrible masters. As one minister said, "My stomach does not tell me when to eat, but I tell my stomach when to eat."

In order for our spirit to be fully developed by the Holy Spirit, it is necessary that there be times of prayer and fasting. This is illustrated over and over again throughout the Bible in the lives of the saints like Moses, David, the prophets, apostles and the leaders of the New Testament Church.

B. Developing Our "spirit" In Worship

As I have stressed over and over, God's ultimate plan and purpose for your life in eternity is as the apostle John writes in Revelation 1:6, "And has made us kings and priests unto God and His Father; to Him be glory and dominion for ever and ever. Amen." As Jesus said in Revelation 3:21, "To him that overcomes will I grant to sit with Me in My throne, even as I also overcame, and am set down with My Father in His throne."

However, God has an even higher purpose for Himself. He wants your love, worship and fellowship. In Luke 10:38-42, we read the story of Mary, Martha and their brother Lazarus who lived in Bethany. Martha had invited Jesus into her home for dinner. While she was busy preparing the dinner, her sister Mary sat at the feet of Jesus listening to Him and fellowshipping with Him. Martha felt overwhelmed with the task of preparing the dinner. In her frustration she turned to Jesus and said, "LORD, do you not care that my sister has left me to serve alone? Bid her therefore that she help me." At the moment, Jesus revealed His heart and the heart of the Father when He said to Martha, "Martha, Martha, you are careful and troubled about many things: But one thing is needful: and Mary has chosen that good part, which shall not be taken away from her" (Luke 10:41-42).

Remember that in Genesis 3:8, we are told that in the cool of the day the LORD God would walk in the Garden of Eden with Adam and Eve to talk and fellowship with them. This is a picture of our Heavenly Father, like an earthly father who looks forward to the end of the day when he can come home to his children to love, fellowship, talk and enjoy them. Just think of the pleasure it brings an earthly father when his children come to him expressing their love and appreciation.

This is the very scene that the apostle John saw when in Revelation 4, he saw a door opened in Heaven and was told to "Come up here and I will show you things which must be hereafter." As John entered Heaven, he saw the throne of God and all the elders, angels and saints worshipping God. John records some of the very words that he heard them speaking, "You are worthy, O LORD, to receive glory and honor and power: for You have created all things, and for Your pleasure they are and were created" (Rev. 4:11). Notice particularly the last few words: "For Your pleasure they are and were created." Your worship and my worship give God "pleasure". What is man that he has this wonderful, wonderful, wonderful privilege of being able to give pleasure to the Creator of the universe!

The apostle John also describes seeing four special angelic beings whom the Church calls "seraphims." They were continually leading the elders, angels and saints in worship. It appears that each time these "seraphims" circled around the Throne of God, they saw or there was revealed to them new dimensions of God and His glory and they would cry "Holy, Holy, Holy, LORD God Almighty." The rest of those before the Throne would respond in worship and praise. One of the most exciting things about God, the Throne and Heaven is that there will be a continuous discovering of new and glorious purposes, understandings, and the revelation of many, many, many things beyond our understanding that have not yet even entered into our imaginations or understanding.

Going back to the Gospel of John chapter 4 when Jesus was talking to the Samaritan woman at Jacob's well, she was asking Jesus about the worshipping of God. She was asking Jesus where God should be worshipped. In His answer to her question, Jesus said it was not where we worshipped God that was important, but how we worshipped God. "But the hour comes, and now is, when the true worshippers shall worship the Father in spirit and in truth: for the Father seeks such to worship Him. God is a Spirit: and they that worship Him must worship Him in spirit and in truth" (John 4:23-24).

There is probably not another field of human activity where there is so much wasted activity as in the field of religion. One of the great leaders of the church in the first half of the twentieth century was A. W. Tozer who wrote:

> "And the church, the poor church! We have banquets, we have conferences, we have Sunday schools, we have morning worship and evening Gospel services, we have everything. We're the busiest crowd of little eager beavers that ever tramped over the North American soil. But we are not worshipers. There is scarcely a church service where we can feel the spirit of worship. . . .the churches are too busy promoting people and things to cultivate the presence of God." (*The Alliance Witness*, June 18, 1958).

Many new converts to Christianity come into the church and never have been taught how to worship. They are like workmen who have been given hammers and saws, but no blue-print or teaching on how to use what they have been given. They have not the remotest notion what they are supposed to build, so they settle down to the dull routine of polishing their tools once each Sunday and then putting the tools back in their boxes.

The early Protestant church had what was named "The Westminster Catechism." It states that the chief end of man is to know God and to enjoy Him forever. I meet many people who know God, but not very many who really enjoy God. For many, church is an endurance contest. They go to church because they have been told that is what you are supposed to do. Others go to a church that helps them have an emotional experience.

The ONE THING THAT MAKES THE DIFFERENCE is whether or not you know how to worship. People can go into a cathedral or beautiful church and sit there and say, "I was worshipping." They may be. For many others, their spirit is not involved, but their soul (emotions, esthetic values, etc.) enjoy the beauty of the building, the sound of a majestic pipe organ, the beautiful stained-glass windows. They may feel strengthened and ministered to. However, if their "spirits" are not involved, they have not truly "worshipped". They have had a "soulish" experience which is good, but they still have not entered into true worship.

Many church services are like a game of volley ball. One of the players or the pastor takes the ball in one hand and throws it up into the air and strikes the ball with the other hand to send it over the net to the other players. Many ministers plan a service and then serve it to the congregation. Many times the motivation is, "Let's see how the congregation receives this one." Most services are prepared for and received by the congregation. Sometimes we talk about a wonderful service saying, "Oh you should have been there. You missed a real blessing." The important question is whether there was real worship or was it just that the music was inspiring, the preacher entertaining, the pews comfortable or the atmosphere just right? In real worship your "spirit" comes out and begins to love and fellowship with the LORD. To worship "in spirit" is to allow the Holy Spirit to move upon the believer's redeemed "spirit" causing love, adoration, devotion, honor and respect to ascend to God.

The writer of the book of Hebrews in the Bible tells us that God has given us a pattern of true worship in the example of the

Tabernacle and later on the Temple, as described in the Old Testament. As the apostle John says in Revelation 1:6, "And has made us kings and priests unto God." As the priest would enter the Holy Place to offer sacrifice and praise to God, it is also a picture of how we as "priests" of God are to worship Him. In quoting the Living Bible from Hebrew 8:5-6, "Their work is connected with a mere earthly model of the real Tabernacle in heaven; for when Moses was getting ready to build the Tabernacle, God warned him to follow exactly the pattern of the heavenly Tabernacle as shown to him on Mount Sinai. But Christ, as a Minister in heaven, has been rewarded with a far more important work than those who serve under the old laws, because the new agreement which He passes on to us from God contains far more wonderful promises".

The apostle Peter writes in 1 Peter 2:5, "You also, as living stones, are built up a spiritual house, an holy priesthood, to offer up spiritual sacrifices, acceptable to God by Jesus Christ." Now in the Old Testament, the priest had two areas of ministry. There was his ministry in the outer court leading the people in repentance (offering the sin offering on the altar of burnt offerings) and leading the people in dedication (offering the burnt offering on the altar of burnt offerings). Now all of this took place in the outer court. However, once a day in the morning and again in the evening, he was to enter the inner court and there at the golden altar of incense offer the incense of praise and worship to God.

This was INNER COURT MINISTRY or ministry to God alone. The priest would enter the INNER COURT alone and there minister only to God. In Ezekiel 44:16, "They shall enter into My sanctuary, and they shall come near to My table, to minister unto Me, and they shall keep My charge." Another picture of this is when Jesus was invited to dinner at the house of Mary, Martha and Lazarus. Martha was busy preparing the dinner, but Mary sat at the feet of Jesus listening to Him and fellowshipping with Him. Martha who felt overwhelmed with the tasks asked Jesus to tell Mary to help her. But do you remember what Jesus said? "Martha, Martha, you are careful and troubled about many things: But one thing is needful: and Mary has chosen that good part, which shall not be taken away from her" (Luke 10:41-42).

Today the emphasis of the church is on the outer court ministry. The Bible colleges, seminaries and minister seminars most always focus on outer court ministry. But God puts the priority on ministry in the inner court. The emphasis of Ezekiel 44:15-16 is you do not have to look for opportunities to minister to human needs, but you do have to make a real effort to minister unto the LORD because of distractions. The Gospel writers tell us Jesus had to face this dilemma also. "But so much the more went there a fame abroad of Him: and great multitudes came together to hear, and to be healed by Him of their infirmities. And He withdrew Himself into the wilderness, and prayed" (Luke 5:15-16). The Gospel writer Mark tells us, "And in the morning, rising up a great while before day, He went out, and departed into a solitary place, and there prayed. . . .And when they had found Him, they said unto Him, all men seek for You" (Mark 1:35-37).

Everybody sees "outer court" ministry but only the LORD, and maybe those close to you, see the "inner court" ministry. Scores of men go into ministry because of "outer court" attention. But only one thing takes you into the "inner court", and that is your love for the LORD.

Some men have real talent and skill in "outer court ministry". It is a pleasure to watch them. They have real skill, grace and finesse with the knife in preparing the sacrifice for the sin offering and the burnt offering, so to speak. Others you are afraid will cut off their thumbs or fingers by accident. But when it comes to the "inner court ministry" or the worship of the LORD, all of us are equal in ability for ministry if we will only do so. All of us can have the same skill. All the LORD wants is our true heart response in love and fellowship. We were all created to have fellowship with Him. Adam walked with God in the cool of the day. Abraham was called the friend of God. David was a man after God's own heart. Many found favor with the LORD. All that God wants from us is our love and fellowship. True worship is simply love, thanks, adoration and fellowship with God.

Going back to Ezekiel 44:15-16, not only was the priest to come into the inner court to minister or worship the LORD, he was to do nothing that would cause him to sweat. Sweat is a symbol of human effort and there is to be no sweat in worship or "inner court" ministry.

"And it shall come to pass, that when they enter in at the gates of the inner court, they shall be clothed with linen garments; and no wool shall come upon them, while they minister in the gates of the inner court, and within. They shall have linen bonnets upon their heads, and shall have linen breeches upon their loins; and they shall not gird themselves with any thing that causes sweat" (Ezek. 44:17-18).

As stated before, in real worship your spirit comes out and begins to love and fellowship with the LORD. To worship "in spirit" is to allow the Holy Spirit to move upon your redeemed spirit causing love, adoration, devotion, honor and respect to ascend to God. It is more than just singing, praising or reading the Bible. Your soul can do all these things. True worship takes place when your very inner being senses the presence of God and there is this spontaneous desire that takes place inside of you that you want to love Him, adore Him, praise Him, minister to Him and fellowship with Him. It is with our "spirit" that we commune with God. The best natural comparison that I know is similar to the spontaneous desire to love and be with the true love of your life.

This is the same type of reaction that the twenty-four elders around the Throne of God in Revelation 4:10-11 have when the angels began to worship God saying, "Holy, holy, holy, LORD God Almighty." Their own spirits responded in true worship as they fell down before Him that sat on the throne and worshiped Him that lives forever and ever saying, "You are worthy, O LORD, to receive glory and honor and power: for You have created all things, and for Your pleasure they are and were created" (Rev. 4:11).

I have found that many people have never had this experience. They equate worship with singing hymns, clapping their hands or praising God. These are all expressions of the soul and they are good and should be done. King David realized that these were the best way to get the inward spirit to stand up (so to speak) and begin to worship. "Bless the LORD, O my soul: and all that is within me, bless His holy name" (Ps. 103:1). "O clap your hands, all you people; shout unto God with the voice of triumph" (Ps. 47:1) "Sing praises to God, sing praises: sing praises unto your King, sing praises" (Ps. 47:6).

As we sincerely seek to enter the "inner court", you will enter and experience the inward man responding in real worship to the

LORD. There is no greater joy and satisfaction when you experience true worship and fellowship with the LORD.

When it comes to worship, there is a very important lesson to learn from a question that God asked Job in the midst of all of his sufferings and trials. In Job 38:1-7, we are told the LORD answered Job out of the whirlwind and said, "Where were you when I laid the foundations of the earth? Declare, if you have understanding. . . .When the morning stars sang together, and all the sons of God shouted for joy?" Music and singing has always been a part of the LORD even before the creation of the world. When the apostle John was caught up into Heaven to the Throne Room of God, they are still singing. In Revelation 5:8-9, we are told when Jesus took the book sealed with seven seals from the right hand of God to open it, "And when He had taken the book, the four beast and four and twenty elders fell down before the Lamb (Jesus), having every one of them harps. . . . And they sung a new song, saying, You are worthy to take the book, and to open the seals thereof."

But even greater than this, there is going to be music and singing that has never been heard before in the universe. The apostle John tells us in Revelation 14:1-3 that he saw the Lamb (Jesus) standing on mount Zion and with Him a 144,000 having His Father's name written in their foreheads (this is during the Great Tribulation that is still to come). Then John says, "and I heard the voice of harpers harping with their harps: And they sung as it were a new song before the throne, and before the four beasts, and the elders: and no man could learn that song but the hundred and forty and four thousand, which were redeemed from the earth."

The apostle Paul exhorts the Church in Ephesians 5:18-19, "be filled with the Spirit; Speaking to yourselves in psalms and hymns and spiritual songs, singing and making melody in your heart to the LORD." Paul further encourages the Church in Colossians 3:16, "Let the word of Christ dwell in you richly in all wisdom; teaching and admonishing one another in psalms and hymns and spiritual songs, singing with grace in your hearts to the LORD."

King David the psalmist probably understood the use of music and singing in the worship of the LORD better than any other man who has lived. When he brought the Ark of the Covenant into

Jerusalem and put it in the Tabernacle of David, there came the sudden prominence of music and singing as a ministry and worship to God (1 Chron. 6:31). According to 1 Chronicles 23:5, David had appointed four thousand Levites to serve in the ministry of music. When the Temple of Solomon was built and the Ark of the Covenant was moved into the Temple, this ministry of song and music continued to be used in the worship of the LORD.

From the preceding Bible references, we know that God is the great originator of all things including music and song. If we will let Him, He can inspire in the hearts of the saints the music of heaven. I personally believe there is a realm of divine music that man has never dreamed or heard of but is available to the Church in these last days and will be so in eternity.

The Bible teaches us there are three aspects of singing that are to be used in worship. As the apostle Paul points out in Ephesians 5:19 and Colossians 3:16, they are (1) psalms, (2) hymns and (3) spiritual songs.

Aspect of Singing	Definitive Distinction	Function of Song
Psalms	Songs of praise from the Bible or songs in the character, spirit or manner of the Psalms in the Bible	Directed primarily to God
Hymns	Songs of praise of human composition or Bible themes	Directed primarily to man as testimonial or in praise to God
and Gospel Songs	Primarily a song of testimony	Directed primarily to man
Spiritual Songs	A song that is quickened by the Holy Spirit that is directed in worship to God	Directed to God

There are three basic parts to music that should be considered in our worship of the LORD which are melody, harmony and rhythm.

Melody

The fundamental part of music is its melody. This is the most creative part of music and should be the strongest consideration. Melody appeals to the spiritual or to the spirit of man. As the apostle Paul said in Ephesians 5:19, "Speaking to yourselves in psalms and hymns and spiritual songs, singing and making MELODY in your heart (or spirit) to the LORD."

Harmony

The next important part of music is its harmony. Harmony is the arrangement of chords which are meant to support the melody. Harmony appeals to the psychological and emotional or soul of man even as a melody appeals to the "spirit" of man. Harmony should follow the melody and should never dominate or subordinate the melodic line. Oftentimes musicians have so great a mass of harmonic sound, it makes it difficult to recognize the melody. The melody should dominate the harmony and not the reverse. One should not get lost in the arrangements and miss the message of the melody.

Rhythm

The third part of music is rhythm. It appeals to the physical, the body. Again, this part should be dominated by the melody. If there is not rhythm, then the music is lifeless and dead. It is like having no pulse. If the beat is throbbing or pulsating then the music is sick. If the beat is concealed in the harmony with the melody dominating, then the music is healthy.

In summarization of this section on DEVELOPING OUR "SPIRIT" IN WORSHIP, let's go back to the fact that man is a triune being with a body, soul and spirit. In worshipping God with music and song, it is important to realize that music which is dominated by the rhythm will appeal to the body. The reason why many people like rock music is because they like the way it affects their body. They like to move their body to the rhythm, but that will not promote worship from their spirit. Music that is dominated by the harmony or harmonics, usually appeals to the emotions and esthetic values which are a part of the soul. There was a song in popular music entitled "I Write the Songs." In the lyrics it talks about that with the rhythm my music makes you dance, I write the song that make the young girls cry. In other words with the harmony I can create the emotions of sentimentalism. Music can be very powerful. However, when we want to enter into true worship, it has to come from our spirit and the spiritual song that brings you into real worship will have a melody that can enter into your spirit.

As a pastor, many times in leading a worship service, we would start with a song with lots of rhythm to get the people awake and doing something together with the rest of the congregation. Then we would move to a song that would get their soul involved. As the psalmist David said in Psalms 103:1, "Bless the LORD, O my soul: and all that is within me, bless his holy name." Once their body and soul were involved, the next step was to lead them in spiritual songs so that the Holy Spirit would quicken their spirits to enter into real worship of the LORD.

C. Developing Our "spirit" In Praise

Not only does God want us to develop our spirit in worship, which gives God pleasure, He wants us to develop our spirit in praise. Remember that He has created us to be kings and priests unto God and His Father (Rev. 1:6). As Jesus told the apostle John in Revelation 3:21, "To him that overcomes will I grant to sit with Me in My throne, even as I also overcame, and am set down with My Father in His throne." King David learned that through praise, he could learn to exercise dominion or rulership.

Read what King David wrote in Psalms 149:1-9, "Praise you the LORD. Sing unto the LORD a new song, and His praise in the congregation of saints. . . . Let the high praises of God be in their mouth, and a two edge sword in their hand; To execute vengeance upon the heathen, and punishments upon the people; To bind their kings with chains, and their nobles with fetters of iron: To execute upon them the judgment written: this honor have all His saints. Praise ye the LORD."

Read what the apostle Paul wrote to the church at Corinth, "It is true that I am an ordinary, weak human being, but I don't use human plans and methods to win my battles. I use God's mighty weapons, not those made by men, to knock down the devil's strongholds. These weapons can break down every proud argument against God and every wall that can be built to keep men from finding Him. With these weapons I can capture rebels and bring them back to God, and change them into men whose heart's desire is obedience to Christ" (2 Cor. 10:3-5 (TLB).

One of these mighty weapons was as King David called it, "Let the high praises of God be in their mouth." Now what did David mean by the term high praises? Here are descriptions of seven different forms of praise:

1. The singing of psalms, hymns and spiritual songs which can be worship, praise or both.
2. The lifting up of the voice with words of praise either by yourself or in unison with other believers.
3. The clapping of hands in expressing praise.
4. The lifting up of hands in an attitude of praise, worship or both.
5. Being joyful either by the expression of the voice (can even be shouting) or in a dance of joy.
6. Personal praise within ourselves or a time of silence in reverence to the LORD.
7. High praise.

The first six forms of praise can be done with the body and the soul. But high praise involves our spirit also. The highest form of praise is when the Holy Spirit of God begins to praise through our spirit. Praises to God begin to flow out of your spirit like an artesian well to God. At times we begin to soar in the spirit. Since the Throne Room of Heaven is filled with praise, there are times when we are able to join with that heavenly host. God takes praises from on high, puts them in our spirits and fills our mouths with praises. It is like speaking in tongues in the Baptism of the Holy Spirit. In high praise, the Holy Spirit is causing the heavenly praises to flow through our mouths. When this happens, THINGS BEGIN TO HAPPEN in the heavenly realm as well as the earthy realm.

As we previously mentioned when the apostle John was caught up to the Throne Room of God in Revelation 4 and 5, he saw in the right hand of God a book sealed with seven seals. When the 24 elders began to worship, Jesus was able to take the book. Then all of heaven went into "high praise" as John writes in Revelation

5:11-13, "And I beheld, and I heard the voice of many angels around about the throne and the beasts and the elders: and the number of them was ten thousand times ten thousand, and thousands of thousand; Saying with a loud voice, Worthy is the Lamb that was slain to receive power, and riches, and wisdom, and strength, and honor, and glory, and blessing. And every creature which is in heaven, and on the earth, and under the earth, and such as are in the sea, and all that are in them, heard I saying, Blessing and honor, and glory, and power, be unto Him that sits upon the throne, and unto the Lamb for ever and ever."

After this time of "high praise", Jesus began to open the seals of the book. As Jesus began to open the seven seals, man's history on earth as we know it, was being brought to a conclusion in preparation for Jesus to return to earth to bring about the millennial or thousand year reign of Christ on this earth.

Another example of "high praise" is when the children of Israel took the city of Jericho as they entered the Promised Land. "So Joshua summoned the priests and gave them their instructions: the armed men would lead the procession followed by seven priests blowing continually on their trumpets. Behind them would come the priests carrying the ark, followed by a rearguard. . . . The ark was carried around the city once that day, after which everyone returned to the camp again and spent the night there. . . . They followed this pattern for six days. At dawn of the seventh day, they started out again, but this time they went around the city not once, but seven times. The seventh time, as the priests blew a long, loud trumpet blast, Joshua yelled to the people, Shout! The LORD has given us the city! . . . So when the people heard the trumpet blast, they shouted as loud as they could. And suddenly the walls of Jericho crumbled and fell before them, and the people of Israel poured into the city from every side and captured it" (Josh. 6:6-20 TLB).

Another example of high praise is when the armies of Ammon, Moab and Mount Seir came against the Kingdom of Judah when Jehoshaphat was king. King Jehoshaphat gathered the people in the Temple at Jerusalem to fast and pray. During this time of prayer and fasting, the prophet Jahaziel proclaimed that they would see an incredible rescue operation by God. Early that next morning the army of Judah went out into the wilderness of Tekoa to meet the advancing armies of Moab, Ammon and Mount Seir.

After consulting with the people, we read in 2 Chronicles 20:21-24, that Jehoshaphat "appointed singers unto the LORD, and that should praise the beauty of holiness, as they went out before the army, and to say, Praise the LORD; for His mercy endures forever. And when they began to sing and to praise, the LORD set ambushments against the children of Ammon, Moab, and Mount Seir, which were come against Judah; and they were smitten." The LORD caused the armies of Ammon, Moab and Mount Seir to begin fighting among themselves and they destroyed each other. When the army of Judah arrived at the watch tower that looks out over the wilderness, as far as they could see there were dead bodies lying on the ground. Not a single one of the enemy had escaped.

Pastor Judson Cornwall tells of a time of "high praise" that the church which he pastored in Eugene, Oregon experienced. They went into a time of "high praise". It was a Sunday morning at 11:15 a.m. Later that day two young men from his church phoned him. One was pastoring another church and one was on the mission field as a missionary.

The phone call from the young man pastoring another church was to find out if it was possible the church in Eugene was in "high praise" at 11:15 a.m. on that day. Pastor Cornwall answered, "Yes, why are you asking?" The young pastor went on to explain how the church was having problems. One of the deacons did not like the pastor's methods and teaching. He said at 11:15 a.m., this deacon came down the aisle pointing his finger saying, "You will resign, you will get out of this church today." The young pastor said he was filled with terror inside and was unable to say a word. Then this deacon stopped at the second row and turned white. Then he pulled out a pen, wrote a note, put it on the pulpit and walked out of the church.

The pastor read the note. To his surprise the deacon had written out his own resignation. Then the glory of the LORD fell upon the congregation. After all was over, the pastor asked the LORD what happened. The LORD answered, "The home church went into "high praise" and I smote him." The young pastor then said to Pastor Cornwall, "I am just calling to verify."

At the same time in a foreign mission field, the other young man experienced the following. It was Sunday evening there during the time of the Sunday morning service in America. There were three town officials who were determined to close the mission church. They had sent out notices to the people not to attend. At the time of the evening service there was no one there except the missionary. He felt impressed of the LORD to go ahead and have the service anyway. He played his accordion and had a song service by himself. Then he had a testimony time which was short since he was the only one there. When it came time for the preaching, he sensed the anointing of the Holy Spirit, so he went ahead and preached the sermon he had prepared. Then he felt impressed to go ahead and give the altar call.

To his utter surprise the three town officials who were determined to close the mission church came through the back foyer door down to the altar. Two of them gave their hearts to the LORD right then and there. Unknown to the missionary, these three officials stood in the foyer watching through a small window to see if their order was going to be obeyed. Instead, the LORD had a special church service for them and as a result, they came to know the LORD and helped to establish a large church.

As we learn to worship and praise and as our spirit is developed through worship and praise, it brings us into God's ultimate plans and purposes for our lives, to be priests and kings taking authority and dominion.

D. Developing Our "spirit" In Taking Authority and Dominion

When you and I learn to move with the Holy Spirit with our spirit in worship and in praise, we are able to enter into the full purpose and plan that God has created for us. Remember that back in chapter one of this book, I pointed out that in Genesis 1:26 that God said, "Let Us make man in our image, after Our likeness: and let them have dominion." At the creation of man, the first two goals were accomplished. First, man was created in God's image as a spirit and second, in God's likeness as a triune being with a body, soul and spirit. The third goal was for man to have dominion with the ability to do, to create (invent) and to rule. This goal was to be learned and developed in our earthly life so that in eternity we would be able to rule and reign with Him and to forever fellowship with Him.

During His ministry on earth, one day Jesus asked His disciples saying, "Whom do men say that I the Son of man am?" (Matt. 16:13). They said, "Some say that you are John the Baptist: some, Elijah. . . or one of the prophets." But then Jesus asked them, "But whom say you that I am?" And Simon Peter answered and said, "You are the Christ, the Son of the living God." And Jesus answered and said unto him, "Blessed are you Simon Bar-jona: for flesh and blood has not revealed it unto you, but My Father which is in heaven. And I say also unto you, That you are Peter, and upon this rock I will build My Church; and the gates of hell shall not prevail against it. And I will give unto you the keys of the Kingdom of Heaven: and whatsoever you shall bind on earth shall be bound in heaven: and whatsoever you shall loose on earth shall be loosed in heaven" (Matt. 16:17-19).

Again Jesus emphasized this to His disciples in Matthew 18:18, "Verily I say unto you, Whatsoever you shall bind on earth shall be bound in heaven: and whatsoever you shall loose on earth shall be loosed in heaven." Again in Mark 11:23 Jesus told His disciples, "For verily I say unto you, That whosoever shall say unto this mountain, Be you removed, and be you cast into the sea; and shall not doubt in his heart, but shall believe that those things which he says shall come to pass; he shall have whatsoever he says."

With this background in mind, look with me at three great men of God who had developed their "spirit" in worship and praise and also learned to take authority and dominion. The first is King David, who as a shepherd boy had learned to play the harp and to enter into worship and praise in the Holy Spirit through his "spirit". (See 1 Samuel 16:14-23.) A number of years later, when David was sent by his father to take food to his older brothers who were in the army of Saul fighting the Philistines, he heard the challenge of the Philistine giant Goliath against the armies of Israel.

> "He was a giant of a man, measuring over nine feet tall! He wore a bronze helmet, a two-hundred-pound

> coat of mail, bronze leggings, and carried a bronze javelin several inches thick, tipped with a twenty-five pound iron spearhead, and his armor bearer walked ahead of him with a huge shield. He stood and shouted across to the Israelis, "Do you need a whole army to settle this? I will represent the Philistines, and you choose someone to represent you, and we will settle this in single combat! If your man is able to kill me, then we will be your slaves. But if I kill him, then you must be our slaves! I defy the armies of Israel! Send me a man who will fight with me."   1 Samuel 17:4-10 (TLB)

The Bible tells us that when all the men of Israel saw the giant, they fled from him and were greatly afraid. But David volunteered to go and fight him. When King Saul heard of David's desire to take up the giant's challenge, his response was, "You are not able to go against this Philistine to fight with him: for you are but a youth, and he a man of war from his youth" (1 Sam. 17:33).

David was able to convince King Saul to let him go against the giant. Since he had never used any armor before, he went dressed like a shepherd with only his shepherd's staff, his sling shot and five smooth stones. When the giant saw this shepherd lad coming at him with only a shepherd's staff and a sling shot, he was highly insulted saying, "Am I a dog, that you come to me with a stick?" The giant cursed David and told him to come on, and that he would give his flesh to the vultures and beasts of the field."

Listen to the authority and dominion that David took over the situation. "You come to me with a sword, and with a spear, and with a shield: but I come to you in the name of the LORD of hosts, the God of the armies of Israel, whom you have defied. This day will the LORD deliver you into my hand; and I will smite you, and take your head from you; and I will give the carcasses of the host of the Philistines this day unto the fowls of the air, and to the wild beasts of the earth; that all the earth may know that there is a God in Israel" (1 Sam. 17:45-46).

Then as David ran towards the giant, he took one of the stones and put it in his sling shot and hurled it from his sling. Like a guided missile, it hit the giant in the forehead and the giant fell upon his face to the ground. Having no sword, David ran to the fallen giant, took the giant's sword and cut off his head. When the Philistines saw that their champion was dead, they turned and ran. The Israeli army had a great victory that day as they pursued the fleeing Philistines.

Here we see David, moved by the Holy Spirit through his "spirit" taking dominion and authority over the situation. This is the LORD's ultimate plan and purpose for you and I, to rule and reign with Him. As a result of this, the LORD made David king over Israel and promised to establish his throne forever. Only the LORD knows what this will mean for King David in eternity.

Then we meet the prophet Elijah who suddenly appears on the scene as recorded in 1 Kings 17:1. Elijah the Tishbite, who was an inhabitant of Gilead, suddenly appeared before King Ahab of Israel and proclaims, "As the LORD God of Israel lives, before whom I stand, there shall not be dew nor rain these years, but according to my word" (1 Kings 17:1). We know nothing about him before this time. He had developed his spirit in worship and praise and now had learned to take authority and dominion by allowing the Holy Spirit to move through his spirit. For three years there was no rain in the land of Israel until the day on Mount Carmel when Elijah called fire down from heaven to consume the offering on the altar as was described earlier in this chapter. Afterwards he prayed and commanded the rain to come for the first time in three years. He was used by the LORD in mighty miracles. When it came time to go to be with the LORD, he was with one of his disciples by the name of Elisha. Then "there appeared a chariot of fire, and horses of fire, and parted them both asunder; and Elijah went up by a whirlwind into heaven" (2 Kings 2:11).

The next time we hear of Elijah was when Jesus took Peter, James and John up to a high mountain "and was transfigured before them: and His face did shine as the sun, and His raiment was white as the light. And behold, there appeared unto them Moses and Elijah talking with Him" (Matt. 17:1-3). These are men who allowed the LORD to prepare them for the plan and purpose He had for their lives.

After the resurrection of Jesus and the outpouring of the Holy Spirit on the day of Pentecost in Acts 2, we read in Acts 3 that Peter and John were on their way to the Temple to pray. Once again we see men who had developed their "spirits" in worship and praise and now had learned to take authority and dominion by allowing the Holy Spirit to move through their spirits. As they were going into the Temple, a certain man lame from his mother's womb sitting at the gate of the Temple asked alms of Peter and John. We read in Acts 3:4-9, "And Peter, fastening his eyes upon him with John, said, Look on us. And he gave heed unto them, expecting to receive something of them. Then Peter said, Silver and gold have I none; but such as I have give I you: In the name of Jesus Christ of Nazareth rise up and walk. And he took him by the right hand, and lifting him up: and immediately his feet and ankle bones received strength. And he leaping up stood, and walked, and entered with them into the Temple, walking, and leaping, and praising God."

It is my sincere prayer as these words are written, that you will understand and embrace the truth that the LORD is preparing you for a special plan and purpose for your life in eternity, that not only have you said yes to Jesus to come into your life, but that you love Him with all your heart, soul and mind, that you are responding with all your heart in faith and obedience, that by the power of the Holy Spirit you are learning to overcome and to prevail in prayer. And above all that you are endeavoring and allowing the Holy Spirit to develop your "spirit" in worship, praise and in taking authority and dominion so that on the day you enter into heaven, He will say unto you, "Well done you good and faithful servant, enter into the plan and purpose that I have for you in eternity."

CHAPTER FOUR

BIBLICAL EXAMPLES OF GOD PREPARING MEN AND WOMEN FOR THE PLAN AND PURPOSE HE HAS FOR THEIR LIVES

The apostle Peter declares in 2 Peter 3:9 that the LORD "is long-suffering to us-ward, not willing that any should perish, but that all should come to repentance." It is important for you and I to understand the difference between the work of saving souls and the work of God in preparing you and me for the plan and purpose He has for our lives. The first and primary step is salvation, but man can stop with salvation and wait for heaven and never do the work God created for him to do. When God created man, He spoke of what He was after, "let them have dominion" (Gen. 1:26). The time we spend on earth is for us to learn how to rule and to take dominion and authority, to prepare us for the plan and purpose He has for us in eternity.

The apostle Paul tells us in Ephesians 2:6-7, "And has raised us up together, and made us sit together in heavenly places in Christ Jesus: That in the ages to come He might show the exceeding riches of His grace in His kindness towards us through Christ Jesus." The apostle Paul acknowledges that he did not understand everything, but he knew this much, "For now we see through a glass, darkly; but then face to face: now I know in part; but then shall I know" (1 Cor. 13:12). Or as Paul writes in 1 Corinthians 2:9, "Eye has not seen, nor ear heard, neither have entered into the heart of man, the things which God has prepared for them that love Him." Paul was quoting the prophet Isaiah who wrote, "For since the beginning of the world men have not heard, nor perceived by the ear, neither has the eye seen, O God, beside You, what He has prepared for him that waits for Him" (Isa. 64:4).

The apostle John wrote: "But as many as received Him, to them gave He power to become the sons of God, even to them that believe on His name" (John 1:12). The apostle Paul adds to this in Romans 8:16-17, "The Spirit itself bears witness with our spirit, that we are the children of God: And if children, then heirs; heirs of God, and joint-heirs with Christ; if so be that we suffer with Him, that we may be also glorified together." Paul takes this a step higher in 1 Corinthians 6:3 where he writes to the Church at Corinth, "Know you not that we shall judge angels?" The writer of Hebrews adds to this as he writes to the Church in Hebrews 1:13-14, "But to which of the angels said He at any time, Sit on My right hand, until I make your enemies your foot-stool? Are they not all ministering spirits, sent forth to minister for them who shall be heirs of salvation?" The above scriptures are imply-ing that we will become "next of kin" to the Trinity. All of history is wrapped up with God preparing a group of people to reign with Him.

The apostle Paul also compares the Church (which is you and me) to a bride. In Ephesians 5:25-27 he writes, "Husbands, love your wives, even as Christ also loved the Church, and gave Himself for it. . . . That He might present it to Himself a glorious Church, not having spot, or wrinkle, or any such thing; but that it should be holy and without blemish." The apostle John takes this a step higher in Revelation 19:7-9, "Let us be glad and rejoice, and give honor to Him: for the marriage supper of the Lamb is come, and His wife has made herself ready. And to her was granted that she should be arrayed in fine linen, clean and white: for the fine linen is the righ-teousness of saints. And he said unto me, Write, Blessed are they which are called unto the marriage supper of the Lamb. And he said unto me, These are the true sayings of God."

Here the Bible pictures the Church as a bride marrying the king. It also pictures the Church as a bride sitting and reigning with Christ. The entire universe is cooperating with God in His purpose to select and train His Church as a bride to reign with Christ. There really is no such thing as "secular history." God is controlling all events, not only on earth but in all realms, to serve His purpose of bringing to maturity and eventually to enthronement the Church with His Son. As the apostle Paul writes in Romans 8:28, "We know that all things (the entire universe) work together (are cooperating) for good to them that love God, to them who are the called according to His purpose (to reign)."

Many times we may be tempted to ask, "Do all things really work together for good?" The truth that all of us need to understand is that this life is our training time. To illustrate this truth, we want to take the lives of Jacob, Joseph, King David, Mary, Peter, John and Paul to illustrate how God prepares men and women for the plan and purpose He has for their lives.

Wherever you turn in your Bible, you come face to face with people who are different. You meet Abraham who quit his job and left his home to follow God into an unknown future. You meet Jacob who had to live in exile about 21 years before he became a "Prince of God." You meet Joseph, who spent 13 years as a slave that he might spend the rest of his life as a king. You meet David, a shepherd boy who killed a giant and established the kingdom of Israel. You meet Daniel, who was a prisoner of war who became a prime minister of Babylon who was his captor. In the New Testament we meet Peter, James and John who were ordinary Jewish fishermen on the Sea of Galilee who conquered the Roman Empire for Christ. Then there is Paul, the brilliant Jewish rabbi who turned the world upside down for Christ.

These are people who were all different. These are people whom God used to make the world different. These are also people who will make a difference in your life, if you will learn from them the secret of their power. These people of the Bible lived at different times in history and belonged to different social levels. But they all had one thing in common. They not only knew the acts of God and the things that He did, but they knew God and His ways personally. They allowed God to work in them that He might work through them. They permitted God to take time to work in their lives at any cost. And because God was permitted to work in them, God was pleased to work through them.

God called Abraham when he was 75 years old when he had no children and promised to make a great nation out of his seed. God spent 25 years preparing Abraham for the birth of Isaac. Then God meets Jacob (the grandson of Abraham) in a dream one night and promises to make a great nation out of him, that all the families of the earth would be blessed through his descendants. God spent the next 21 years preparing him in exile away from his parents. After this God promised Joseph (the son of Jacob) that one day he would be a king. Joseph spent 13 years as a slave in preparation to equip him for this great ministry.

Christ called His disciples and schooled them for three years before sending them out as His representative to a lost world. Even the great apostle Paul, trained in the finest schools of his day, spent approximately three years in the Arabian desert and another six or seven years in his hometown of Tarsus in preparation for his life work establishing New Testament churches and writing many of the books of the New Testament.

The principle is obvious. God must work in us before He will work through us. "And even though Jesus was God's Son, He had to learn from experience what it was like to obey, when obeying meant suffering. It was after He had proved Himself perfect in this experience that Jesus became the Giver of eternal salvation to all those who obey Him" (Heb. 5:8-9 TLB).

If God has chosen us to be His own people, and it is His will that we all be, then we need to ask ourselves what history we must pass through under His hand to develop us into His own people. As we study the lives of these great people of God, we find the answer to our question. Must we also go through trials and discipline? Do not think you can have a unique history with God?

Most of us want God. The trouble is that we don't want to do things God's way but our own way. We act in self-will, depending on our own energy and wisdom. Never has there been a time when people have had a greater mania for success than we do today. The reading material on most bookstands is slanted to exploit the desire in men to achieve, to be successful, to be prosperous, to influence people, to be popular and to have magnetic personalities. The Bible says, "There is a way which seems right unto a man; but the end thereof are the ways of death" (Prov. 14:12). In contrast, Jesus said, "I am the way, the truth, and the life: no man comes unto the Father, but my Me" (John 14:6).

The key to the whole problem is that we really fail to understand what God wants from us. Many of us stop with the thought that God created us to be good, and God does want us to be good. However, we were created for a far higher purpose than just being good. We were created to be indwelt by God, to contain Him so that we could be like Him. Then we might be exalted and brought into His plan and purpose for our lives.

The Bible records the lives of Abraham, Jacob, Joseph, Moses, David, Mary, Peter, John, Paul and many others to illustrate this process. As God dealt with them, so will He deal with us. This is how we learn to know God and His ways, by observing His dealings with them. Remember Jesus said, "If any man will come after Me, let him deny himself, and take up his cross, and follow Me" (Matt. 16:24). The great apostle Paul said, "I am crucified with Christ: never-the-less I live; yet not I, but Christ lives in me" (Gal. 2:20).

The normal tendency is to think of men like Abraham, Jacob, Joseph, Moses, David, Peter, John, Paul and others as always being saints. Because they are always so revered and so honored, it is easy to look upon them as some sort of "super believers" or saints, thinking that they were paragons of perfection who always automatically did what God wanted them to do. But when we begin to take a close look at the Biblical account of their lives, the Bible shows that they were very much like us. They experienced times of growth, times of standing still, times of failure and even times of slipping back in their relationship with God. Many of them would be the last ones we would call if we were God. However, there is one thing that they all did. They responded to God when He came their way. They said, "Yes."

God is not expecting to find those who are "born good." He knows full well that they are not to be found. But God chooses ordinary people, like you and me, who are willing to respond to His call, who are willing to allow Him to indwell them, to be changed into His likeness and to fellowship with Him.

A. JACOB

When we begin to look at Jacob the man, we discover how strikingly his history is like our own. In fact, before God started to deal with Jacob, we might be inclined to feel that we are superior. However, when you and I begin to see our own weaknesses and sinfulness and how self-willed we are, we begin to see Jacob in ourselves. When you and I see how wondrously God worked with this man until he came to be a "prince with God", it should give us all hope that we can also become a "prince with God". God changed Jacob's name to Israel, the name Israel is a combination of two words "Isra" meaning prince and "el" meaning God.

As we look at the life of Jacob, we can recognize four stages in Jacob's life:
1. The man Jacob was.
2. His testing and discipline through the events of his life.
3. When he allowed God to change his life.
4. The prince of God.

As we go into the man Jacob was, do not lose sight of the fact that Jacob became one of the greatest men in the Old Testament. All the promises of God made to his grandfather Abraham were passed on by God to Jacob. The nation that God would raise up would be called Israel, and Jacobs's twelve sons would become the head of the twelve tribes of the nation Israel.

When we first look at Jacob, he was like most of us self-centered, always looking out for number one, a schemer and plotter, and clever, wily and confident that he could do anything. His attitude was, "Show me once LORD and I'll take it from there." Yet no one was more sincere in wanting God's purpose in his life. He wholeheartedly pursued his objective to be the heir to God's promises to Abraham. This goal fit in with his desires. He wanted God's will, but not particularly God Himself.

Jacob was a twin with his brother Esau. While in the womb of his mother Rebekah, the twins struggled and his mother Rebekah inquired of the LORD what was happening to her. The LORD said unto her, "Two nations are in your womb, and two manner of people shall be separated from your womb; and the one people shall be stronger than the other people; and the elder shall serve the younger" (Gen. 25:23).

The first twin to be born was Esau, but immediately after came Jacob, whose hand took hold of Esau's heel. Therefore, he was given the name "Jacob" which means the "supplanter." His name was a prophetic description of his character, that he would always be trying to take things by his own natural strength and wit. Brother Esau became a cunning hunter, while Jacob was a quiet sort who liked to stay at home.

One day Esau overdid his hunting, came home exhausted from the hunt and was on the verge of collapsing. Jacob was cooking stew when Esau arrived. Esau begged for some food. Jacob saw an opportunity and said, "All right, trade me your birthright for it." Esau replied, "When a man is dying of starvation, what good is his birthright?" Jacob then said, "Well then, vow to God that it is mine!" And Esau vowed, thereby selling all his eldest son rights to his younger brother. Jacob then gave Esau the food. When Esau had eaten and recovered, he went about his business, indifferent to the loss of the rights he had thrown away. (See Genesis 25:27-34 TLB.)

When Jacob's father Isaac became very old and his eyes were dim so that he could not see, he called for his oldest son Esau in order to give him the family blessing before he died. Father Isaac loved the venison that his son Esau hunted and how Esau prepared it for a meal. Isaac instructed him to go out and hunt for venison, come home and prepare it, and after eating it, Isaac would give the family blessing to Esau. Jacob's mother, Rebekah overheard these instructions and called Jacob to go into the flock and get two young goats so she could prepare his father's favorite dish. She instructed Jacob to "take it to your father, and after he has enjoyed it he will bless you before his death, instead of Esau" (Gen. 27:8-10 TLB).

Jacob liked the idea, but he had a problem. "Father won't be fooled that easily. Think how hairy Esau is, and how smooth my skin is! What if my father feels me? He'll think I'm making a fool of him, and curse me instead of blessing me!" (Gen. 27:11-12 TLB). Mother Rebekah took some of Esau's clothes and put them upon Jacob along with the skins from the goats upon his hands and upon the smooth of his neck.

Jacob went into his father, claimed to be Esau, and told Jacob that God had given him good success in finding the venison so quickly. Since Isaac could no longer see, he asked him to come near to be able to touch his hands, feel the back of his neck and to sniff his clothes. Even though he was not sure of the voice, Isaac concluded that it was Esau and gave him the family blessing.

A short time later, Esau came in. Both he and his father realized that Jacob had deceived them. Esau cried bitterly, "No wonder they call him The Cheater: For he took my birthright, and now he has stolen my blessing. Oh, haven't you saved even one blessing for me?" Isaac answered, "I have made him your master, and have given him yourself and all of his relatives as his servants. I have guaranteed him abundance of grain and wine – what is there left to give?" (Gen. 27:36-37 TLB).

Now we come to an important question. How could God use such a man as this, one who would become a prince with God? Jacob was the classic example of Dr. Jekyll-Mr. Hyde in the Bible. If Jacob had died at that time, he was so crooked you couldn't have buried him. Instead you would have had to screw him into the ground. What use was such a man to God? By nature he was not suited. Jacob's cleverness and his talent for self-advancement had no place in the will and plan God had for him.

But there was a desire and response in his heart for God. And that is what God needs first of all to even begin to work in our hearts and lives. As Jesus said in Revelation 3:20, "Behold, I stand at the door, and knock: if any man hear My voice, and open the door, I will come in to him." Jacob had already answered "YES". Now let us see how God began preparing Jacob for the plan and purpose for his life. Jacob was seeking God and God wanted him. But Jacob neither knew God nor himself. During the next 21 years of his life, God took Jacob through what you might call the "school of the spirit", or a time of testing and discipline.

Brother Esau's reaction to all of this was that he was determined to kill Jacob after father Isaac died. Mother Rebekah heard what Esau intended to do and told Jacob to flee to her brother's place in Haran and stay there until Esau would get over his anger. Rebekah told Isaac that she was weary of the life, and if Jacob married one of the local girls as Esau had done, it would be more than she could stand. She convinced Isaac to send Jacob back to her ancestral home to find a wife, which Isaac did.

As Jacob began traveling back to Haran, God started to prepare Jacob for the plan and purpose He had for Jacob's life. That first night he lay down on the ground and went to sleep. In a dream he saw a ladder that reached from the earth to heaven and he saw the angels of God going up and down upon it. The LORD stood above it and said, "I am the LORD God of Abraham, and of your father Isaac. The ground you are lying on is yours! I will give it to you and to your descendants. . . . What's more, I am with you, and will protect you where ever you go, and will bring you back safely to the land; I will be with you constantly until I have finished giving you all I am promising" (Gen. 28:13-15 TLB).

Now you would think that God would have rebuked him for all his deceit and what he had done. Yet God made no mention of what had happened. God knew what Jacob was like and that he was determined to reach his goal, no matter the means he would use. It would have been no use to rebuke him. He was like that, he could not change. But what Jacob could not do, God Himself could. God knew He would have to let Jacob come to the place where he would allow God to change him.

This experience made a profound impression on Jacob but it did not change him. He made a vow saying, "If God will help me and protect me on this journey and give me food and clothes, and will bring me back safely to my father, then I will choose the LORD as my God. . . . And I will give you back a tenth of everything you give me" (Gen. 28:20-22 TLB).

That was Jacob. He even wanted to do business with God. Everything for him was on a commercial basis. However, the LORD knew Rebekah and her brother Laban, and Jacob had inherited their character. He knew Jacob would be spending the next 20 years with Uncle Laban. A lot of corners had to be rubbed off of Jacob. What brother Esau was unable to do, Uncle Laban certainly would be able to do so.

When Jacob arrived at Haran, Uncle Laban welcomed him. "Surely you are my bone and my flesh. And he abode with him the space of a month" (Gen. 29:14). After Jacob had been there a month, it no longer was "my bone and my flesh." Now it was, "You work and I'll pay you." This was a polite way of telling Jacob, "You can't live here for nothing." At home Jacob was a son but now he was just a servant under a hard taskmaster. Now we see God's chastening hand was at work.

Laban had two daughters. The oldest was Leah and the younger one was Rachel. Jacob had fallen in love with Rachel. He agreed to work for Uncle Laban seven years and then be given Rachel for wife. Jacob spent the next seven years working to pay for Rachel, but he was so much in love they seemed to him but a few days. Finally the time came for him to marry her. Uncle Laban made a big wedding feast. That night, when it was dark, Laban took Leah instead of Rachel to Jacob. In the morning when it was light, to his utter surprise, Jacob saw that he had been given Leah instead of Rachel.

Jacob went to Uncle Laban in a rage, "What sort of trick is this? I worked for seven years for Rachel. What do you mean by this trickery?" "It's not our custom to marry off a younger daughter ahead of her sister," Laban replied smoothly. "Wait until the bridal week is over and you can have Rachel too – if you promise to work for me another seven years!" (Gen. 29:25-27 TLB). It is always bitter to have to take your own medicine. So Jacob worked another seven years because of his love for Rachel.

Uncle Laban could scheme and plan even better than Jacob. After 14 years of service for his two wives, Jacob continued to work another six years in order to gain enough substance to support his own family. Even during this time, Uncle Laban changed his wages ten times. Jacob begins to recognize God's hand upon his life and he begins to change. Before he wanted God and the things of God for his own good, but now he was advancing to the place where he wanted God. In earlier years, Jacob only wanted God's will because it fit in with his own desire. Now he wanted God Himself.

After being with Uncle Laban for over 20 years, Jacob noticed a change of attitude on Uncle Laban's part. At first he was welcomed by his uncle, but no longer. The LORD spoke to Jacob saying, "Return unto the land of your fathers, and to your kindred; and I will be with you" (Gen. 31:3). Jacob obeyed the LORD and took his wives, children and all his possessions to return to his father Isaac.

Jacob also sent messengers before him to his brother Esau to inform him of his return, hoping for a friendly meeting. The messengers returned with the news that Esau was on the way to meet Jacob with an army of 400 men. Jacob was frantic with fear. He began to pray, "O LORD, please deliver me from destruction at the hand of my brother Esau, for I am frightened – terribly afraid that he is coming to kill me and these mothers and my children. But you promised to do me good, and to multiply my descendants until they became as the sands along the shores – too many to count" (Gen. 32:11-12 TLB).

Jacob was making progress in the development of his life in serving the LORD. Now he was praying and asking for God's help. However, there was still a little bit of Jacob left. He now started to scheme how he would meet Esau. He would send a present on before him to Esau of 550 animals divided into nine different groups. The men driving these groups of animals were to tell Esau upon meeting him, "These belong to your servant Jacob. They are a present for his master Esau! He is coming right behind us" (Gen. 32:18 TLB). Jacob was hoping that these presents would soften up Esau and that their meeting would be friendly. Then Jacob took his wives and children, passed over the ford Jabbok and returned to the camp alone that night. If all failed, Jacob still had strong legs and could run.

The Bible tells us as Jacob was alone that night, a man wrestled with him until the breaking of day. It was not Jacob who wrestled, but God who came and wrestled with him to bring about his complete surrender. The object of wrestling is to pin a man down so he cannot move and make him yield. When Jacob would not yield, God touched the hollow of his thigh and put it out of joint. Jacob's last means of escape was gone. A lame man cannot run. Now it was going to be God delivering him or perish. As day was breaking, Jacob was commanded to let go, but Jacob said, "I will not let you go, except you bless me" (Gen. 32:26). Jacob realized he was wrestling with the LORD and was determined not to let go. Then the LORD said to Jacob, "Your name shall be called no more Jacob (the heel-grabber or the supplanter), but Israel (a prince with God): for as a prince have you power with God and with men, and have prevailed" (Gen. 32:28).

As the sun arose, Jacob called the brook "Peniel" which means, "for I have seen God face to face, and my life is preserved" (Gen. 32:30). As he crossed the brook, he was now a prince with God who had learned to "prevail in prayer". Jacob had taken one of the most valuable steps that the LORD wants every one of us to take in preparation for our future rulership with Christ in eternity.

The striving, scheming Jacob now became the cleaving Jacob. The one who so persistently held onto himself now held on to God. He had seen the helplessness of self. Now he realized it was God that he had to depend on and not himself, that God must dwell within and that he must be changed into God's likeness. The first time God came his way at Bethel, while he was running away from home, he didn't know what to do. The second time God came his way, Jacob knew not to let Him go, "I will not let you go, unless you bless me."

The change in his name from Jacob to Israel describes the change that took place in him. Now he was a prince with God, one who rules with God. THIS IS THE EXPERIENCE THAT GOD WANTS FOR ALL OF US.

That morning the sun came up, and Jacob crossed over the brook, a lame man stepped out to meet his brother Esau and his 400 warriors. However, it was not just a lame man. It now was a "prince of God" in whom God dwelt. As this "prince of God" approached his brother, the reaction of Esau was as the Bible describes: "to run to meet him, and embrace him, and fell on his neck, and kissed him; and they wept" (Gen. 33:4).

In Genesis 49 we read about the end of Jacob's earthly life. We are able to look back and see how God prepared Jacob for the plan and purpose for his life that will be lived out in eternity. It all started with Jacob's desire for God and how he took that first step of saying "YES" to God's plan. Then we see the development of his LOVE and FAITH as God teaches him to OBEY. Finally we see how God put him to the test to prove him and as he became an OVER-COMER at Peniel, where he also learned to PREVAIL IN PRAYER as he wrestled with God.

As we come to Genesis 49, we see the DEVELOPMENT OF

HIS SPIRIT THAT GOD HAD GIVEN HIM AS HE LEARNED TO WORSHIP, TO PRAISE AND TO TAKE AUTHORITY AND DOMINION. On his death, "Jacob called unto his sons, and said, Gather yourselves together, that I may tell you that which shall befall you in the last days. Gather yourselves together, and hear you sons of Jacob; and harken unto Israel your father" (Gen. 49:1-2).

Then he prophesied what would happen to each of his twelve sons. To his son Judah, he prophesied that the symbol of kingship would not depart form his descendants and that from his descendents would "SHILOH" come. This was the prophecy that the kings of Israel would come from his descendants and the greatest coming would be that of Jesus the Messiah who would reign forever.

B. Joseph

Jacob's favorite son Joseph was very different from his father as far as his character and moral values were concerned. Therefore, God prepared Joseph differently for the plan and purposes He had for him. From this we learn that God deals with each one of us according to what is needed to accomplish His plan and purpose for our individual lives.

One of the most fascinating things about the Bible is that almost every truth in the New Testament is pictured in the Old Testament. The angel that appeared to Mary announcing the birth of Jesus as we read in Luke 1:32-33, "and the LORD God shall give unto him the throne of his father David: And he shall reign over the house of Jacob for ever; and of his kingdom there shall be no end."

When Joseph was still a young lad, God gave him a dream, which he promptly shared with his eleven brothers. "Listen to this dream I had: We were binding sheaves of grain out in the field when suddenly my sheaf rose and stood up right, while your sheaves gathered around mine and bowed down to it" (Gen. 37:6-7 NIV). The brothers retorted to him, "Shall you indeed reign over us? or shall you indeed have dominion over us?" (Gen. 37:8). His brothers were already jealous over the fact that Joseph was his father's favorite son. This caused them to hate him even more.

Then Joseph had another dream and he told it to his brothers. "Listen, he said, I had another dream, and this time the sun and moon and eleven stars were bowing down to me" (Gen. 37:9 NIV). His father rebuked him, but his brothers were fit to be tied concerning this affair. His father gave it quite a bit of thought and wondered what it all meant.

In a sense, Joseph was a picture of Jesus in the Old Testament – a man of good character destined for a throne. It is also a picture of the throne you and I are destined for. As Jesus said in Revelation 3:21, "To him that overcomes will I grant to sit with Me in My throne, even as I also overcame, and am set down with My Father in His throne."

Joseph was a person of almost perfect character. Like us, God had to prepare him for the plan and purpose He had for Joseph, not only in this life, but also in eternity. Joseph had already responded to God by a big "YES" in his life and he "loved" God. The next step for him was to have "faith" in what God said and "obey".

Just as Israel was taken into the wilderness where God would "prove" them, so was Joseph taken into a time of "proving" to see if he would obey and be an overcomer. When he received his dreams Joseph did not fully comprehend God's purposes.

God was going to let Joseph go through a time of proving and preparation. It would be like getting caught in the ocean waves on the sea shore with one wave after another catching him and rolling him over and over again.

While Joseph was still a teenager, his father Jacob sent him to Shechem to see how his brothers were doing in feeding their father's flock of sheep. When his brothers saw him coming, they conspired to kill Joseph and then tell their father that a wild animal had devoured him. The oldest brother, Reuben, convinced them not to slay him but put him into a deep pit. Later on he planned to come back and rescue Joseph. After they put Joseph into the pit, Reuben left for a short time. While he was gone, a group of Midianite merchants came by on their way to Egypt. The brothers decided that instead of killing Joseph, they would sell him as a slave to this band of merchants on their way to Egypt.

Joseph was sold for twenty pieces of silver and taken to Egypt. The brothers took Joseph's coat of many colors, killed a goat, dipped the coat in the blood of the goat and took it back to their father

Jacob. They let Jacob believe that Joseph was slain by a wild animal.

At this time it would have been normal for Joseph to begin to complain to God and remember all the dreams. "Thanks a Lot God! What about Your promises?" But instead, Joseph did what the apostle Paul writes in Ephesians 6:13, "Wherefore take unto you the whole armor of God, that you may be able to withstand in the evil day, and having done all, to stand."

When the Midianites arrived in Egypt, they sold Joseph as a slave to Potiphar, an officer of Pharaoh and a captain of the guard. As Joseph continued to have faith in God and make the best of his situation, the LORD was with him and made all he did prosper. Joseph found favor in the sight of Potiphar, who made Joseph overseer over his house and all that he owned.

After a period of time, Potiphar's wife began to lust after Joseph. She tried to entice him to have a sexual affair with her, but he fled from her. She caught his coat as Joseph fled. She used this coat to claim to her husband that Joseph had attempted to rape her, and because she cried out, he fled and left his coat.

Potiphar believed his wife and put him in the king's prison. It would have been easy for Joseph to say, "Thanks a lot God! What about Your promises?" However, he did what the apostle Paul said, "Wherefore take unto you the whole armor of God, that you may be able to withstand in the evil day, and having done all, to stand." As Joseph continued to have faith and to obey the LORD, the LORD granted him favor with the chief jailer. In fact the jailer soon handed over the entire prison administration to Joseph so that all the other prisoners were responsible to him. The chief jailer had no more worries after that, for Joseph took care of everything. The LORD was with him so that everything ran smoothly.

Sometime later the king of Egypt became angry with his chief baker and wine taster and imprisoned them both. Joseph was assigned to wait upon them. After a period of time, these two men both had dreams. They told Joseph there was no one there to tell them what the dreams meant. Joseph told them God had given him skill in interpreting dreams and asked them to tell him what they dreamed. The king's wine taster told Joseph his dream. Joseph said the dream meant that in three days, Pharaoh was going to give the wine taster his job back. Joseph asked the wine taster to please remember me when he was back in favor, and ask Pharaoh to release him. For I was kidnapped from my homeland among the Hebrews, and now I am in jail when I did nothing to deserve it.

This interpretation encouraged the chief baker to tell his dream to Joseph. The interpretation was that in three days Pharaoh would have him put to death.

Three days later it was Pharaoh's birthday. Just as Joseph had interpreted, the wine taster was restored to his position and the chief baker was put to death. However, Pharaoh's wine taster promptly forgot all about Joseph, never giving him a thought.

One night two years later, Pharaoh had two dreams and was troubled as to what the dreams meant. He called for all the magicians and sages of Egypt and told them the dreams. Not one of them could suggest what his dreams meant. The King's wine taster suddenly remembered Joseph and told Pharaoh about Joseph and his ability to interpret dreams.

One of the hardest things to suffer is when time begins to drag on. During those two years, Joseph could have lost all hope in God's promises, but he continued to have "faith" and to "obey" the LORD. He continued to stand strong during those years, still believing in God's promises.

Upon hearing the account of the king's wine taster, Pharaoh sent for Joseph at once. He was brought hastily from the dungeon, and after a quick shave and change of clothes, came before Pharaoh. Pharaoh told Joseph, "I have heard that you can interpret dreams, and that is why I have called you." Joseph answered Pharaoh saying, "It is not in me: God shall give Pharaoh an answer of peace" (Gen. 41:16).

Pharaoh told the dreams to Joseph. "I was standing upon the bank of the Nile River," he said, "when suddenly seven fat, healthy-looking cows came up out of the river and began grazing along the river bank. But then seven other cows came up from the river, very skinny and bony – in fact, I've never see such poor-looking specimens in all the land of Egypt. And these skinny cattle ate up the seven fat ones that had come out first, and afterwards they were still as skinny as before! Then I woke up."

"A little later I had another dream. This time there were seven heads of grain on one stalk, and all seven heads were plump and full. Then, out of the same stalk, came seven withered, thin heads. And the thin heads swallowed up the fat ones! I told all this to my magicians, but not one of them could tell me the meaning."

"Both dreams mean the same thing," Joseph told Pharaoh. "God was telling you what he is going to do here in the land of Egypt. The seven fat cows (and also the seven fat, well-formed heads of grain) mean that there are seven years of prosperity ahead. The seven skinny cows (and also the seven thin and withered heads of grain) indicate that there will be seven years of famine following the seven years of prosperity."

"So God has showed you what he is about to do: The next seven years will be a period of great prosperity throughout all the land of Egypt; but afterwards there will be seven years of famine so great that all the prosperity will be forgotten and wiped out; famine will consume the land."

"The famine will be so terrible that even the memory of the good years will be erased. The double dream gave double impact, showing that what I have told you is certainly going to happen, for God had decreed it, and it is going to happen soon."

"My suggestion is that you find the wisest man in Egypt and put him in charge of administering a nationwide farm program."

"Let Pharaoh divide Egypt into five administrative districts, and let the officials of these districts gather into the royal storehouses all the excess crops of the next seven years, so that there will be enough to eat when the seven years of famine come. Otherwise, disaster will surely strike" (Gen. 41:17-36 TLB).

Pharaoh said to Joseph, "For as much as God has shown you all this, there is none so discreet and wise as you are: You shall be over my house, and according unto your word shall all my people be ruled: only in the throne will I be greater than you. And Pharaoh said unto Joseph, See, I have set you over all the land of Egypt" (Gen. 41:39-41).

Joseph not only said "yes" to God, but he "loved" God with all his being and had an enduring "faith" and "obedience" to God. After years of being tried, he became an "overcomer" and was promoted to the throne of Egypt. As James writes in James 1:2-4, "My brethren, count it all joy when you fall into divers temptations; Knowing this, that the trying of your faith works patience. But let patience have her perfect work, that you may be perfect and entire, wanting nothing."

After Joseph was second in command on the throne of Egypt for seven or eight years, what God had shown him in dreams as a boy came to pass. Famine came upon Egypt and countries surrounding Egypt. One day he saw ten of his brothers bowing down before him asking for bread during the famine that had come upon that part of the world.

Joseph was not only a king, but now a mature saint. Listen to Joseph as he talks to his brothers after not seeing them for over twenty or more years. They had not seen him since he was a teenager and now he was a mature king at least 36 or 38 years old.

"And Joseph said unto his brethren, Come near to me, I pray you. And they came near. And he said I am Joseph your brother, whom you sold into Egypt. Now therefore be not grieved, nor angry with yourselves, that you sold me here: for God did send me before you to preserve life. . . . And God sent me before you to preserve you a posterity in the earth, and to save your lives by a great deliverance. So now it was not you that sent me here, but God: and He has made me a father to Pharaoh, and lord of all his house, and a ruler throughout all the land of Egypt" (Gen. 45:4-8).

Joseph is a picture of how God wants you and I to run the race set before us and to finish the course, so He can bring us into the plan and purpose He has for us in eternity, that is to sit with Him on His throne and to reign with Him.

C. David

David has the very unusual distinction of being described by God as "a man after my own heart" and that "I will establish his throne forever." The apostle Paul tells us in Acts 13:22, "God raised up unto them David to be their king; to whom also He gave testimony, and said, I have found David the son of Jesse, a man after mine own heart, which shall fulfill all my will." In Psalms 89:36-37, the LORD said, "His (David's) seed shall endure for ever, and his throne. . . . It shall be established for ever." When the angel appeared unto Mary announcing the birth of Jesus, the angel said: "The LORD God shall give unto Him the throne of his father David: And He shall reign over the house of Jacob for ever; and of His kingdom there shall be no end" (Luke 1:32-33).

In the last chapter, we have already talked about David who had allowed his spirit to be developed to worship, to praise and to take authority and dominion. Now let us take a closer look at how God prepared David for the plan and purpose He had for David. In 1 Chronicles 29 we read the account of King David passing the crown of his kingship over Israel on to his son Solomon. What a tremendous moment when David had climbed that last highest mountain of his earthly life and looked back over the last 70 years of his life. Today you and I have the advantage of being able to stand with David upon that mountain top, to look back with him at all those things that made him a man after God's own heart, in spite of his failures.

We are able to see in 1 Chronicles 29:29-30, "Now the acts of David the king, first and last. . . are written. . . . With all his reign and his might, and the times that went over him."

What were the times that went over him? What times?
1. The shepherd boy
2. The soldier
3. The fugitive
4. The king
5. The saint
6. The sinner
7. The time when he died an old man

As we look back over these times, we see the making of a man of God. We see the exact process that God uses. It takes but a moment to make a convert, but for most of us it takes a lifetime to make a saint. Just what made David a man after God's own heart? We will see the same seven steps outlined for us in chapter three: to say "YES" to God, to "LOVE" God, to have "FAITH", to "OBEY", to "OVERCOME", to "PREVAIL IN PRAYER", and the DEVELOPMENT OF THE SPIRIT" that God has given us.

The first quality that we see in David's life that made him a man after God's own heart appears when he is just a shepherd boy. The LORD had sent the prophet Samuel to the town of Bethlehem to anoint the future king of Israel. The only clue God gave to Samuel was that the man would be of the family of Jesse. As the family of Jesse gathered together that day, nobody would have guessed it would be David. As the family was gathered together, Samuel thought it was surely the oldest son Eliab, who looked like every inch a king. When the seven sons of Jesse passed before Samuel, the LORD told Samuel that He does not look at the outward appearance of man, but looks on the heart. At this point, Samuel was bewildered and then asked Jesse if these were all his sons.

To his family, David was only a little boy who watched the sheep. They probably thought he was naïve and a fanatic who played his harp, sang songs and meditated day and night upon the LORD. So small was David in his father's esteem that he didn't even consider it necessary to include him in the family when the prophet of God called them to a sacrifice.

When Samuel found out there was still one more son, he gave the command to go and bring him in to the sacrifice. As soon as David walked in, the LORD said to Samuel, "Arise, anoint him: for this is he" (1 Sam. 16:12). And the SPIRIT OF THE LORD came upon David from that day forward.

We would also miss the whole meaning of this story in 1 Samuel 16 if we were to imagine that this was the first time God had spoken to David's heart. The public anointing was the outcome of what had taken place in private between God and David for a long time. The God who sees and discerns the hearts of all men knew that David's heart had not only said "YES" long before to Him, but that also David "LOVED" the LORD with all his heart. Perhaps one night while David was taking care of the sheep and lying on the ground on his back looking up into the stars, he learned the following truths. "When I consider Your heavens, the works of Your fingers, the moon and the stars, which You have ordained; What is man, that You are mindful of him? and the son of man, that You visited him? For You have made him a little lower than the angels, and have crowned him with glory and honor. You have made him to have dominion over the works of Your hands: You have put all things under his feet" (Ps. 8:3-7). Then David mentions the sheep, oxen, and beasts of the field which give us the clue that he thought this while still a shepherd.

David loved God with all his heart and sought to please Him. God's presence was the most important thing to him in life. David did not have a fickle heart, but one that believed, meditated, set itself on holiness and righteousness, grateful and fixed upon God.

The third quality in David that made him a man after God's own heart is first seen when he began his career as a soldier. As we talked about the giant Goliath and David in chapter three, we see the giant Goliath challenging the armies of Israel. He is a picture of how Satan comes at us at various times, always challenging God's people. The armies of Israel were afraid of him because of a lack of faith and trust in God. This is often a picture of the Church today, unable to conquer Satan and his forces because of a lack of faith and trust.

The Bible tells us that when the men of Israel saw the giant, they fled from him and were greatly afraid. But David volunteered to go and fight him. When King Saul heard of David's desire to take up the giant's challenge, his response was, "You are not able to go against this Philistine to fight with him: for you are but a youth, and he a man of war from his youth" (1 Sam. 17:33).

David was able to convince King Saul to let him go against the giant. Since he had never used any armor before, he went dressed like a shepherd with only his shepherd's staff, his sling shot and five smooth stones. When the giant saw this shepherd lad coming at him with only a shepherd's staff and a sling shot, he was highly insulted saying, "Am I a dog that you come to me with a stick? And the giant cursed David and told him to come on and that he would give his flesh to the vultures and beasts of the field."

Listen to the authority and dominion that David took over the situation. "You come to me with a sword, and with a spear, and with a shield: but I come to you in the name of the LORD of hosts, the God of the armies of Israel, whom you have defied. This day will the LORD deliver you into my hand; and I will smite you, and take your head from you; and I will give the carcasses of the host of the Philistines this day unto the fowls of the air, and to the wild beasts of the earth; that all the earth may know that there is a God in

Israel" (1 Sam. 17:45-46).

As David ran towards the giant, he took one of the stones, put it in his sling shot and hurled it from his sling. Like a guided missile, it hit the giant in the forehead and the giant fell upon his face to the ground. Having no sword, David ran to the fallen giant, took the giant's sword and cut off his head. When the Philistines saw that their champion was dead, they turned and ran. The Israeli army had a great victory that day as they pursued the fleeing Philistines.

Here we see David, moved by the Holy Spirit through his "spirit" taking dominion and authority over the situation. This is the LORD's ultimate plan and purpose for you and me, to rule and to reign with Him. As a result of this, the LORD made David king over Israel and promised to establish his throne forever. Only the LORD knows what this will mean for King David in eternity.

Here we have seen how David said "YES" to God and the "love" and "faith" that had been developed in his life. Now we see David learning to "obey" and to "overcome". David described the times that went over him as, "All Your waves and Your billows are gone over me" (Ps. 42:7). He said, "My times are in Your hand" (Ps. 31:15).

This reminds me of the time I was a teenager and loved to surf the ocean waves as they came into the shore. Many times the waves would break over you and dash you to the bottom and roll you over in the sand.

All these times that went over David was like the writing of God upon his life, making him into a man after God's own heart. These were God's times. By them, He wrote upon David's heart the pattern of His will and purposes. You and I have been chosen by God. He allows times to pass over you as He develops you for His plans and purposes for your life. What sort of times are you going through just now? Remember the Bible tells us, "And we know that all things work together for good to them that love God, to them who are called according to His purpose" (Rom. 8:28).

Following David's victory over the giant Goliath, King Saul made David a leader in his army. David behaved himself wisely and God's favor was upon him. David received great favor with the people as he would return from battles with Israel's enemies. The women would come out of the cities of Israel singing and dancing as the army returned from battle. The women would be singing, "Saul has slain his thousands, and David his ten thousands" (1 Sam. 18:7). This made King Saul jealous of David. As time went on, King Saul not only became jealous of David, but his jealousy turned to hatred. Eventually the hatred turned into a crusade to murder David.

Finally at dinner one night, Saul threw a spear at David endeavoring to pin him to the wall. David escaped and fled to stay with Samuel the prophet. When Saul came looking for him, David fled from where he was staying with Samuel. He secretly met with Jonathan, the son of Saul, to learn what Saul was really trying to do. Jonathan told David to hide himself in a certain place while he found out his father's real intentions. At an appointed time he would come with a little lad to do archery practice where David would be hiding. If he shot the arrows near David, it would be a signal that everything would be alright. But if he shot the arrows way beyond David, it would mean that David should flee for his life.

David waited for the appointed time and the flight of an arrow that would determine his destiny. To his disappointment, the flight of the arrow went beyond him. Now he had no choice except to leave his home, his wife, his friends and flee into the desert wilderness as a fugitive. He was anointed to be king, but was running for his life. Destined to be master over a great kingdom, he would now go begging for bread. It seems that all the providences of God were running completely counter to His promises. It was as if a huge wave had hit David and rolled him down under the water into the sand.

Fear seized David's heart and it lead him to do wrong. He stopped at the Tabernacle in Nob and lied to the priest about what he is doing in order to obtain a sword for protection and food to survive. Then David fled to one of the cities of the Philistines, the city of Gath, thinking he could hide from Saul there. The people there recognize him. In fear, David acted like a crazy mad man. Insane people were usually treated like they were possessed of gods and put out of the city. David then fled to a cave that he knew about deep in the desert wilderness.

You and I may find it easy to criticize David at this point. But remember as David was destined to be the king of Israel, you and I are destined to share the throne of Christ one day. It was during this time David would be learning some very important lessons, learning to look to the LORD "to obey" and "to overcome". For the next six years of his life, David went from one desperate situation to another desparate situation. As we look at what he was going through, we know God was preparing him for the throne. However, David did not see it this way. All he knew was that he was in deep trouble.

Here he was despised and rejected by the "right" people of his day, hiding in a cave in the wilderness. Other men that were in distress, in debt or discontent for other reasons joined up with David. It became a "rag-tag" band of men that were considered the rejects of society. Some would say, "What a pathetic group of men that will never accomplish anything."

King Saul continued to pursue David with an army of three thousand soldiers, chasing David like a partridge around the desert wilderness. This is the way David lived for almost six long years.

During this time it would have been very easy for David to become very embittered against Saul and seek personal vengeance. However, David was learning to look to the LORD for his help and endeavoring to "obey" the LORD in all things. On two different occasions, David was presented with golden opportunities to take vengeance upon Saul and get rid of him.

One hot summer afternoon, David and his men were in a cave where it was cool. To their surprise, Saul and some of his men stopped at the cave to go in, cool off and take an afternoon nap. David and his men could have easily slain Saul, but David refused to take vengeance and touch God's anointed King Saul. David chose to "obey" God and not take advantage of his opportunity for vengeance. David had the opportunity to do the same thing a number of months later. But David was learning to obey God rather than do his own thing.

Here we see a man who has followed God's will, but life even becomes more difficult. It seems that life could not get much worse for him as he looks at the bewildering circumstances that surrounded him. David takes his eyes off the LORD and begins to look at the circumstances. Listen to David, "And David said in his heart, I shall now perish one day by the hand of Saul: there is nothing better for me than that I should speedily escape into the land of the Philistines; and Saul shall despair of me, to seek me any more in any coast of Israel: so shall I escape out of his hand" (1 Sam. 27:1). In a fit of depression David goes to Achish, king of Gath, to dwell in the land of the Philistines.

The LORD had promised David that he would be king of Israel. Now David was doubting God's promises and saying in effect, "I am afraid the LORD has undertaken something more than He can accomplish. I have waited for the LORD long enough, and I am weary of waiting. It is time I took things into my own hands and use my own wits to get out of the situation."

Listen to the actual words of David as recorded in the Bible in Psalms 10:1, "Why stand You afar off, O LORD? Why hide Yourself in times of trouble?" We also read, "How long will You forget me, LORD? Forever? How long will You look the other way when I am in need? How long must I be hiding daily anguish in my heart? How long shall my enemy have the upper hand? Answer me, O LORD my God; give me light in my darkness lest I die" (Ps. 13:1-3 TLB). "My God, my God, why have You forsaken me? Why do You refuse to help me or even to listen to my groans? Day and night I keep on weeping, crying for Your help, but there is no reply" (Ps. 22:1-2 TLB).

King Achish of Gath welcomed David and his men and gave them the little town of Ziklag in which to dwell. At this time David had over 600 men with him. Achish thought they could be used against King Saul in case of war. In order to get provisions to support his 600 men and their families, David and his men made raids upon various enemies of Israel in the southern areas. To keep word from getting back to Achish and the Philistines, they killed men, women and all. When Achish asked where he had made the raids, David replied, "Against the south of Judah," leaving Achish to believe it was against the people of Israel, an outright deception.

After over a year's time, the Philistines were going to battle against Israel. King Achish asked David and his men to join with him. When the other leaders of the Philistines saw David and his men, they commanded Achish to send David and his men back to Ziklag. David felt humiliated. To make things even more disastrous, when David and his men got back to Ziklag, a band of Amalekites had destroyed the town. Their wives, children and possessions were gone. The Bible says the men "lifted up their voice and wept, until they had no more power to weep. . . . And David was greatly distressed; for the people spake of stoning him, because the soul of all the people was grieved, every man for his sons and for his daughters" (1 Sam. 30:4-6).

Could the hour ever have been darker for David? King Saul wanted him dead, the Philistines did not want him, all the wives, children and possessions were gone, and his men wanted to stone him. David was going through the darkest hour of his life. Here was David standing among the ruins of his own self-will and the result of giving into a fit of depression and compromise, despised by his enemies, blamed by his own men, feeling down and out and miles away from God. Can anybody be lower than that? Could any of us be in a worse plight than David? What does one do when he gets to such a place? What can he do?

In 1 Samuel 30:6-8 tells us that David encouraged himself in the LORD. He inquired of the LORD, asking, "Shall I pursue after this troop? shall I over take them?" If David had not turned to the LORD and repented, it would probably have been total failure for David's life.

What did the LORD answer David?
1. "David, I can't trust you now." No, He did not.
2. "David, I am going to keep you on probation at least six months." No, not that.
3. "David, you have to go back in training for a long time before I can trust you in My army." No, not that threat of punishment either.
4. God answered him: "Pursue, you shall surely overtake them and without fail recover all."

David had learned the lesson. When David hit rock bottom, he turned back to God. When he lifted up that tear stained face, the LORD looked down and saw His broken hearted child weeping until he could weep no more. God answered with power and victory and sent him out to conquer. This was a gateway to victory and the accomplishment of God's purpose for his life. This is an Old Testament illustration of what God will do for you.

The Bible tells us David and his men pursued the Amalekites, found them and recovered all the wives, children and possessions and they all returned to Ziklag. After they had been in Ziklag for two days, David received the news that King Saul was killed in battle with the Philistines on Mount Gilboa to the north. Upon receiving this news, David and his men took time to mourn for King Saul and his son Jonathan. After a period of mourning, David wondered if it would be safe to return to his native land of Israel. He inquired of the LORD saying, "Shall I go up into any of the cities of Judah? And the LORD said unto him, Go up. And David said, Where shall I go up? And He said, unto Hebron" (2 Sam. 2:1).

It seems that the darkest hour in a man's experience is always just before the dawning of new light. This was certainly true in David's life. His life had come extremely close to total failure. He found himself on the wrong side, wanting to march with the wrong army and about to fight the wrong people (Israel). Had he gone to battle with Achish and the Philistines against Israel, he would have been involved in the battle in which King Saul was killed. In his darkest hour, David had given up in absolute frustration, despair and discouragement. However, David had turned it all over to the LORD and inquired of the LORD what to do.

This is not just a historical story, but a picture of life today. Many of us give up in a fit of depression and despair. We wonder why there is sickness instead of health, why there is inactivity instead of activity, why we are forgotten by friends rather than receiving help. Do you wonder why God allows discouragement, delays, desperation, financial difficulties and marital problems to come your way? As you read these pages, you are learning how God deals with man.

If you desire to be a man after God's own heart like David, if you have responded to Him with all your heart, there will be a time of testing and preparation. The LORD is refining you and preparing you for His plans and purposes. According to the apostle Peter,

"These trials are only to test your faith, to see whether or not it is strong and pure. It is being tested as fire tests gold and purifies it – and your faith is far more precious to God than mere gold: so if your faith remains strong after being tried in the test tube of fiery trials, it will bring you much praise and glory and honor on the day of His return" (1 Peter 1:7 TLB).

During this time of testing and preparation, God first seeks a vital union with man's inner being or what we call man's "spirit" or heart. As we come into this vital union with God, He enrolls us in what we can call the "school of the Spirit". Remember as you complete school, there comes a time of graduation or for the believer's "exaltation" to the plan and purpose that God has for you.

Wouldn't it be helpful if the LORD would always tell us before-hand how He is going to deal with us and how He wants us to react? However, God never comes to a servant of His and says, "Now I am going to take you through a certain experience which will be of this particular character, and the reason for this is so and so. The usual experience is that without any intimation from the LORD, we find ourselves in a difficult situation which altogether confounds us and puts us beyond the power of explaining that experience. God takes us through without any explanation whatever until the purpose for which that experience was given is reached. Then we have the explanation. Often the most severe discipline is to cheerfully follow God's leading – especially when we cannot understand the purpose of His dealings.

We all want an understanding of God's times that pass over our lives like the waves of the ocean, the times of bereavement, the times of temptation, the times when His billows go over me until I feel I can't take it any more. I want to be able to say "LORD Jesus, my times are in Your hands" – the times when I suffer pain, afflic-tion, loneliness, misunderstanding, persecution, joy, blessings, victory.

These are God's times. If they come from His hand, we can have faith the waves will never overwhelm, the hurricane will never uproot, the floods will never drown – because our times are in His hand.

Now the time for David to become king had arrived. As David

had inquired of the LORD whether to return unto the area of his boyhood, God had told him to return and go to Hebron, which was only about 12 miles south from Bethlehem where David was born. There the men of the tribe of Judah came and anointed David to be king over the house of Judah. Seven years later all the elders of Israel came to Hebron and anointed David king over all Israel.

After becoming king over all Israel, David made Jerusalem his capital. He took an insignificant nation and within a few years, built it into a mighty kingdom completely subduing all neighboring nations from the River of Egypt to almost the great river, the Euphrates River. Although it did not become a world empire, it did become probably one of the most powerful kingdoms on earth at that time. This goes back to the covenant that God made with Abraham in Genesis 15:18, "In the same day the LORD made a covenant with Abraham, saying, Unto your seed have I given this land, from the river of Egypt unto the great river, the river Euphrates."

David took the Ark of the Covenant that Moses made for the Tabernacle in the wilderness when Israel was at Mt. Sinai and brought it from its present place in Kirjath-jearim in Judah and placed it in a Tabernacle on Mt. Zion in Jerusalem. He drew up the plans for the Temple that would be built in Jerusalem by his son Solomon in which the Ark of the Covenant would come to rest.

In my opinion, David's greatest accomplishments were the choirs, orchestras, and the priesthood that he organized for the continual worshiping of God in the Tabernacle of David on Mount Zion as well as later on in the Temple to be built by his son Solomon. Many of the Psalms also were written by David.

Now we come to one of the most difficult and sorrowful times in David's earthly life. It also is a time when we see the LORD's great love and mercy being show to man. As the apostle John writes in 1 John 2:1-2, "My little children, these things write I unto you, that you sin not. And if any man sin, we have an advocate with the Father, Jesus Christ the righteous. And He is the propitiation for our sins: and not for ours only, but also for the sins of the whole world."

We have no record of any great failures in the John's life, yet he encourages the Church by saying, "If we say that we have no sin, we deceive ourselves, and the truth is not in us. If we confess our sins, He is faithful and just to forgive us our sins, and to cleanse us from all unrighteousness. If we say that we have not sinned, we make Him a liar, and His word is not in us" (1 John 1:8-10).

At the zenith of David's earthly life the kingdom of Israel had been established and became a mighty kingdom. In a moment of rest and relaxation, David committed adultery with a neighbor's wife. David already had a number of wives. There was no reason for him to desire another man's wife.

After the affair, the woman sent David word that she was with child. Her husband was a loyal soldier in David's army and was away in battle. In an effort to cover up his sin, David sent a command to the general to send the woman's husband to report on the progress of the battle. The goal was to bring the husband back so that he could be with his wife, and the expected child would be considered his own child. However, the husband was an extremely loyal soldier. After reporting to David, he would not go home. David asked him why he would not go home. The loyal soldier replied, "The ark, and Israel, and Judah, abide in tents; and my lord Joab, and the servant of my lord, are encamped in the open fields; shall I then go into mine house, to eat and to drink, and to lie with my wife? As you live, and as your soul lives, I will not do this thing" (2 Sam. 11:11).

The next morning, David wrote a letter to General Joab, put it under seal and sent it with this loyal soldier back to the battlefield. In the letter, David gave Joab the following instructions: "Set this man in the forefront of the hottest battle, and retire you from him, that he may be smitten, and die" (1 Sam. 11:15).

General Joab sent word back to David that his instructions were accomplished. After an appropriate time of mourning for the death of her husband, David brought his neighbor's wife to the palace. She became one of his wives and gave birth to his son. However, the LORD was displeased with what David had done. A whole year went by and David did not face his sin. God in His love and mercy sent the prophet Nathan to David to help David to face up to his sins and deal with them. The prophet Nathan tells David the following account of an injustice:

"There were two men in a certain city, one very rich, owning many flocks of sheep and herds of goats; and the other very poor, owning nothing but a little lamb he had managed to buy. It was his children's pet and he fed it from his own plate and let it drink from his own cup; he cuddled it in his arms like a baby daughter. Recently a guest arrived at the home of the rich man. But instead of killing a lamb from his own flocks for food for the traveler, he took the poor man's lamb and roasted it and served it."

1 Samuel 12:1-4 TLB

David's anger was greatly kindled against this man and he said to Nathan "As the LORD lives, the man that has done this thing shall surely die. And he shall restore the lamb fourfold, because he did this thing, and because he had no pity" (2 Sam. 12:5-6).

The prophet Nathan then said to David, "You are the man." The prophet recounted all that God had done for David, how God saved David from Saul and made him king of Israel, how David and the kingdom had prospered. If David needed more, God would have given David more. Then came a hard and direct question, "Why, then, have you despised the laws of God and done this horrible deed? For you have murdered Uriah and stolen his wife" (2 Sam. 12:9 TLB).

David acknowledges his sins and confesses to Nathan, "I have sinned against the LORD." Listen to David's prayer in Psalm 51, "Have mercy upon me, O God, according to Your loving kindness: according unto the multitude of Your tender mercies blot out my transgressions. Wash me thoroughly from my iniquity, and cleanse me from my sin. For I acknowledge my transgressions: and my sin is ever before me. . . . For You desire not sacrifice; else would I give it: You delight not in burnt offerings. The sacrifices of God are a broken and contrite heart, O God, You will not despise" (Ps. 51:1-3,16-17).

David had already pronounced judgment upon himself when he said that the man who has done this thing shall surely die and shall restore the lamb fourfold. However, because David had confessed his sin and asked for forgiveness, the prophet Nathan said unto

David, "The LORD also has put away your sin; you shall not die" (2 Sam. 12:13).

Although God forgives sin with its guilt and penalty, it does not erase the consequences that follow sin. If you have murdered someone, forgiveness does not bring the murdered victim back to life. If you have stolen an item, forgiveness does not mean you get to keep the stolen goods, they are to be returned if possible. For the sin of adultery and the sin of murder, David was forgiven of the penalty (which is death) and the guilt. However the consequences were fourfold for each sin.

For the sin of murder, the child that was born as a result of his adultery died. The seeds from his sin of murder resulted in the death of his three sons, Ammon, Absolom and Adonijah. The seeds from his sin of adultery resulted in one of his daughters being raped, his wives defiled by his neighbor, the rebellion of his son Absolom. This sin gave occasion to the enemies of the LORD to blaspheme a man of God and the Bible.

However, our LORD is a God of infinite love and mercy. David continues to be a "man after God's own heart" (Acts 13:22). The promises God made to David still stand.

God made this promise to David in 2 Samuel 7:16, "And your kingdom shall be established for ever before you: your throne shall be established for ever." The angel Gabriel came to Mary, as recorded in Luke 1:30-33, and said, "Fear not, Mary: for you have found favor with God. And, behold, you shall conceive in your womb, and bring forth a son, and shall call his name Jesus. He shall be great, and shall be called the Son of the Highest: and the LORD God shall give unto Him the throne of His father David."

D. MARY

One of the greatest lessons we can learn about how God is preparing us for the plan and purpose for our lives is from the life story of Mary. Her simple love, faith, trust and obedience to the LORD illustrates how the LORD would have us respond. Many artists picture Mary as something less than a woman, untouchable, sexless, floating around the Holy Land in one idealized pose after another. Pictured as the "lovely lady," dressed in blue, awaiting a painless child birth, not-quite-woman and almost divine. However, as we look closely at her life, we will understand why Mary found favor with God.

As we first meet Mary, she was a normal teenage girl maybe only sixteen or seventeen years of age from a poor Jewish family in the town of Nazareth. Like the other teenage girls in her town, she probably worked hard gathering wood, washing clothes, helping to take care of the herds of sheep and goats, cooking in the hot summers and cold winters. If you lined up fifty young ladies from Nazareth, you likely could not have picked Mary out from among them. There is no indication that she was a beauty queen.

Like all the other young ladies, she was looking forward to being married. She was engaged to a man named Joseph. The marriage contract was already drawn up and signed. All that was left was the final marriage ceremony to be conducted before they came together as husband and wife. When I think of Mary, I think about the prophet Samuel who God sent to the house of Jesse to anoint the future king of Israel. You remember that David was the last one to be chosen that day as Samuel reviewed all the sons of Jesse. In fact, Samuel earned the rebuke of the LORD when the LORD said, "For the LORD sees not as man sees; for man looks on the outward appearance, but the LORD looks on the heart" (1 Sam. 16:7). I am afraid if you or I had to choose a young lady to be the mother of Jesus, we would have made a similar mistake.

When the angel Gabriel came to Mary, he told us what the LORD saw when He looked at Mary. The first words of the angel were: "Hail, you who are highly favored, the LORD is with you: blessed are you among women" (Luke 1:28). At first Mary was speechless and wondered why she should be addressed in such exalted terms. The angel then assured her not to be troubled, that she had found favor with God. Then the angel told her she would have a son who would be named Jesus (Yahweh is salvation). He would be called the Son of God, would be given the throne of His ancestor King David, and would reign forever.

Mary's first response was a very normal question. "How shall this be, seeing I am a virgin?" The angel answered that this would be a miracle brought about by the Holy Spirit, for with God nothing shall be impossible. Mary's response to the angel was the startled, flushed, joyously shocked, explosively excited "yes" of a teenage girl, "Behold I am the servant of the LORD, be it unto me according to Your word" (Luke 1:38).

Mary gave a total response to God's call in "love" and "faith" without knowing all the facts. She did not fully understand. But if God was speaking to her, that was all that was necessary. Her heart responded in "faith" and "obedience" because she loved and believed the LORD.

The angel also told Mary that her cousin Elizabeth was with child for the first time in her old age. Mary went immediately to a city in Judea to be with her. When Mary entered the door of the home and her voice was heard, the baby in Elizabeth's womb (now in the sixth month) leaped for joy in the womb of Elizabeth. Prophetically, Elizabeth knew the child Mary would bear would be the Messiah. Elizabeth made this proclamation, "Blessed is she that believed: for there shall be a fulfillment of those things which were told her of the LORD" (Luke 1:45).

Here we not only see Mary saying yes to the LORD, but she "loved" the LORD, had "faith" and was "obedient" to the LORD. As the writer of Hebrews says, "Without faith it is impossible to please him" (Heb. 11:6). Are you beginning to see why Mary was so highly favored? When God speaks to you, do you believe and obey? Or do you question and doubt? Without faith it is impossible to please Him.

In response to Elizabeth, Mary responds in a song of praise, which is evidence that Mary loved God very deeply and that she knew the Word of God. Her song of praise is composed entirely of parts of the Bible. Mary must have committed much of the Word of God to her heart in hours of youthful Bible study. Like David, she could say, "Your word have I hid in mine heart, that I might not sin against You" (Ps. 119:11). Not only did Mary know God's word, but she knew how to worship. As she says in her song, "My soul does magnify the LORD" (Luke 1:46). However, her worship went even deeper than the soul, for her spirit had been developed to worship God in spirit and truth as she sings, "And my "spirit" has rejoiced in God my Savior" (Luke 1:47). Then Mary goes on to praise God for His goodness, mercy and justice. Here is just a teenage girl praising and worshipping the LORD as a seasoned saint. Do you see why God highly favored Mary?

How about your own life? Do you really love Jesus? Do you continually magnify Him in your soul? Do you rejoice in your spirit and give thanks and praise? Or do you continually complain and bemoan your lot in life, or your health or your work? You will not find favor with God if this is true.

After three months with Elizabeth, Mary returns home to Nazareth. Now it would be evident that she was with child. What would she tell Joseph? She loved Joseph. She had given her heart to Joseph. I am sure she wondered, "What will I tell Joseph when he learns that I am going to have a child and he is not the father?" But God had first place in her heart. As the Bible says, "And you shall love the LORD your God with all your heart, and with all your soul, and with all your mind, and with all your strength: this is the first and great commandment" (Mark 12:30). Do you see why Mary was favored so highly by God?

I believe there was a normal, fully developed love life between Joseph and Mary. Can you imagine the hurt in Joseph when he found that Mary was expecting a child that was not his? However, Joseph was a loving and just man and he did not want to hurt Mary in any way. He wanted to dissolve the betrothal in a private manner. While Joseph was thinking on these things, the angel of the LORD appeared unto him in a dream and explained to Joseph what was taking place, how prophecy was being fulfilled. He was told not to be afraid to take Mary as his wife, and that she was to be a virgin until she had brought forth her first born child, who would be named Jesus. Immediately Joseph woke up and did as the angel of the LORD instructed him.

As I pointed out in the last chapter, all of us will be put to the test at various times to see if we will be "overcomers". Remember Jesus told the apostle John in Revelation 3:21, "To him that overcomes will I grant to sit with Me in My throne, even as I also overcame, and am set down with My Father in His throne." At the birth of Jesus in Bethlehem and all the events that took place, Mary did not understand them all but the Bible says, "Mary kept all these things, and pondered them in her heart" (Luke 2:19). When Jesus was twelve years old and stayed behind at the Temple when the rest of the family headed back to Nazareth, Joseph and Mary were almost frantic until they found him in the Temple. Mary asked him, "Why have you done this to us?" (Luke 2:48). Jesus answered, "How is it that you sought Me? did you not know that I must be about My Father's business?" (Luke 2:49). Mary and Joseph did not understand what Jesus was saying, but Mary kept all these sayings in her heart.

When Jesus began His public ministry, He and His disciples were invited to a wedding at Cana. During the wedding, they ran out of wine. Mary came to Jesus asking for His help. Jesus answered her, "Woman what have I to do with you? My hour is not yet come" (John 2:4). Mary showed no offense but turned to the servants and told them, "Whatsoever He says to you, do it" (John 2:5).

As Mary suffered through the arrest, trial and crucifixion of Jesus, we can all imagine her grief, sorrow and pain. Never once did she complain. While on the cross, Jesus looked down on her standing there with His disciple John and said, "Woman, behold your son: and to John He said, Behold your mother" (John 19:26-27). Mary was with the disciples at the resurrection, she was with them in the upper room on the day of Pentecost when the Holy Spirit came upon all of them. She went on to be a vital part of the New Testament Church.

Today Mary has a special place in all of our hearts and has been greatly blessed by the Church. Like Jacob, Joseph and David, she allowed God to prepare her for the plan and purpose He has for her in eternity.

E. PETER

Peter first appears in the Bible when his brother Andrew, who had spent the day with Jesus and was convinced that Jesus was the Messiah, went and found his brother Peter. Andrew proclaimed he had found the Messiah and brought Peter to meet Jesus. Jesus spent a few moments looking at Peter and then said, "You are Simon the son of John, you shall be called Cephas (Peter), which is by inter-pretation, A stone" (John 1:42).

This was a new experience for Peter to have someone stand there and read him like a book. The name Simon represented who he actually was, but Peter is the name that proclaimed the man who he would become. First, let us look at the man that Simon Peter was. Along with his brother Andrew, he was the son of John. He was involved in a fishing business on the Sea of Galilee near Capernaum with Zebedee and his sons, John and James. It was a large business requiring a crew of hired servant. John had business connections in Jerusalem. Historians tell us at that time mule pack trains would gather up snow and ice on Mt. Hermon to the north, then come to Galilee, take the fish catches, put them under ice and take the fish to Jerusalem for market distribution. Peter was known as the "big fisherman," a tall, strong, gruff, blustering and dominating man who could easily handle the hired servants and deal with his business associates. He was a man's man and men liked him. The oaths and swearing that came from his lips the night he denied Christ were not his first. They used to be his natural speech.

It is evident that religion had not been primary in his life. He was content to leave religious matters to the religious leaders. His concept of the Messiah was the same as his contemporaries, who believed one day a great man of God would come and become king of Israel and make Israel the leading nation of the world. Now he was too busy with business to pay attention to religion. Besides, Andrew was the religious one. As Jesus stood there looking at Peter, this was a new experience for the swaggering Simon, who always considered himself superior and worthy.

As Jesus looked at him, he saw a man who was impetuous, stubborn, over-confident, boastful, full of pride and thought he was self-sufficient. They say that when the great artist Michelangelo saw a rugged block of marble, he could also see as he began to sculpture that block of marble, the famous statue of King David that would be the results. In the same way Jesus saw what Peter would become after the dross, flaws and impurities were cleared away. Jesus saw that no one man would be more prominent in His life, that no one man would be present in the crucial hours of His life more often than Peter, that Peter would be the first of the disciples to proclaim that Jesus was God manifested in the flesh, that Peter's name would appear first in the lists of the apostles.

Jesus saw what Peter would become after he had gone through

God's steps of preparation for the plan and purpose He had for Peter's life. He saw that there would be a total "YES" or acceptance of Jesus into his life. That he would "love" God with heart, soul, mind and all his strength. That in days to come, Peter would respond in total "faith" and "obedience". That he was a man who would "overcome" the tests in his life, who would "prevail in prayer" and whose "spirit" would completely be developed in worship, praise and taking dominion and authority. Jesus knew he would become one of the foundation stones on which the New Testament Church would be built.

At the end of his earthly journey, Peter wrote to the Church at large, "So be truly glad! There is wonderful joy ahead, even though the going is rough for a while down here. These trials are only to test your faith, to see whether or not it is strong and pure. It is being tested as fire tests gold and purifies it – and your faith is far more precious to God than mere gold; so if your faith remains strong after being tried in the test tube of fiery trials, it will bring you much praise and glory and honor on the day of His return" (1 Peter 1:6-7 TLB).

Several times Jesus had to rebuke Peter. On one occasion Jesus was telling His disciples how He must go to Jerusalem and how He would suffer and be killed, but be raised again the third day. Peter took Jesus aside and began to rebuke Jesus saying, "Be it far from You, LORD: this shall not be unto You. But Jesus turned, and said unto Peter, Get you behind Me Satan: you are an offense unto Me: for you savorest not the things that be of God, but those that be of men. Then Jesus said unto His disciples, If any man will come after Me, let him deny himself, and take up his cross, and follow Me" (Matt. 16:22-24).

At the Last Supper on the night before His crucifixion, Jesus told all His disciples that they all would be offended (made to stumble) because of what was going to happen to Him. Listen to Peter, "Though all men shall be offended because of You, yet I will never be offended. . . . Though I should die with You, yet will I not deny You"(Matt. 26:33-35). With Peter it was still: "I. . . I. . . I. . . I."

Jesus told Peter that before the rooster would crow in the morning that Peter would have denied Him three times. Peter replied,

"Though I should die with You, yet I will not deny You" (Matt. 26:35). That same night Jesus went with His disciples to the Garden of Gethsemane to pray. Jesus asked all of His disciples to pray with Him. He went a short distance from them to pray to His Father. When He returned, all of his disciples were asleep. Jesus said to Peter, "What, could you not watch with me one hour?" (Matt. 26:40).

At this time Judas came leading a group of the chief priests and a band of soldiers into the Garden of Gethsemane to point out Jesus so they could arrest Him. As they began to take hold of Jesus, Peter thought he could handle the situation. He drew his sword and aimed for the neck of the high priest's servant. Evidently the man ducked the coming sword enough to miss having his neck cut off, but had his ear cut off instead. Jesus rebuked Peter for trying to do things in his own strength. He tells Peter that He could have called for twelve legions of angels, but He was there to fulfill God's plan and purpose. Then Jesus touched the man's ear and made him whole again. At this point all the disciples forsook Him and fled. But Peter followed at a distance as did John.

Jesus was being tried before the high priest, elders and scribes. John had connections with the high priest and went in. He brought Peter into the palace courtyard. As the trial proceeded, a number of people recognized Peter and began to accuse him of being with Jesus. Peter began to deny the accusations. He cursed and swore he did not know the man Jesus. Just then Peter heard the rooster crowing. Jesus turned and looked at Peter, and Peter remembered Jesus saying, "Before the rooster crows today, you will deny me three times." Peter went out and wept bitterly. Would Peter give up and go his own way, or would he go on to become an "overcomer"? For the first time, Peter comes to see himself as he really is.

Notice how Jesus continued to deal with Peter. After the trial and crucifixion of Jesus, Peter remained in the company of the disciples. He repented of all his pride, self-confidence and boastfulness. Now he had become as clay ready for the master potter (Jesus) to mold him into the man God had planned for him to become.

On the morning of the resurrection, the women came to the tomb and found it empty. Two angels were standing there. The angels asked them why they were seeking the living among the dead. The angels reminded the women that Jesus told them He would arise on the third day. Then the women remembered the words of Jesus. The angel told them to go tell His disciples and Peter. That evening Jesus appeared to ten of the disciples, who were assembled in a secure place because they still feared the Jews. Jesus stood in the room with them and the disciples were overcome by wonder and joy. Eight days later Jesus appeared to all the eleven in the same house.

The third time Jesus appeared to His disciples was a number of days later by the Sea of Galilee. The disciples had spent the night fishing and caught nothing. In the morning there was a man standing on the shore who asked them had they caught any fish. They replied that they had not. He told them to cast their net on the other side of the boat. When they did, the net was immediately full of fish. Then John recognized that it was Jesus. When the disciples got to the shoreline, Jesus had already prepared breakfast and they ate together that morning.

Then Jesus began to minister to Peter. He said, "Simon, son of John, do you love me more than these?" (John 21:15). Notice, He did not say "Peter" but "Simon." Jesus was making sure the old "Simon" had now really overcome and was really "Peter." The old proud, boastful, willful Simon was gone. Now it was Peter saying, "Yes, LORD, You know that I love You" (John 21:15). Then Jesus said, "Feed my sheep." Twice more Jesus questioned Peter, and Peter gave the same basic answer.

Peter had now been prepared for the plan and purpose that God had for him not only in this life, but for eternity. It was Peter who led the Church on the day of Pentecost when they were all filled with the Holy Spirit. He preached a sermon that brought three thousand souls into the Kingdom of God that day. Peter was the leader in the early Church and one of the first to preach to the Gentiles. According to Acts 12, after King Herod had the apostle James martyred, he had Peter arrested and put in prison with a guard of sixteen soldiers, and was chained to the guards.

If he was the old Simon, he would have clanged the chains, pulled bars, shouted, started fights with the soldiers, and cursed everyone. But the "overcomer" Peter just went to sleep and left it with the LORD. An angel of the LORD came and tapped Peter on the shoulder, picked him up off the floor and led him out of the prison. All this time Peter thought he was having a good dream. When he was about a block away out in the night air he realized an actual angel had come and delivered him out of prison.

From that time he was one of the main leaders of the New Testament Church, not only in Jerusalem but in other parts of the world including Rome. In Matthew 19:27-28, Peter asked Jesus, "Behold, we have forsaken all, and followed You; what shall we have therefore? And Jesus said unto them, Verily I say unto you, That you which have followed Me, in the regeneration when the Son of man shall sit in the throne of His glory, you also shall sit upon twelve thrones, judging the twelve tribes of Israel."

F. JOHN

Previously it was mentioned that the third time Jesus appeared to His disciples after His resurrection was when seven of them decided to go fishing on the Sea of Galilee. After fishing all night and catching no fish, that morning they saw Jesus standing on the shore. Because of the distance, they did not recognize Him at first. Jesus called out to them to ask if they had caught any fish. They replied that they had not. Jesus told them to cast their nets on the other side of the boat. Suddenly the net was so full of fish that they could not draw it into the boat. They brought the boat to the shore line about 100 yards away. As they approached the shore, John realized that it was Jesus standing on the shore. When they came ashore, Jesus had prepared a fire and was fixing breakfast for them. This is when Jesus began to ask Peter, "Do you love Me more than these?" When Jesus had asked the question three times and told Peter to feed His sheep, Jesus told Peter that when he was old that he also would be crucified. Then He gave Peter the command, "Follow Me."

Peter turned and saw John. He asked Jesus, "What shall this man do?" (John 21:21). Peter was actually asking Jesus what John would have to go through. The answer that Jesus gave Peter might be quoted as, "Peter, how I deal with John is not your problem.

Your problem is to respond to Me and follow Me." God endeavors to work in every one of our lives according to what the needs are, if we will only respond to Him.

In John's life we will see how the LORD wants us to respond in:

1. Saying "Yes
2. Love
3. Faith
4. Obedience
5. To Overcome
6. Prevail in Prayer
7. Development of our "spirit"

So let us take a close look at John's life for God wants the very same thing from you.

As we look at John, he also was a fisherman in the full sense that Peter was a fisher of men. He was no less a builder of the Church than Paul was a builder of the Church. In the book of Acts we read that John was right along Peter in preaching and bringing people into the Kingdom of God. John also wrote a good portion of the New Testament. In the Bible we read that John and Andrew were the first ones to believe and accept Jesus as the "CHRIST". They began as disciples of John the Baptist. When John the Baptist pointed out who Jesus was, they answered with an emphatic "yes" and responded to Jesus with all their hearts.

John, along with his brother James and his father Zebedee, were all involved in a family fishing business with hired servants. They were also in partnership with Andrew and Peter. John was often referred to as the disciple Jesus loved and also as the apostle of love. However, until his life had been changed by Jesus, a number of times Jesus had to rebuke John in no uncertain terms.

During the earthly ministry of Jesus, John rebuked a man casting out demons in the name of Jesus because the man was not among the company of disciples traveling with Jesus. This earned John a rebuke. Jesus said to John, "Forbid him not; for he that is not against us is for us" (Luke 9:50). It is interesting that John did not record this incident in the Gospel of John.

On another occasion when Jesus was traveling to Jerusalem through Samaria, He sent some of His disciples into a village of Samaria to make preparations for an overnight stop. The Samaritans refused to receive Jesus. John and his brother James said, "Master, shall we order fire down from heaven to burn them up?" (Luke 9:54 TLB). Jesus turned and rebuked them, and said, "You know not what manner of spirit you are of. For the Son of man is not come to destroy men's lives but to save them" (Luke 9:55-56). Neither does John record this incident in the Gospel of John. In the Gospel of Mark, when Mark lists the twelve disciples in Mark 3:17, "And James the son of Zebedee and John the brother of James; and He (Jesus) surnamed them Boanerges, which is, The sons of thunder."

A short time before the crucifixion of Jesus, James and John along with their mother came to Jesus with a request. Jesus asked them what their request was. They answered, "Grant unto us that we may sit, one on Your right hand, and the other on Your left hand, in Your glory" (Mark 10:37). When the other ten disciples heard this, they began to be much displeased with James and John. Jesus had to gather all twelve disciples together to explain to them that even though those who rule over the Gentiles lord it over them and their great men exercise authority over them, but it shall not be so among them. Jesus said, "Whosoever of you will be the chiefest, shall be servant of all. For even the Son of man came not to be ministered unto, but to minister, and to give His life a ransom for many" (Mark 10:44-45).

Jesus also told James and John they did not understand what they were asking and asked them, "Can you drink of the cup that I drink of? and be baptized with the baptism that I am baptized with?" (Mark 10:38). Both James and John answered Jesus saying, "We can." Jesus then told them that they indeed would drink of the cup that He would drink of; and be baptized with the baptism He would be baptized with, but to sit on His right hand and on His left hand was not His to give, but it shall be given to them for whom it is prepared.

Both James and John accepted what Jesus told them and went on to love and obey Jesus with all their whole being (body, soul and spirit). John, James and Peter became an inner circle with Jesus.

They were on the Mount of Transfiguration when Jesus was transfigured for a moment back to His former glory (Matt. 17:1-8). When Jesus went to pray in the Garden of Gethsemane, He took Peter, James and John to pray especially with Him.

James became the first disciple to be martyred. Although John lived longer than all the other disciples, he knew what it was to suffer for Jesus Christ. According to church tradition, John was once plunged into boiling oil, but lived through that experience only to be exiled later to the island of Patmos off the coast of Asia Minor. It is there that the Church believes John received the revelations that he wrote in the Book of Revelation.

There are two outstanding qualities that we see in the life of John. His "love" for the LORD and His Church and the tremendous "faith" that he had. Through "faith" John had tremendous understanding of God, to recognize and see God in those things happening around him, and to glorify God. The Church often refers to John as the Disciple of Love. There is no record of anyone having a greater love for the LORD and His Church than John.

The other Gospel writers wrote primarily the historical facts concerning the life of Christ. Matthew and Luke record the historical facts of the birth of Jesus, the announcement of the angel to Mary, the birth in Bethlehem, being born in a manager, the shepherds and the wise men. But listen to John, "In the beginning was the Word, and the Word was with God, and the Word was God" (John 1:1). "And the Word was made flesh, and dwelt among us, and we beheld His glory, the glory as of the only begotten of the Father, full of grace and truth" (John 1:14).

When John looked at the manger, he saw more than just a baby, shepherds, wise men or angels. He saw God come in the flesh, by whom all things were made, who formed this world, put the mountains in their places, whose finger traced the course of the rivers down the mountains, across the plains and to the sea, who created all the stars, put them in their places and called them by name.

Here John saw the Creator who took upon Himself humanity to live a perfect human life without sin so that He would die on a cross to pay for the sins of the whole world. We would not have to pay for our sins in an eternal hell, but would receive eternal life and dwell with Him forever in eternity.

When Jesus called John to be a full-time disciple, it was while John was mending fishing nets beside the Sea of Galilee. What John was doing at that time was also a prophetic picture of what would be John's main ministry, which would be that of a "mender of the nets." John writes more about love in his Gospel and letters to the Church than all the other writers put together. This is the same disciple who originally wanted to call fire down from heaven on those who rejected him, the one who originally wanted first place for himself on the right hand of Jesus. He had been transformed into the apostle of love by the Holy Spirit. He learned that God is love.

Jesus said in John 13:34, "A new commandment I give unto you, That you love one another; as I have loved you, that you also love one another." John always obeyed and practiced this. Church tradition tells us that when John was in his nineties, he lived in Ephesus. Although he was old and to feeble to walk, they would carry him to church on a bed. You can imagine how the congregation wanted to hear from the last living disciple of the LORD. His main message to the Church was, "Little children, love one another." When asked why he always repeated the same words he replied, "It is the LORD's commandment, and enough is done when this one commandment is obeyed."

G. PAUL

One lesson I trust that you are learning from the lives of the various people who have been described is how differently we look at men in comparison to how God looks at men. When the prophet Samuel anointed Saul as the first king of Israel, Saul was head and shoulders above the rest of the men, he was strong, good looking, impressive. Looking at him, he looked every inch like a king. Yet Saul proved to be a man God could not use because he would not let God prepare him for the plan and purpose He had for him. As far as eternity is concerned, Saul was an utter failure.

In contrast as we look at the apostle Paul, probably most of us would have written him off at the beginning. Many New Testament scholars would describe Paul as a man of small stature, weak voice, a "skinny little runt of a Jew" with no sense of humor. Paul was all business, never got married and probably was never sought after as husband material. Yet we read in the Bible that when the LORD spoke to Ananias (a devout man according to the law, having a good report of the Jews which dwelt in Damascus, Acts 22:12) to go to Paul and lay hands on him so that he would receive his eye sight again and be filled with the Holy Spirit, Ananias was afraid at first to go. The LORD said to him, "Go your way: for he is a chosen vessel unto Me, to bear My name before the Gentiles, and kings, and the children of Israel: For I will show him how great things he must suffer for My name's sake" (Acts 9:15-16). The apostle Paul acknowledges in Galatians 1:15, "it pleased God, who separated me from my mother's womb, and called me by His grace."

When Ananias came to Paul, Paul's immediate reaction was "YES" and he was immediately baptized in water and filled with the Holy Spirit. Let us take a look at how God prepared Paul for the plan and purpose He had for Paul in this life and eternity.

Paul was born into a godly Jewish family that had moved to Tarsus, a Roman city in Cilicia. His birth name was Saul. After his conversion, his name was changed to Paul. His father brought Paul up in the strict observance of the Hebrew faith and traditions. Somehow his father had obtained Roman citizenship, in addition to being a Jew. Therefore, Paul was not only a Jew but also born as a citizen of Rome.

At an early age, Paul was sent to Jerusalem to be educated. He had for one of his teachers one of the most learned and distinguished rabbis of the day, Gamaliel, who was the grandson of another great rabbi, Hillel. It was Gamaliel whose speech, recorded in Acts 5:34-39, prevented the Sanhedrin from attempting to slay the apostles. As a result of Paul's education and training, he gained a position of large influence. Opportunities of honor and gain had been open to him. As we read in Acts 22:5 and Acts 26:10, Paul received great authority from the high priest and the council of the elders to persecute and imprison the followers of Jesus.

Paul was active in the persecution of Stephen, the first Christian martyr. As the people stoned Stephen, they "laid down their clothes at a young man's feet, whose name was Saul (Paul)" (Acts 7:58).

However, as Stephen was dying, he prayed for Paul and those stoning him (Acts 7:60). Immediately after Stephen's death, we find Paul taking a leading part in the persecution of Christians. He became fanatical about trying to stamp out this new Christianity. He was consumed with great zeal and totally blind to what he was doing.

In the Acts 9, we read that he was on his way to Damascus to arrest Christians and bring them back to Jerusalem to be dealt with. In order for God to get Paul's attention, He had to knock Paul off his donkey. At high noon, a bright light shined down from heaven and Paul fell down on the ground. God spoke to him audibly saying, "Saul, Saul; (Paul), why do you persecute Me?" (Acts 9:4). Paul answered, "Who are you LORD?" The LORD replied, "I am Jesus who you persecute, it is hard for you to kick against the pricks" (Acts 9:5). At that moment we see that Stephen's prayer for God to forgive Paul was answered when Paul, who now was trembling and astonished, said, "LORD what will You have me to do?" The LORD answered, "Arise, and go into the city, and it shall be told you what you must do" (Acts 9:6). That is when Ananias came and prayed for Paul and baptized him.

Paul had now taken the first step to say "YES". Next, the LORD would continue to prepare Paul for the plan and purpose He had for Paul – to "love" God with all his heart, to develop "faith" and "obedience", to be an "overcomer", to "prevail in prayer", to develop his "spirit" in worship and praise and to "take authority" and "dominion".

Paul immediately began to evangelize and preach Jesus Christ in Damascus, which caused the Jews to make plans to kill Paul. During the night the Christians at Damascus let him down in a basket over the city wall. In Galatians 1:17-18, Paul said that he spent the next three years in Arabia. This was a time of God developing "love", "faith" and "obedience" in Paul. After this period of time, he went up to Jerusalem to see Peter. It appears that the Christians in Jerusalem were still afraid of him because of his former reputation. Paul directed his efforts especially towards his former friends, the Greek-speaking Jews. Because Paul boldly spoke about Jesus, within fifteen days they went about to kill Paul.

The threatening danger caused the brethren to send him away. They took him to Caesarea and sent him from there back to the city of Tarsus, where he was born, and he spent the next six or seven years there. Paul was forgotten about until Barnabas went to Tarsus looking for Paul to come and help him with the Church at Antioch, which was now basically a Greek-speaking Gentile congregation.

The three years in Arabia and another seven years back in Tarsus was a ten-year training and preparation time for Paul before he would begin the ministry the LORD had planned for him. When Barnabas and Paul returned to Antioch, a great outpouring of the Holy Spirit took place. Many Gentiles became believers. It was here at Antioch that believers were first called Christians (Acts 11:26).

During the next twenty plus years of Paul's life, we see the life of an "overcomer", one who "prevailed in prayer", a mighty man of God who in "spirit" knew how to worship, praise and take dominion and authority. After several fruitful years of ministry in Antioch, the Holy Spirit said, "Separate Me Barnabas and Paul for the work whereunto I have called them" (Acts 13:2).

After a time of prayer and fasting, the Church at Antioch sent Paul and Barnabas on their first missionary journey. It was approximately two years in duration. They traveled through the southern part of Asia Minor establishing new churches. Their customary practice was to go first to the Jewish synagogue in a city and share the Gospel with the Jews first. When the Jews would no longer receive their ministry, then they would turn to the Gentiles who believed and start a New Testament type of Church. The opposition of the unbelieving Jews grew so strong and vehement that in the city of Lystra, they were able to persuade the people to stone Paul. They dragged his body out of the city, supposing that he was dead. However, as an "overcomer", Paul got up and went on to the next city to preach the Gospel. Whether Paul actually died is unclear; however, the people knew that he had been definitely injured to the point where they thought he was dead.

After returning to Antioch for a period of time, Paul began a second missionary journey to visit the churches that had been established on the first missionary journey and to establish new churches in Asia Minor, Macedonia and Greece. On this second missionary journey we see an example of how Paul's "spirit" had been developed to worship, to praise and to take authority and dominion. In the city of Philippi there was a certain young woman who was possessed by an evil spirit of divination or fortune-telling. After a number of days of this young woman harassing Paul and his companions, Paul rebuked the evil spirit to come out of her. When her masters saw that she had lost the spirit of fortune-telling, they stirred up the people and the city magistrates against Paul and his companions. As a result Paul and his companions were beaten and then cast into an inner prison and their feet made fast in stocks.

At about midnight as Paul and Silas began to lift up their "spirits" in prayer, singing praises and worship, the LORD responded by sending an earthquake that not only shook the prison, but caused all the locked doors to open and the chains to fall off the prisoners. When the head jailor awoke from his sleep and saw all that had happened, he assumed that all the prisoners had escaped. He was ready to commit suicide, since he would be put to death for allowing the prisoners to escape. The apostle Paul stopped him from killing himself and told him all the prisoners were still there. When the jailer realized how God had intervened for Paul, he asked Paul how to become a Christian. That night the jailer and all his household accepted Jesus Christ and were baptized.

As the apostle Paul wrote to the Church at Corinth, "For though we walk in the flesh, we do not war after the flesh: For the weapons of our warfare are not of the flesh, but mighty through God to the pulling down of strongholds; Casting down imaginations, and every high thing that exalts itself against the knowledge of God, and bringing into captivity every thought to the obedience of Christ" (2 Cor. 10:3-5). Here we see that Paul's "spirit" had been so developed in the LORD in worship and praise that he was able to take authority and dominion in this situation.

There are many other journeys that the apostle Paul made as well as years spent in imprisonment. We could well ask ourselves the question, "How many happy days did Paul have?" Read a description that the apostle Paul wrote concerning his own life. "I have worked harder, been put in jail oftener, been whipped times without number, and faced death again and again and again. Five different times the Jews gave me their terrible thirty-nine lashes. Three times I was beaten with rods. Once I was stoned. Three times I was shipwrecked. Once I was in the open sea all night and the whole next day. I have traveled many weary miles and have been often in great danger from flooded rivers, and from robbers, and from my own people, the Jews, as well as from the hands of the Gentiles. I have faced grave dangers from mobs in the cities and from death in the deserts and in the stormy seas and from men who claim to be brothers in Christ but are not. I have lived with weariness and pain and sleepless nights. Often I have been hungry and thirsty and have gone without food; often I have shivered with cold, without enough clothing to keep me warm" (2 Cor. 11:23-27 TLB).

Church history tells us that the apostle Paul was beheaded as a martyr in Rome in 67 or 68 A.D. Some of his last words were written to his son in the LORD, Timothy. "For I am now ready to be offered, and the time of my departure (death) is at hand. I have fought a good fight, I have finished my course (race), I have kept the faith: Henceforth there is laid up for me a crown of righteousness, which the LORD, the righteous judge, shall give me at that day: and not to me only, but unto all them also that love His appearing" (2 Tim. 4:6).

As you look back over the Paul's life, no one has been able to calculate how many souls he introduced to Jesus Christ. There were probably hundreds of churches established as a result of his ministry. Conservative scholarship attributes fourteen books of the New Testament as being written by the apostle Paul. There is definitely one certain thing we can say about the Paul's life. It is a detailed example of how God prepares a man for the plans and purposes He has for his life.

Through the illustrations of the lives of Jacob, Joseph, David, Mary, Peter, John and Paul, we are able to see the different needs, the shortcomings of individual lives and how God works in various ways in different lives to prepare us for the plan and purpose He has for our lives in time and more importantly for eternity.

CHAPTER FIVE

KINGDOM OF GOD, KINGDOM LIVING, THE TRIUMPH OF THE KINGDOM OF GOD

A. KINGDOM OF GOD

During His earthly ministry, Jesus spoke many things to the multitudes in parables. This puzzled His disciples so they came to Him and asked Him, "Why do You speak to them in parables?" Jesus answered, "Because it is given unto you to know the mysteries of the Kingdom of Heaven, but to them it is not given" (Matt. 13:10-11). The Gospel writer Mark recorded the words of Jesus, "Unto you it is given to know the mystery of the Kingdom of God: but unto them that are without, all these things are done in parables" (Mark 4:11).

Matthew uses the term "kingdom of heaven" while Mark uses the term "kingdom of God." Both phrases mean the same thing. Matthew was writing his Gospel to the Jews who never used the name God because they never wanted to be guilty of taking the name of God in vain so they would only say LORD or Heaven. Mark was writing his Gospel primarily to Gentiles who never thought in terms of the commandment, "You shall not take the name of the LORD your God in vain" (Exod. 20:7)

What did Jesus mean by the MYSTERY OF THE KINGDOM OF GOD? Why did He refer to it as a MYSTERY? The apostle Paul also uses the same term MYSTERY in his letter to the Church in Rome in Romans 16:25-26, "Now to Him that is of power to establish you according to my Gospel, and the preaching of Jesus Christ, according to the revelation of the MYSTERY, which was kept secret since the world began, But now is made manifest."

All of the New Testament was originally written in New Testament Greek. The word translated as "mystery" from the Greek into English does not mean something that is mysterious, but means knowledge that is made known in a manner and time appointed by God. At the time of man's creation, God did not reveal all the plans and purposes that He had for man. He did reveal that man was created in His image and likeness and that man was to have dominion. To the prophet Daniel, God revealed even more of His plans and purposes for man. However, when Daniel wanted to know more, the LORD said to Daniel, "Go your way, Daniel: for the words are closed up and sealed till the time of the end" (Dan. 12:8-9). As we progressively go through the Bible, more and more of God's plans and purposes for man are revealed.

As John the Baptist began his ministry, he began preaching in the wilderness, "Repent you: for the kingdom of heaven is at hand" (Matt. 3:2). As Jesus began His preaching and healing ministry in Galilee, the people sought for Him to stay with them, but Jesus said to them, "I must preach the kingdom of God to other cities also: for therefore am I sent" (Luke 4:43).

When Jesus sent His disciples out to preach for the first time, what did He tell them to preach? Most of us would say that He sent them out to preach "Jesus saves." However, when you turn to Luke 9, after He gave them power and authority over all the devils and to cure diseases, He told them what to preach, "Preach the kingdom of God, and to heal the sick" (Luke 9:2).

In Luke 10, we read that the next step was that Jesus appointed seventy other disciples and sent them out two and two. He told them to heal the sick, cast out demons, raise the dead and tell them what? The message was, "say unto them, the kingdom of God is come nigh unto you" (Luke 10:9).

Jesus made the Kingdom of God the center of His message. If you go back through the four Gospels, it is emphasized over a hundred times. Jesus said, "The law and the prophets were until John: since that time the kingdom of God is preached, and every man presses into it" (Luke 16:16). During the last days of His ministry before the crucifixion, Jesus was telling His disciples about the end times and told them, "And this Gospel of the kingdom shall be preached in all the world for a witness unto all nations; and then shall the end come" (Matt. 24:14).

Even after the resurrection, when the risen Jesus was appearing to the disciples, we read, "To whom also He showed Himself alive after His passion by many infallible proofs, being seen of them forty days, and speaking of the things pertaining to the kingdom of God" (Acts 1:3). When the early Church began to spread the Gospel, we read in Acts 8 that Philip went to Samaria and preached. "But when they believed Philip preaching the things concerning the kingdom of God, and the name of Jesus Christ, they were baptized, both men and women" (Act 8:12).

In the last years of the apostle Paul's ministry while he was under arrest in Rome, we read in Acts 28:23, "there came many to him into his lodging, to whom he expounded and testified the kingdom of God, persuading them concerning Jesus, both out of the law of Moses, and out of the prophets, from morning till evening." Then the book of Acts concludes with this statement, "And Paul dwelt two whole years in his own hired house, and received all that came in unto him, Preaching the kingdom of God, and teaching those thing which concern the LORD Jesus Christ, with all confidence, no man forbidding him" (Acts 28:30-31).

Author's Note: Since Jesus made the "KINGDOM OF GOD" the center of His teaching along with salvation, I believe we should reverance the Kingdom of God as a proper name.

If Jesus made the Kingdom of God the center of His message and commanded His disciples to preach the Kingdom of God, the greatest need of men is to seek to understand and enter into the Kingdom of God. When the disciples asked Jesus to teach them how to pray, He gave them the model of the Lord's Prayer. The first petition in this prayer after addressing the Father is, "Your Kingdom come, Your will be done on earth as it is in Heaven." Prayer is the deepest thing we do, and in the deepest thing we do, the coming of His Kingdom is the most important. It is to be foremost and uppermost in our lives here on earth and in eternity. In the Sermon on the Mount, the most important lesson that Jesus taught was, "Seek you first the Kingdom of God, and His righteousness; and all these things shall be added unto you" (Matt. 6:33).

In the book of Acts, the very first chapter tells how Jesus appeared to His disciples after His resurrection to give them final instructions before ascending back to His Father in Heaven. The very first question of the disciples was, "LORD, will You at this time restore again the Kingdom to Israel?" (Acts 1:6). The heart of Jesus must have sunk within Him. Jesus had spent three years of intensive teaching and illustrating the Kingdom of God to His disciples. After His resurrection, He had spent 40 days dotting His "i's" and crossing the "t's" of His message on the Kingdom of God. And their very first question was, "Do we get back our self-government?" They didn't reject the Kingdom, they reduced it to a political kingdom.

However, the Church as a whole has made the same mistake. We have not rejected the Kingdom, but we have reduced it. We have reduced it to the "church" or to the "second coming" or to "heaven" one day.

Going back to God's original plan and purpose for your life as stated in Genesis 1:26, were these goals: "Let us make man,"
1. In Our image
2. After Our likeness
3. Let them have dominion (authority)

As was explained in chapter one of this book, the "image" would be a "spirit" as God is a SPIRIT. The likeness would be a "trinity" as God is Father, Son and Holy Spirit, man would be body, soul and spirit. The first two goals were accomplished at creation; however, authority is only learned and obtained through obedience. THIS IS WHERE THE KINGDOM OF GOD COMES INTO THE PLANS AND PURPOSES GOD HAS FOR MAN, NOT ONLY IN TIME BUT MORE SO IN ETERNITY.

I used to think that seeking the Kingdom of God was seeking to go to Heaven. However, God is not primarily interested in getting us to Heaven, as He is interested in getting Heaven into us. In Heaven, God's will and rule is absolutely done without exception. When Satan and the angels that followed Satan decided they wanted to do their own thing, they were cast out of Heaven.

The Kingdom of God is when Jesus comes and sets up His throne and rule in our lives. It is not something off in the future, but it is NOW! I always used to think of the Kingdom as a future or a place. It is not just Heaven or the Millennium. The Kingdom of God has always existed and Heaven and the Millennium will be a part of the Kingdom of God. The Kingdom of God is a condition of God's WILL AND RULE being absolute, before it is a place. God is not trying to get us to Heaven, but trying to get Heaven or His Kingdom into us. This is what Jesus taught in the Lord's Prayer "Your Kingdom come. Your will be done, as is in Heaven, so in earth" (Luke 11:2).

One day during the earthly ministry of Jesus, one of the scribes asked Jesus what the greatest commandment was. When the scribe heard the answer Jesus gave, he repeated it as follows, "to love Him (God) with all the heart, and with all the understanding, and with all the soul, and with all the strength. . . is more than all whole burnt offering and sacrifices. And when Jesus saw that he answered discreetly, He said unto him, You are not far from the Kingdom of God" (Mark 12:33-34).

The word "kingdom" in the Greek New Testament is a word used 932 times in the New Testament Greek. It is primarily an abstract noun denoting "sovereignty, royal power, dominion." The Kingdom of God is the sphere of God's rule. Where the King is, there is the Kingdom. (See Endnote 1.)

From the use of this word in the New Testament, the Kingdom of God has to do with a reign and not necessarily with a place. The important question is not only have you heard the Gospel, not only have you believed and been saved, BUT HAS THE GOSPEL BROUGHT YOU UNDER THE RULE OF GOD? The following illustration depicts three different states. The circle depicts a person's heart, the chair depicts the seat or throne of a person's will and spirit, and the "E" depicts the person's ego or the center of his being and the cross depicts whether Jesus is outside of our heart or has been accepted into our life. The most important question is who sits on the throne of our lives?

The Kingdom of God

The Unbeliever

*A Believer
but not under
Rule of God*

*A Believer
under the
Reign of God*

*Does
Jesus
sit on
the
throne
of your life?*

The Heart

The Chair
represents a
Person's Will
and Spirit

The Person's Ego
or center of
his being

The Cross
represents
Jesus Christ

In the Book of Acts, people understood exactly what the apostles meant by the Kingdom of God. When the apostle Paul and Silas were preaching the Kingdom of God in Thessalonica, a number of the people dragged Paul and Silas before the rulers of the city crying, "These that have turned the world upside down are come here. . . and these all do contrary to the decrees of Caesar, saying that there is another king, one Jesus" (Acts 17:6-7).

It is important to not only understand the Kingdom of God, but that we are to seek His rule, reign, government and the sovereignty of God ruling our lives. It is also important to understand that the CHURCH in of itself is not the Kingdom, but part of the Kingdom of God. The Church is not an end in itself; the end is the Kingdom of God. In the Lord's Prayer, it does not say, "May Your Church come on earth as it is in Heaven." The prayer is, "Your Kingdom come. . . on earth as it is in Heaven."

Today the Holy Spirit is saying that where the Kingdom of God is in authority, there will the true Church be built up. It is the presence of the Kingdom of God that produces the Church. The Church is to do the work of the Kingdom of God. Jesus said the Kingdom of God is like unto a grain of mustard seed (an unusually small seed) which a man took and sowed in his field. However, when it is grown, it is the greatest among herbs, and becomes a tree, so that the birds of the air come and lodge in its branches. (See Matthew 13:31-32.)

Jesus took twelve men and discipled them for over three years until the Kingdom of God became established in their lives. From that small seed, the Church was established on the day of Pentecost with a group of 120 believers in Acts 2. Today the Church has grown to over several billion believers. Later on in this chapter, we will see that at the second coming of Christ and in the millennial reign of Christ the King, the Kingdom of God will be brought to full maturity and perfection. The prophet Daniel and the apostle John saw this in their visions. The apostle Paul declares in 1 Corinthians 15:24 that after the second coming of Christ, "Then comes the end, when He shall have delivered up the Kingdom to God, even the Father; when He shall have put down all rule and all authority and power. For He must reign, until He has put all enemies under His feet. The last enemy that shall be destroyed is death."

However, before we come to the consummation of the Kingdom of God, let us seek to understand how we are to enter into the Kingdom of God. The apostle Paul said in Romans 14:17, "For the Kingdom of God is not meat and drink; but righteousness, and peace, and joy in the Holy Spirit." A religion of "meat and drink" is a system of rules and commandments and merit is earned by a system of works. When the Pharisees, the religious leaders of his day, asked Jesus when the Kingdom of God should come, He answered them and said, "The Kingdom of God comes not with observation: Neither shall they say Lo here! or, lo there! for, behold, the Kingdom of God is within you" (Luke 17:20-21). The apostle Paul said, "Now this I say, brethren, that flesh and blood cannot inherit the Kingdom of God" (1 Cor. 15:50).

The apostle John tells us very simply in John 3 how to enter the Kingdom of God. It is in the story of a man who was a ruler of the Jews, a master teacher of the Jewish religious system. His name was Nicodemus. He came to Jesus secretly by night (probably he feared criticism from other Jewish leaders) because he realized Jesus was of God and he wanted to be a part of what Jesus was doing. Some people believe that Nicodemus was just a nasty old sinner, but he was a holy man of God. He saw that Jesus was walking in the Kingdom, that a river of life was flowing out of the life of Jesus. Wherever Jesus went, life flowed from him. When Jesus reached out His hand to the sick, healing took place. Whenever Jesus spoke, life came forth.

Use your imagination with me for a moment. I believe that Nicodemus was thinking, "I am a teacher of God, but my ministry is not like that." He said, "Master, we know you are a holy man of God and that no man can do these things unless God is with Him." The implied question from Nicodemus was, "Master, how do I get in on what you are doing?"

Nicodemus was not asking how to go to Heaven. He wanted to get in on what Jesus was doing. Jesus told him very simply how to do it. Jesus said, "Verily, verily, I say unto you, Except a man be born again, he cannot see the Kingdom of God" (John 3:3). When Jesus said, "Cannot see" this was not a prohibition, but a statement that he would not have the ability to see or would not even know the Kingdom of God was there. The next question that Nicodemus asked demonstrated that he had no idea what Jesus was talking about. His question was, "How can a man be born when he is old? Can he enter the second time into his mother's womb and be born?" (John 3:4).

Jesus answered, "Verily, verily, I say unto you, Except a man be born of water and of the Spirit, he cannot enter into the Kingdom of God. That which is born of the flesh is flesh; and that which is born of the Spirit is spirit. Marvel not that I said unto you, You must be born again" (John 3:5-7).

Then a few verses later in John 3 we come to the "Golden Text" of the Bible, John 3:16, "For God so loved the world, that He gave His only begotten Son, that whosoever believes in Him should not perish, but have everlasting life." We enter the Kingdom of God by being "born again."

A step-by-step way of entering into the Kingdom of God comes from how Jesus dealt with the apostle Peter. In Matthew 16:15, Jesus was asking the disciples, "But whom say you that I am?" Simon Peter answered, "You are the Christ, the Son of the living God" (Matt. 16:16). Jesus told Peter that flesh and blood or human ability had not revealed that truth to him, but the Heavenly Father. Then Jesus said to Peter, "And I will give unto you the keys of the Kingdom of Heaven; and whatsoever you shall bind on earth shall be bound in Heaven; and whatsoever you shall loose on earth shall be loosed in Heaven" (Matt. 16:19).

So what are the exact keys to the Kingdom of God? In Acts 2 we read how on the day of Pentecost that Peter "opened up the gates of the Kingdom" to about three thousand souls (Acts 2:41). When the Holy Spirit filled the 120 disciples that were gathered together in an upper room on the day of Pentecost, thousand of pilgrims were in Jerusalem for the Feast of Pentecost. They witnessed the coming of the Holy Spirit on the 120 and began to ask what it all meant. Peter preached his famous sermon about Jesus and the outpouring of the Holy Spirit. As they heard the message, they asked, "Men and brethren what shall we do?" (Acts 2:37). Peter gave them the three keys to the Kingdom of God in

Acts 2:38:

Peter said to them,

1. REPENT,
2. and be BAPTIZED every one of you in the name of Jesus Christ for the remission of sins,
3. and you SHALL RECEIVE THE GIFT OF THE HOLY SPIRIT."

Peter unlocked the door to the Kingdom of God. The Bible says, "Then they that gladly received his word were baptized: and the same day there were added unto them about three thousand souls" (Acts 2:41).

An illustration of the three keys to the Kingdom of God can also be illustrated as the three steps into the Kingdom of God.

Enter the Kingdom of God

3. Baptism of Holy Spirit

2. Water baptism

1. Repentance

For a moment, let us go back to a question that was raised at the beginning of this chapter. What did Jesus mean by the term "MYSTERY" OF THE KINGDOM OF GOD? Why did the apostle Paul use the same term MYSTERY in Romans 16:25-26, "and the preaching of Jesus Christ, according to the revelation of the MYSTERY, which was kept secret since the world began, But now is made manifest." As was stated previously, the word translated as "mystery" from the New Testament Greek into English does not mean something that is mysterious, but means knowledge that is made know in a manner and time appointed by God.

When God created Adam and Eve and put them in the Garden of Eden, they were without sin. As God gave them a free will and allowed them to be tested, they chose the wrong way and ate of the Tree of Knowledge of Good and Evil that God commanded them not to touch. As sin entered the picture, God immediately told Adam and Eve of His plan of redemption for man as was explained in chapter one of this book. However, God's plans for the Kingdom of God and His plans and purposes for man in that Kingdom had to be put on hold.

As we open the pages of the New Testament, we have John the Baptist preaching, "Repent you: for the Kingdom of Heaven is at hand" (Matt. 3:2). As Jesus began His public ministry He said, "I must preach the Kingdom of God. . . for therefore am I sent" (Luke 4:43). Why now was the Kingdom of God being proclaimed? The answer is because Jesus was here to take upon Himself the form of a servant and to be made in the likeness of man. "And being found in fashion as a man, He humbled Himself and become obedient unto death, even the death of the cross" (Phil. 2:8). Jesus died on the cross to pay for the penalty of our sins so that we would not have to pay the penalty for our sins and we could have everlasting life. However, there was an even greater purpose that Jesus had for us by paying the penalty of sin for us. That greater purpose was what God had planned for you before creation, that you would be able to enter into the fullness of the Kingdom of God, not only in time but also for all eternity.

Back in the Garden of Eden when Adam and Eve had sinned, God in His love and wisdom did not reveal His plans and purpose for man regarding the Kingdom of God. Until man's sin problem had been paid for, it was a plan and purpose for man that could not be fulfilled. In His love God would not offer or dangle, like a carrot, a plan and purpose that man could not receive until the time that it would become possible. The death of Jesus on the cross not only made it possible, but made it a FREE GIFT to man if man would receive it.

There would have been no purpose to proclaim the Kingdom of God before this time, but now you and I can enter into the fullness of the Kingdom of God. All through the New Testament Jesus proclaimed it, and the disciples and apostles preached the Kingdom of God. Let us look at and receive what God wants for all of us.

As we take the three keys to the Kingdom of God or the steps of repentance, water baptism, and the baptism of the Holy Spirit, we enter the Kingdom of God at ground level. The next step is "obedience", that Jesus reigns as the sovereign King of our lives. The

Gospel calls people not only to "believe", but also asks to "obey". The greatest of God's demands on man is not for him to bear a cross, to serve, make offerings or deny himself. The greatest demand is for him to simply "obey". Most of the time we think we are obeying and fail to see that we are really "self-willed" or "rebellious".

Jesus said in Matthew 7:21, "Not everyone that says unto me, LORD, LORD, shall enter into the Kingdom of Heaven; but he that does the will of my Father which is in Heaven." The basic controversy of the universe is centered on who shall have authority?

God?   Satan?   Ourselves?

Remember when God put Adam and Eve in the Garden of Eden and told them that they could eat of the trees in the Garden except of the Tree of Knowledge of Good and Evil. He also warned them that the day they ate of the Tree of Knowledge of Good and Evil, they would surely die. Would they obey God or listen to Satan and do what they wanted to do? The crux of this charge was more than the forbiddance to eat a certain fruit. It was that God was putting Adam under His authority so that Adam might learn obedience.

One of the most graphic illustrations of obedience I have seen is a picture of a police dog being trained. Picture with me a beautiful well-groomed German shepherd dog that is brimming with vitality and strength. The dog has been brought to a training school for a nine-week course in preparation for police duty. Lessons in obedience are necessary before he can be of any value in his assignment.

The trainer throws a stick into an open field with the command "Fetch!" The dog takes off in a cloud of dust, grabs the stick and trots back triumphantly. The trainer throws a purse with the same command and off goes the dog again. There is seemingly no thought on the dog's part. "Should I go or should I not go?" Instead the immediate reaction is "there it goes, here I go!"

After several runs, the trainer throws the purse once more; only he follows the act with the command, "Heel!" This requires some shifting of gears by the dog. The dog almost ruptures a blood vessel trying to follow the change in the command. So many times the dog has gone off after the object, but obedience to the order to stay or heel demands an act of definite effort and discipline.

The goal is not the stick or purse but obedience. Just where do you and I fit into this picture? As children of God, the object in all of His dealings with us is to bring us into an obedient spirit, a heart that is perfect towards Him. Going back to Matthew 7:21-23, "Not everyone that says unto me, LORD, LORD, shall enter into the Kingdom of Heaven; but he that does the will of My Father which is in Heaven. Many will say to Me in that day, LORD, LORD, have we not prophesied in Your name? and in Your name have cast out devils? and in Your name done many wonderful works? And then will I profess unto them, I never knew you: depart from Me, you that work iniquity." When we see the word "iniquity" we immediately think of sins like adultery, stealing and lying. The New Testament Greek word for iniquity is "anomia" it means one that is not subject to law or that they were doing what they wanted to do rather than what the LORD asked them to do. When we read the words "I never knew you," we also miss the true meaning of what Jesus was saying. The LORD is omniscience or knows all things. A more accurate translation would be "I never approved of what you were doing."

If we enter into the Kingdom of God, it means we will be obedient to the King and that we seek to do His will and not to do our own thing. A very free translation of Matthew 7:21- 23 could be, "Why do you call Me LORD when you do not want to do the things I tell you to do? If you are going to call me LORD, then you must come under a spirit of obedience. You see, it is not what needs to be done, but it's what I tell you to do. But you call me LORD, LORD, and you take the things of the Spirit and use them to your own promotion, to do your own thing, to go your own way and build something for Me when you are really endeavoring to build your own kingdom."

For many years, I really thought salvation, Heaven and the Kingdom of God were all the same thing. I used to think that seeking the Kingdom of God was the same thing as seeking to go to Heaven. However, Romans 10:13 very clearly and explicitly says, "For whosoever shall call upon the name of the LORD shall be saved." Salvation is the first step. Salvation, eternal life and Heaven are gifts of God. The Kingdom of God is a realm that you and I can enter into right now. The Kingdom of God comes when the King

(Jesus) comes into our hearts and lives right now and sets up His rule and reign. It is a realm that you and I can enter right now and not just off in the future. This is why Jesus commands us, "Seek you first the Kingdom of God and His righteousness; and all these things shall be added unto you" (Matt. 6:33).

I trust that you are beginning to understand that the Kingdom of God is the RULE, REIGN, GOVERNMENT, AND SOVEREIGNTY OF GOD RULING YOUR LIFE. Our prayer should be:

- "LORD Jesus rule over me"
- "Conquer me"
- "Deal in my life"
- "Conquer this rebel will"

All of us need to face the fact that we have an inward condition that insists on our:

- Own ways
- Own methods
- Own ideas

Nobody has trouble "obeying" until God's will crosses our own will. When God's will crosses our will is when we discover the spirit within us that responds: "But I want to do my own thing." It would be wonderful if "obedience" was a gift of the Holy Spirit like the gift of salvation. However, the Bible teaches us in Hebrews 5:8-9, "Though He were a Son, yet learned He obedience by the things which He suffered. And being made perfect, He became the author of eternal salvation unto all them that obey Him." Wouldn't it be wonderful if obedience could be imparted as a gift like salvation or eternal life? But God made obedience something to be learned. It does not come naturally, but is a learned accomplishment. That is why Jesus said, "Seek you first the Kingdom of God" or His rule and reign over our lives.

B. KINGDOM LIVING

Now the apostle Paul spent a great deal of time in writing about Kingdom living. As we seek the Kingdom of God and take the steps to enter into the Kingdom of God, it will result in Kingdom living. As stated before, the apostle Paul wrote in Romans 14:17, "For the Kingdom of God is not meat and drink; but righteousness, and peace, and joy in the Holy Spirit." A religion of "meat and drink" is a religion of rules and commandments where merit is earned by a system of works. "Meat and drink" religion never brought anyone righteousness, peace and joy.

I was raised in a holiness background and I thank God for it. But I also thank God for deliverance from meat and drink religion. It was a system of do's and don'ts. How long is your hair? How long is your dress? Do you eat pork? But the more abundant life is entering the Kingdom of God where there is true righteousness, peace and joy. When you accept Jesus into your heart and life, He counts your faith as righteousness. As the apostle Paul writes in Romans 4:1-3, "What shall we say then that Abraham our father, as pertaining to the flesh, has found? For if Abraham were justified by works, he has whereof to glory (or boast); but not before God. For what says the scripture? Abraham believed God, and it was counted unto him for righteousness."

When you and I first come to Jesus, we know that we are sinners and that our lives are a mess. However, Jesus says that if we will open the door of our life to Him, He will come into our lives and live with us, that our faith will be counted as righteousness. I remember the birth of one of my daughters. As we arrived at the hospital, the mother was immediately taken into the delivery room. In a few minutes, a nurse came out into the hallway with a baby wrapped in a blanket. She asked, "Do you want to see your new daughter?" As a father, I was anxious to see her, so the nurse opened up the blanket and I was able to examine a little baby daughter for the first time. She was still covered with blood and mucus. Then I will never forget how the nurse said, "Now we will wrap her back up in this blanket and take her to the nursery and wash and clean her up so that she will be clean and beautiful." As the nurse walked to the nursery, the LORD spoke to me and said, "Son, that is a picture of you when you first allowed Me to come into your heart. I forgave you of all your sins and wrapped you up in My righteousness. Then I brought you into My nursery and began to cleanse and sanctify your life and bring My righteousness into your life." As you and I enter into the Kingdom of God, He brings all of our acts and conduct under His rule and brings His righteousness into our lives.

As we enter the Kingdom of God, and realize that we are under the sovereignty and rule of Jesus, there comes a real peace in spite of what may be happening around us, knowing that He is in control. It does not mean there will be an absence of difficulty or trouble, but there will be a confident assurance that Jesus has everything under control. As the psalmist David wrote, "The LORD is my shepherd; I shall not want. He makes me to lie down in green pastures: He leads me beside the still waters. He restores my soul: He leads me in the paths of righteousness for His name's sake. Yes, though I walk through the valley of the shadow of death, I will fear no evil: for You are with me; Your rod and Your staff they comfort me. You prepare a table before me in the presence of mine enemies: You anoint my head with oil, my cup runs over. Surely goodness and mercy shall follow me all the days of my life: and I will dwell in the house of the LORD for ever" (Ps. 23).

One of the most beautiful pictures of "peace" that I have seen was a picture of a mother bird nesting on a nest at the end of the limb of a tree that stretched out over a waterfall. Her head was tucked underneath one of her wings as the water was crashing down all around her. At the bottom of the picture was the inscription, "Hallelujah! My Father takes care of me." As you and I live in the Kingdom of God, we can experience this type of peace.

The apostle Paul tells us the Kingdom of God is joy in the Holy Spirit. Joy is a mark of maturity. You will never see anyone except the spiritually mature with real joy. A lot of people have fun. I have fun when I go water skiing or flying. However, those living in the Kingdom of God are able to experience a real joy that only the LORD gives. We often call it the joy of the LORD.

One of the greatest benefits of Kingdom living according to the apostle Paul in Romans 5:17, "For if by one man's offense death reigned by one; much more they which receive abundance of grace and of the gift of righteousness shall reign in life by one, Jesus Christ." Where did Paul say they would reign?

- In the Millennium?

- In Heaven?

Paul says they shall reign in LIFE by Jesus Christ. When is that? It is now in this life. If we have entered into the Kingdom of God and are living in the Kingdom, we are able to reign over life rather than life reigning over us.

Many times people will ask you, "How are you doing?" Many times we answer back, "Fine under the circumstances." But for a person living in the Kingdom of God, we then should ask them, "What are you doing under there?" If you are living in the Kingdom, we should not be under the pile or circumstances but on top reigning over the situation.

The writer of Hebrews tells us in Hebrews 4:9, "There remains therefore a rest to the people of God." Rest here involves more than inactivity. It follows the satisfactory completion of a task.

In Romans 8, the apostle Paul lists twenty-one promises to those who walk after the Spirit or who are walking in Kingdom living.

1. You MAY live without condemnation (8:1).
2. You CAN be free from the law of sin and death (8:2).
3. You CAN have the law fulfilled in you (8:4).
4. You CAN be spiritually minded (8:6).
5. The Spirit of God MAY dwell in you (8:9).
6. The Spirit WILL heal your mortal body (8:11).
7. You CAN (through the Spirit) mortify the deeds of the flesh (8:13).
8. You CAN be led of the Holy Spirit (8:14).
9. You CAN experience the spirit of adoption to cry "Father" (8:15).
10. You CAN know the Spirit bearing witness to your spirit (8:16).
11. You CAN be a joint-heir with Jesus Christ (8:17).
12. You CAN know the glorious liberty of the children of God (8:21).
13. Experience the redemption of your physical bodies (in the future) (8:23).
14. The Spirit CAN lend you a hand with your weaknesses

(8:26).

15. You CAN know all things work together for your good (8:28).
16. You CAN be conformed to the image of God's Son (8:29).
17. God will (with His Son) freely give you ALL things (8:32).
18. Jesus ALSO will make intercession for you (8:34).
19. You CAN know inseparable love (8:35).
20. You CAN be more than a conqueror (8:37).
21. You CAN experience the love of God in Christ Jesus (8:39).

With all the forgoing descriptions of the Kingdom of God, one can see why Jesus said, "Seek you first the Kingdom of God, and His righteousness; and all these things shall be added unto you" (Matt. 6:33).

Jesus said, "The Kingdom of Heaven is like unto treasure hid in a field; the which when a man has found, he hides, and for joy thereof goes and sells all that he has, and buys that field" (Matt. 13:44). Picture in your mind a man plowing out in a field from sun up to sun down saying to himself, "What a miserable life. I just pray God would take me home to glory." Suddenly the plow hits something. When he bends down to see what he hit, he discovers a buried treasure. He covers it up, runs home and tells the wife to get everything they have and sell it so they can buy the field and own the treasure.

Again Jesus said, "The Kingdom of Heaven is like unto a merchant man, seeking goodly pearls. Who, when he had found one pearl of great price, went and sold all that he had and bought it" (Matt. 13:45-46).

C. THE TRIUMPH OF THE KINGDOM

During the last week of the ministry of Jesus before His crucifixion, the disciples came to Him on the Mount of Olives and asked Him very directly what would be the sign of His coming and of the end of the world. Jesus replied, "And this Gospel of the Kingdom shall be preached in all the world for a witness unto all nations; and then shall the end come" (Matt. 24:14).

Both the prophets, Daniel and John, had visions of the triumph and establishment of the Kingdom of God on earth. During the days of Daniel in the Kingdom of Babylon, King Nebuchadnezzar dreamed a dream that greatly troubled his spirit. However, when he awoke, he could not remember the contents of the dream, but his spirit was greatly troubled. Nebuchadnezzar summoned the astrologers, magicians and wise men in his Kingdom to tell him what the dream was and what the dream meant. They all replied that what the king was asking of them, to tell him the contents of the dream and then to give him the interpretation, was something only the gods could do. King Nebuchadnezzar was furious with them and said that if they could not tell him the dream and the interpretation, they would all be put to death.

Since Daniel was one of the wise men, he asked the king to give him and his companions time to pray and that God would give them the contents of the dream and the interpretation of the dream. Daniel and his three friends set about in prayer. That night, "Then was the secret revealed unto Daniel in a night vision" (Dan. 2:19). Daniel blessed the God of heaven who "reveals the deep and secret things" (Dan. 2:22). The "deep and secret things" would also be the same as the "mystery" of the Kingdom of God.

Daniel went into King Nebuchadnezzar to tell him what the dream was and the interpretation of the dream. As we carefully look at the dream, it deals with the mystery of the Kingdom of God. Daniel told Nebuchadnezzar, "There is a God in heaven that reveals secrets, and makes known to the king Nebuchadnezzar what shall be in the latter days" (Dan. 2:28).

Then Daniel says, "You, O king, saw and beheld a great image. This great image, whose brightness was excellent, stood before you; and the form thereof was awesome. This image's head was of fine gold, his breast and his arms of silver, his belly and his thighs of brass. His legs of iron, his feet part of iron and part of clay. You saw (the image) until that a stone was cut out without hands, which smote the image upon his feet that were of iron and clay, and break them to pieces. Then was the iron, the clay, the brass, the silver, and the gold, broken (crushed) to pieces together, and became like the chaff of the summer threshing floors; and the wind carried them away, that no place (trace) was found for them: and the stone that smote the image became a great mountain, and filled the whole earth" (Dan. 2:31-35).

Daniel gave the interpretation, "You, O king, are a king of kings: for the God of Heaven has given you a kingdom, power, and strength, and glory. . . . You are this head of gold. And after you shall arise another kingdom inferior to you, and another third kingdom of brass, which shall bear rule over all the earth. And the fourth kingdom shall be strong as iron: forasmuch as iron breaks in pieces and subdues all things: and as iron that breaks all these, shall it break in pieces and bruise (crush). And where as you saw the feet and toes, part of potter's clay, and part of iron, the kingdom shall be divided; but there shall be in it of the strength of the iron, forasmuch as you saw the iron mixed with miry clay. And as the toes of the feet were part of iron, and part of clay, so the kingdom shall be partly strong, and partly broken (brittle or fragile). And whereas you saw iron mixed with miry clay, they shall mingle themselves with the seed of men: but they shall not cleave one to another, even as iron is not mixed with clay" (Dan. 2:37-43).

Then Daniel gives the conclusion, "And in the days of these kings shall the God of Heaven set up a Kingdom, which shall never be destroyed: and the Kingdom shall not be left to other people, but it shall break in pieces and consume all these kingdoms, and it shall stand forever" (Dan. 2:44).

Most Bible scholars and history shows that the head of gold was the kingdom of Babylon. The shoulders and arms of silver was the kingdom of the Medes and Persians. The belly and thighs of brass was the kingdom of Alexander the Great or the Grecians. The legs of iron were the kingdom of Rome. The feet and ten toes of part iron and part clay would be the last world kingdom or empire before the second coming of Christ. But the stone that smote the image and became a great mountain and shall fill the whole earth will be Jesus Christ, who will return to this earth as King of Kings and LORD of Lords and His Kingdom will become as a great mountain that shall fill the whole earth.

You may wonder why Jesus Christ was pictured in the dream as a "stone cut out without hands." Jesus was not the result of human or man's efforts, but was God come in the flesh. "And the Word was made flesh, and dwelt among us" (John 1:14). As the apostle Paul says, "And are built upon the foundation of the apostles and prophets, Jesus Christ Himself being the chief corner stone" (Eph. 2:20). Or as the apostle Peter writes, "Behold, I lay in Zion a chief corner stone, elect, precious: and he that believes on Him shall not be confounded (put to shame)" (1 Pet. 2:6). This is also a quotation from Isaiah 28:16, "Therefore this says the LORD God, Behold, I lay in Zion for a foundation a stone, a tried stone, a precious corner stone, a sure foundation."

It is important to understand that "Zion" is one of the hills on which Jerusalem stood. King David captured this real estate and changed its name to the City of David. On this hill, King David pitched a tent for the Ark of the Covenant and from that time forth, it became sacred. David's son, Solomon, built the Temple on the hill next to it, known as Mt. Moriah. After the Temple was built, Solomon transferred the Ark of the Covenant from Mt. Zion to the Temple and the name Zion was extended to comprehend the Temple. This accounts for the fact that while Zion is mentioned between 100 and 200 times in the Old Testament, Mt. Moriah is named only two times in the Old Testament. Therefore, Zion is also known as the "Mountain of the LORD."

King Nebuchadnezzer saw in his dream the stone cut out without hands which smote the image and broke it in pieces, then became a great mountain and filled the whole earth. The Old Testament prophets had much to say about this stone that became a great mountain. Zechariah 8:3, "This says the LORD; I am returned unto Zion, and will dwell in the midst of Jerusalem: and Jerusalem shall be called a city of truth; and the mountain of the LORD of hosts the HOLY MOUNTAIN." The prophet Zechariah goes on to proclaim, "Yes, many people and strong nations shall come to seek the LORD of hosts in Jerusalem, and to pray before the LORD" (Zech. 8:22). Then Zechariah proclaims, "And the LORD shall be king over all the earth: in that day shall there be one LORD, and His name one" (Zech. 14:9).

The prophet Isaiah prophesied, "And it shall come to pass in the last days, that the mountain of the LORD's house shall be established in the top of the mountains, and shall be exalted above the hills; and all nations shall flow unto it. And many people shall go and say, Come you, and let us go up to the mountain of the LORD, to the house of the God of Jacob; and He will teach us His ways, and we will walk in His paths: for out of Zion shall go forth the law, and the word of the LORD from Jerusalem. And He shall judge among the nations, and shall rebuke many people: and they shall beat their swords into plowshares, and their spears into pruning hooks: nation shall not lift up sword against nation, neither shall they learn war any more" (Isa. 2:2-4).

The prophet Micah prophesied, "But in the last days it shall come to pass, that the mountain of the house of the LORD shall be established in the top of the mountains, and it shall be exalted above the hills; and people shall flow unto it. And many nations shall come, and say, Come, and let us go up to the mountain of the LORD, and to the house of the God of Jacob; and He will teach us of His ways, and we will walk in His paths: for the law shall go forth of Zion, and the word of the LORD from Jerusalem" (Mic. 4:1-2). Then the prophet Micah proclaims, "And the LORD shall reign over them in mount Zion from hence forth, even forever" (Mic. 4:7).

The prophet Habakkuk proclaims: "For the earth shall be filled with the knowledge of the glory of the LORD, as waters cover the sea" (Hab. 2:14).

As was stated at the beginning of this section, both the prophets Daniel and John had visions of the TRIUMPH AND ESTABLISHMENT OF THE KINGDOM OF GOD. In the Book of Revelation, the apostle John saw in a vision a door that was opened in Heaven. He heard the voice of Jesus saying, "Come up here, and I will show you things which must be hereafter" (Rev. 4:1). Here John saw the Throne of God and Jesus invested with the authority to establish the Kingdom on earth because of His redeeming work as the Lamb. In the next chapter we will talk about what John was shown. However, at this time, the focus will be in the triumph and establishment of the Kingdom of God.

In Revelation 10:7, John writes: "But in the days of the voice of the seventh angel, when he shall begin to sound, the mystery of

God should be finished, as He has declared to His servants the prophets." In Revelation 11:15, John writes, "And the seventh angel sounded (blew his trumpet); and there were great voices in Heaven, saying, THE KINGDOMS OF THE WORLD ARE BECOME THE KINGDOMS OF OUR LORD, AND OF HIS CHRIST; AND HE SHALL REIGN FOR EVER AND EVER."

The seventh trumpet results in the second coming of Jesus Christ and the establishment of the millennial Kingdom of Christ. The kingdoms of this world will be completely overthrown and Jesus Christ will reign as King of Kings and LORD of Lords. In Revelation 20, the apostle John tells us that he saw an angel come down from Heaven, having the key of the bottomless pit and a great chain in his hand. The angel takes a hold of Satan and binds him up and shuts Satan up for thousand years in the bottomless pit so that he could not deceive the nations any more until the thousand years be passed. During this thousand years, Christ reigns and brings His Kingdom to full maturity. THEN THE FINAL TRIUMPH WILL TAKE PLACE.

In Revelation 21:1 the apostle John says, "And I saw a new Heaven and a new earth: for the first Heaven and the first earth were passed away; and there was no more sea." However, just before this takes place, the apostle Paul declares unto us the ULTI-MATE TRIUMPH that has to take place before God brings about the NEW HEAVEN AND THE NEW EARTH as we will discuss in chapter seven.

Read the declaration of the ULTIMATE TRIUMPH, "Then comes the end, when He (Jesus) shall have delivered up the Kingdom to God, even the Father; when He (Jesus) shall have put down all rule and all authority and powers. For He (Jesus) must reign, till He has put all enemies under His feet. The last enemy that shall be destroyed is death. . . . And when all things shall be subdued unto Him, then shall the Son also Himself be subject unto Him (the Father) that put all things under Him, that God may be all in all" (1 Cor. 15:24-28).

The apostle John saw the end of the last enemy "death". John writes in Revelation 20:14, "And death and hell were cast into the lake of fire. This is the second death." Once this final judgment occurs, there is no longer any further need for either death or hell. An eternal separation is now made between those who have LIFE and those who have DEATH. As you and I enter that NEW HEAVEN and NEW EARTH, we enter into God's ultimate plan and purpose for our life.

ENDNOTES:

[1] W.E. Vine, et al, *Vine's Complete Expository Dictionary of Old and New Testaments Words*, (Thomas Nelson Publishers 1985) p.344 New Testament Section.

CHAPTER SIX

THE LAST DAYS or THE FINAL DAYS
(Day 6 and Day 7)

A. WHAT TIME IS IT?

What time is it? This is the <u>BIG QUESTION</u> as we learn about God's plan and purpose for our lives. As was stated in the introduction, Genesis 1 tells us that God created this present world as we know it in seven days. It was a prophetic picture of man's time on earth. The apostle Peter writes in 2 Peter 3:8, "But, beloved, be not ignorant of this one thing, that one day is with the LORD as a thousand years and a thousand years as one day." Man's time on this earth would be seven thousand years.

Why would God create "TIME" if He Himself were a part of ETERNITY? As explained in chapter one, God wanted a being that was created in His image and likeness. Even more important was that man would be a "free moral" being with a "free will" who had the capacity and ability to choose to love God and fellowship with God because he wanted to do so. However, if man would have a "free will", whatever way he chooses or whatever direction he would choose to go, if it took place in eternity, it is FIXED and FINAL FOREVER. Only in a temporal environment can we put things behind us, change directions and turn as the Bible so often exhorts us to do.

God showed His love to man by creating this earth in six days and resting on the seventh day. In other words, He created TIME and put man in it to prepare man for the eternal purpose and plan that He had for man. That if man failed, rebelled or sinned, he would still be in TIME and could repent and return. As the Bible says in Hebrews 9:27, "And as it is appointed unto men once to die, but after this the judgment." At death, TIME is no more for a man, now it is eternity.

The apostle John tells us in one of his visions recorded in Revelation 10:5-7, "And the angel which I saw stand upon the sea and upon the earth lifted up his hand to the Heaven, And sware by Him that lives for ever and ever, who created Heaven, and the things that therein are, and the sea, and the things which are therein, THAT THERE SHOULD BE TIME NO LONGER. . . the mystery of God should be finished, as He has declared to His servants the prophets."

The apostle Peter graphically describes the end of TIME in 2 Peter 3:10-13, "But the day of the LORD will come as a thief in the night; in the which the Heavens shall pass away with a great noise, and the elements shall melt with fervent heat, the earth also and the works that are therein shall be burned up. . . . Never the less we, according to His promise, look for new Heavens and a new earth, wherein dwells righteousness."

GOD'S TIME CLOCK - 7 DAYS
"a day with the Lord is as a 1,000 years"
2 Peter 3:8, Psalms 90:4

A Prophetic Picture of God's Time Clock of 7,000 Years

4,000 B.C.	3,000 B.C.	2,000 B.C.	1,000 B.C.	B.C./ A.D.	1,000 A.D.	2,000 A.D.	3,000 A.D.
Adam	Noah	Abraham	David	Jesus		Millennium	
DAY 1	DAY 2	DAY 3	DAY 4	DAY 5	DAY 6	DAY 7	

According to the graphic on "God's Time Clock – 7 Days", you can see that our generation is at the end of day 6 and day 7 is soon to begin. Thus, you can see that the final days are what is left of Day 6 and all of Day 7. Most students of Bible prophecy try to put all events in a chronological order. However, rather, than focus on the chronology, I would like to focus upon SEVEN MAJOR AREAS:

1. God's Time Clock
2. Order of events
3. Restoration of Israel
4. The CHURCH – The Proclamation of Kingdom of God, and the GLORY OF THE LORD
5. The Secular World – Rise of Last World Empire and the Antichrist
6. The Second Coming
7. The Millennium

1. GOD'S TIME CLOCK

What time is it? Where are we on God's time clock? In 1650 A.D. Archbishop Usher worked out dates from Adam through Christ to his day. He dated Adam at 4004 B.C., Abraham's birth at 1996 B.C., Solomon's Temple at 1012 B.C. and the birth of Jesus at B.C./A.D. In the early Church, the epistle of Barnabas, in the beginning of the Christian era, mentioned a belief then held that, even as there had been two thousand years from Adam to Abraham, and two thousand years from Abraham to Christ, so there would be two thousand years for the Christian era. Then would come the Millennium even as the six days of creation were followed by the seventh day of rest. Although there is not exact agreement between scholars, we do know we are now drawing toward the close of the sixth day and the beginning of the seventh day.

In the Book of Daniel, the prophet Daniel began to search the writings of the prophets in order to determine where he and his generation were in relationship to God's time clock. Daniel 9:1-3, "In the first year of Darius the son of Ahasuerus, of the seed of the Medes, which was made king over the realm of the Chaldeans; In the first year of his reign I Daniel understood by books the number of the years, whereof the word of the LORD came to Jeremiah the prophet, that he would accomplish seventy years in the desolations of Jerusalem. And I set my face unto the LORD God, to seek by prayer and supplications, with fasting, and sackcloth, and ashes:"

The events in this scripture (first year of Darius) occurred in 539 B.C. after the Medes-Persians had conquered Babylon. Daniel began to search the Scriptures to determine the prophetic significance of the capture of Babylon by the Persians. His search revealed the prophet Jeremiah had prophesied the captivity of the Jews by Babylon would only last 70 years and time was up. His prayer was simply, "Now what LORD?" While Daniel was fasting and praying, the angel Gabriel came to Daniel and said, "I am now come forth to give you skill and understanding" (Dan. 9:22).

Daniel was going to be given an accurate look at God's time clock. Read the words of the angel Gabriel in Daniel 9:24 -27. The translation of these verses in the New International Version is one of the best English translations of the Hebrew. "Seventy 'sevens' are decreed for your people and your holy city to finish transgression, to put an end to sin, to atone for wickedness, to bring in everlasting righteousness, to seal up vision and prophecy and to anoint the most holy. Know and understand this: From the issuing of the decree to restore and rebuild Jerusalem until the Anointed One (Messiah), the ruler, comes, there will be seven, 'sevens' and sixty-two 'sevens.' It will be rebuilt with streets and a trench, but in times of trouble. After the sixty-two 'sevens,' the Anointed One (Messiah) will be cut off and will have nothing. The people of the ruler who will come will destroy the city and the sanctuary. The end will come like a flood: War will continue until the end, and desolations have been decreed. He will confirm a covenant with many for one 'seven.' In the middle of the 'seven', he will put an end to sacrifice and offering. And on a wing of the Temple, he will set up an abomination that causes desolation, until the end that is decreed is poured out on him."

According to the *Analytical Concordance to the Bible* by Robert Young, the Hebrew word "shabua" can be translated as seven, a week (which is seven days) or seven times or the seventh. Most scholarship agrees that when this word as used here in Daniel, that the week stands for seven years and that seventy weeks stands for 70 sets of weeks, each of seven years or 70 x 7 = 490 years. The 70 weeks began from the only Biblical decree authorizing the rebuilding of Jerusalem and its walls as recorded in Nehemiah 2 when the king Artaxerxes, King of Persia, decreed for Nehemiah to return to Jerusalem to begin rebuilding the city walls of Jerusalem on March 14, 445 B.C.

From the date of March 14, 445 B.C., the anointed one (Messiah) would be cut off after 69 weeks of years or 69 x 7 = 483 years. Using the Jewish calendar of the 360-day year, this would be 173,880 days. Using these days and correcting for leap years, this would take us from March 14, 445 B.C. to April 6, 32 A.D. which was the Palm Sunday before the Crucifixion of Jesus. This was the time the Messiah or Anointed One was cut off. Then the angel Gabriel told Daniel that following this event that the people of the prince that shall come (the prince being referred to here is the "Antichrist" and the people who he would come from would be those out of the Old Roman Empire) would destroy the city of Jerusalem and the Temple which was done by the Roman Army in 70 A.D. Following that, the world would have floods, wars and desolations until God's time clock would start ticking again for Daniel's seventieth week or the last seven years before Jesus would return back to earth as King of Kings and LORD of Lords.

At the future time of the last week or seven years, when God's time clock would start ticking again, a last world empire would arise out of the old Roman Empire. Over it an evil prince, the Antichrist will gain control and would make a seven year covenant with the nation of Israel for their protection. However, in the middle of that seven year covenant, he will set himself up in the Jewish Temple as God and demand to be worshipped.

Jesus says in Matthew 24:15, "When you therefore shall see the ABOMINATION OF DESOLATION, spoken of by Daniel the prophet, stand in the holy place (whoso reads, let him understand)." Then Jesus goes on to say, "For then shall be great tribulation, such as was not since the beginning of the world to this time, no, nor ever shall be" (Matt. 24:21).

Now with this look at God's time clock, what time is it? With a day being a thousand years and a thousand years being a day, and there being two thousand years between Adam and Abraham and another two thousand years between Abraham and Jesus, the question is: "Did DAY FIVE begin at the birth of Christ or at His crucifixion and resurrection?" All of us know that the Bible tells us that no man knows the day or the hour of Christ's return. However, common sense would indicate that DAY FIVE would begin after the completed work of Christ or His crucifixion and resurrection. That would indicate that DAY SIX would end at 2032 A.D. That would also be the beginning of DAY SEVEN. We also know that Daniel's seventieth week or the last seven years of what the angel Gabriel told him in Daniel 9 has yet to take place and would take place prior to the beginning of DAY SEVEN. Although Jesus made it very clear that no man knows the day or hour of His second coming, He did say we could know the season which is very close at hand.

Another very important look at God's time clock is what Jesus told the disciples in Luke 21 when they asked Him, "Master, but when shall these things be? And what sign will there be when these things shall come to pass?" (Luke 21:7). Jesus then told the disciples a number of things that would happen to the Jews as a people and what would take place in the world. Jesus gave them three signs.

1. The Jews will be led away captive into all nations: "and Jerusalem shall be trodden down of the Gentiles, until the times of the Gentiles be fulfilled" (Luke 21:24).
2. Then Jesus gave them the parable of the fig tree which is a symbol of the Jewish nation. "Behold the fig tree, and all the trees: When they now shoot forth, you see and know of your own selves that summer is now nigh at hand. So likewise you, when you see these things come to pass, know you that the Kingdom of God is nigh at hand" (Luke 21:29-31).
3. Then Jesus said when you see these signs, "This generation shall not pass away, till all be fulfilled" (Luke 21:32).

In the two thousand years after crucifixion and resurrection of Jesus Christ, the Jewish people have been scattered through out the whole earth. However, they never lost their identity. A miracle took place on May 14, 1948 when a nation was born in a day. On November 29, 1947, the United Nations (UN) voted to end British control of Palestine and divide the country into a Jewish state and an Arab state. On May 14, 1948 the last British high commissioner, General Sir Alan Cunningham, left Palestine. On the same day the State of Israel was proclaimed as a nation. Within a few hours Israel won de facto recognition from President Truman of the United States. This was the "budding of the fig tree".

The city of Jerusalem was still a divided city until June 1967 when in the Six-Day War, Israel not only gained its present territory, but for the first time in 2,500 years, Israel gained complete control of the city of Jerusalem as a sovereign nation. This was the fulfillment of the sign that Jerusalem would be trodden down by the Gentiles until the time of the Gentiles would be fulfilled.

Of the three signs Jesus gave, only the last remains to be fulfilled, "This generation shall not pass away, till all be fulfilled" (Luke 21:32). There are two questions still to be answered: (1) Does the generation begin in 1948 or in 1967? (2) How long is a generation? Some scholars believe a generation is approximately forty years because in many of the Biblical genealogies descendents are listed approximately every forty years. Or is it as King David said in Psalms 90:10, "The days of our lives are seventy years: and if by reason of strength they be eighty years." If a generation is 40 years, then it would not be possible for a generation to see all these events fulfilled. If you use 1948 as a start date, it would require the above signs to be fulfilled by 1988. If you use 1967, it would not leave enough time for Daniel's seventieth week (or the last seven years of his prophecy) to be fulfilled. Logic would point to the length of the generation being 70 to 80 years.

If the length of a generation is as King David said, 70 to 80 years, then it would be possible to use a start date of 1948 or 1967. However, Jesus put the emphasis on Jerusalem being under the control of a Jewish nation or Israel. If you use the start date of 1967 and a generation of 70 years, it would take you to 2037 A.D. If you take the prophecies of Daniel 9, the indication is that DAY SIX would end and DAY SEVEN would begin in 2032 A.D. These time periods come very close to each other.

HOWEVER, WE MUST BE VERY CAREFUL because Jesus said concerning His second coming, "But of that day and that hour knows no man, no, not the angels which are in Heaven, neither the Son, but the Father" (Mark 13:32). But Jesus did say that we could know the "season". Jesus said, "And when these things begin to come to pass, then look up, and lift up your heads; for your redemption draws near" (Luke 21:28).

Events that we are looking for are the (1) Rapture of the Church, (2) Daniel's seventieth week and (3) Jesus' return to rule the earth as King of Kings and LORD of Lords. We know that we are in the season and that the "Rapture of the Church" could occur at any time. Remember Jesus did not say that this season would be a generation in length of time, but that these events would take place in this generation, whether it was 40 or 70 years long. A reasonable conclusion could be that THIS GENERATION started in 1967 and that many in THIS GENERATION would live to see all these events fulfilled. Now let us take a look at what remains to be fulfilled.

2. ORDER OF EVENTS

For a moment, imagine that you and I are standing on the mountains of Israel along with the prophets, King David, Isaiah, Micah, Hosea and others looking down through the corridor of time six hundred to one thousand years before the first coming Jesus Christ. As they looked, they saw good things as well as fearful and terrible things. They saw "good things" such as (1) a virgin who would conceive the Anointed One that would be known as Jesus Christ, (2) that He would be born in Bethlehem, (3) that He would be called out of Egypt, and (4)that He would be called the Nazarene. As they looked, they also saw fearful and terrible things such as (1) the slaughter of babies in Bethlehem, (2) that Jesus would be rejected, (3) that Jesus would be crucified, (4) that Jesus would have His body pierced, and (5) Jesus would cry out,"My God, My God, why have You forsaken Me?" At that time would we have been able to fit all these things together in "chronological order"?

The truth of the matter is that many of these prophecies could not be put in chronological order until the events took place. In looking back over the events after they happened, we have no problem connecting the dots. Jesus would be born in Bethlehem, Joseph and Mary would flee to Egypt to avoid the slaughter of the babies in Bethlehem. A few years later, God tells Joseph, Mary and Jesus to return to Israel. Instead of going back to Bethlehem, they go to Nazareth where Jesus was raised and after which He was called the Nazarene.

As we now look at all the events that have been prophesied for the last days or for the rest of DAY SIX and all DAY SEVEN, what chronological order should they be put in? How can we connect all the dots in chronological order? The reality of the matter is that we will not be able to connect all the dots in chronological order until the actual events take place. Some of the dots we are able to connect, but for many all we can do is make an attempt to understand what God is doing and where He is going.

The diagram that follows is an attempt to do this. A number of the major events that have been prophesied or foretold are put in a "flow chart" in an attempt to understand what God's purposes and plans are for us. In reality, we will only know the true chronological order as the events take place. Later on in this chapter, we will go into a more detailed discussion concerning these events.

The chart starts out with the fulfillment of the prophecy concerning Jerusalem when it came back under the control of Israel in 1967. Then it branches out into three time lines, one for Israel, one for the Church and one for the secular world. Then the time lines merge back into one time line at the time of Daniel's seventieth week when the Antichrist makes a seven-year covenant with Israel.

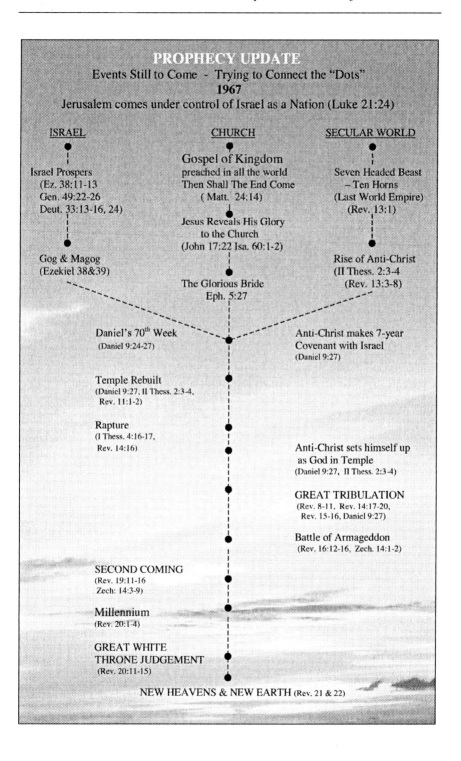

PROPHECY UPDATE
Events Still to Come - Trying to Connect the "Dots"
1967
Jerusalem comes under control of Israel as a Nation (Luke 21:24)

ISRAEL   CHURCH   SECULAR WORLD

Gospel of Kingdom
preached in all the world
Then Shall The End Come
(Matt. 24:14)

Israel Prospers
(Ez. 38:11-13
Gen. 49:22-26
Deut. 33:13-16, 24)

Seven Headed Beast
– Ten Horns
(Last World Empire)
(Rev. 13:1)

Jesus Reveals His Glory
to the Church
(John 17:22 Isa. 60:1-2)

Gog & Magog
(Ezekiel 38&39)

Rise of Anti-Christ
(II Thess. 2:3-4
(Rev. 13:3-8)

The Glorious Bride
Eph. 5:27

Daniel's 70th Week
(Daniel 9:24-27)

Anti-Christ makes 7-year
Covenant with Israel
(Daniel 9:27)

Temple Rebuilt
(Daniel 9:27, II Thess. 2:3-4,
Rev. 11:1-2)

Rapture
(I Thess. 4:16-17,
Rev. 14:16)

Anti-Christ sets himself up
as God in Temple
(Daniel 9:27, II Thess. 2:3-4)

GREAT TRIBULATION
(Rev. 8-11, Rev. 14:17-20,
Rev. 15-16, Daniel 9:27)

Battle of Armageddon
(Rev. 16:12-16, Zech. 14:1-2)

SECOND COMING
(Rev. 19:11-16
Zech: 14:3-9)

Millennium
(Rev. 20:1-4)

GREAT WHITE
THRONE JUDGEMENT
(Rev. 20:11-15)

NEW HEAVENS & NEW EARTH (Rev. 21 & 22)

3. RESTORATION OF ISRAEL

All of the "end-time" prophecies focus on the nation Israel. As Israel became a sovereign nation again in 1948 with Jerusalem as its capital city in 1967, all of this is the fulfillment of God's promises to Abraham, Isaac, Jacob, Moses, Joshua, King David and the last of the Old Testament prophets as well as Jesus Christ and the writers of the New Testament.

Approximately two thousand years before Jesus was born in Bethlehem, God made a covenant with Abraham, "In the same day the LORD made a covenant with Abraham saying, Unto your seed have I given this land, from the river of Egypt unto the great river the river Euphrates" (Gen. 15:18). The river of Egypt does not refer to the Nile River, but to a watercourse normally dry, but which after heavy rains, runs north from the desert, being fed by tributaries from the desert area of the Peninsula of Sinai. It empties into the Mediterranean Sea about 50 miles south of the Gaza Strip. The modern name of this watercourse is Wadi el-Arish. The northern border would be the Euphrates River which is also approximately the northern border of the country of Syria. This would be an area of about 400 miles from south to north. The land would also cover both side of the Jordan River. On today's map, this would include (1) all of present day Israel, (2) the land claimed by the Palestinian Liberation Organization, (3) Lebanon, (4) a major portion of Syria and (5) a major portion of Jordan. In Genesis 15:19-21, the ancient countries that occupied these lands are listed.

After Abraham had entered into a "blood covenant" relationship with God as described in chapter two of this book, God promised, "And I will give unto you, and to your seed after you, the land wherein you are a stranger, all the land of Canaan, for an everlasting possession; and I will be their God" (Gen. 17:8). After Moses led the Children of Israel out of Egypt across the Red Sea to Mount Sinai, where he received the Ten Commandments, God renewed His promise. In Exodus 23:31, "And I will set your bounds (boundaries) from the Red Sea even unto the sea of the Philistines (Mediterranean), and from the desert (Peninsula of Sinai) unto the river (Euphrates): for I will deliver the inhabitants of the land unto your hand; and you shall drive them out before you."

Prior to the defeat of Israel by the Assyrians in 721 B.C. and the captivity of Jerusalem by the Babylonians in 606 B.C.-586 B.C., the prophet Amos warned of the coming defeats and captivity. Yet there was God's promise, "And I will bring again (back) the captivity of my people Israel, and they shall build the waste cities, and inhabit them; and they shall plant vineyards, and drink the wine thereof; they shall also make gardens, and eat the fruit of them. And I will plant them upon their land, and they shall no more be pulled up out of their land which I have given them, says the LORD your God" (Amos 9:14-15).

Even after Jerusalem had been destroyed by the Babylonians and many of the Jews carried off into captivity, the prophet Ezekiel prophesied in Babylon, "And I will bring them out from the people, and gather them from the countries, and will bring them to their own land, and feed them upon the mountains of Israel by the rivers, and in all the inhabited places of the country" (Ezek. 34:13).

In 70 A.D., the Romans under General Titus completely destroyed Jerusalem. For almost 1,900 years the land of Israel lay in ruins and desolation. The Jewish people had been scattered abroad around the world. After World War II, what the prophets had prophesied began to take place. What the prophet Isaiah had prophesied almost 2,700 years earlier came to pass. Isaiah 49:14-16, "But Zion said, The LORD has forsaken me, and my LORD has forgotten me. Can a woman forget her sucking child, that she should not have compassion on the son of her womb? yes, they may forget, yet I will not forget you. Behold, I have graven you upon the palms of My hands; your walls are continually before Me."

In answer to the prophesy of Isaiah, the prophet Ezekiel prophesied, "And I will make them one nation in the land upon the mountains of Israel; and one king shall be king to them all. . . . And they shall dwell in the land that I have given unto Jacob My servant, wherein your fathers have dwelt; and they shall dwell therein, even they, and their children, and their children's children" (Ezek. 37:22-25).

The prophet Ezekiel goes on to describe their prosperity

before Gog and Magog come against Israel as will be explained later. "And you shall say, I will go up to the land of unwalled villages; I will go to them that are at rest, that dwell safely (securely), all of them dwelling without walls, and having neither bars nor gates. To take a spoil (plunder), and to take a prey (booty); to turn your hand upon the desolate places that are now inhabited, and upon the people that are gathered out of the nations, which have gotten cattle and goods, that dwell in the midst of the land. Sheba, and Dedan, and the merchants of Tarshish, with all the young lions thereof, shall say unto you, Are you come to take a spoil? have you gathered your company to take a prey? to carry away silver and gold, to take away cattle and goods, to take a great spoil? . . . In that day when My people of Israel dwell safely?" (Ezek. 38:11-14).

According to the prophet Ezekiel, a great time of prosperity and a false sense of peace are coming to the nation Israel. Upon his deathbed Jacob also prophesied of the coming prosperity. Jacob prophesied over all twelve of his sons, "And Jacob called unto his sons and said, Gather yourselves together, that I may tell you that which shall befall you in the last days (day six and day seven)" (Gen. 49:1). For example, let us take two of his sons, Joseph and Asher. In Genesis 49:22-26, "Joseph is a fruitful bough, even a fruitful bough by a wall; whose branches run over the wall. . . . Even by the God of your father, who shall help you; and by the Almighty, who shall bless you with blessings of Heaven above, BLESSINGS OF THE DEEP THAT LIE UNDER (BENEATH), blessings of the breast, and of the womb: The blessings of your father have prevailed (excelled) above the blessings of my progenitors (ancestors) unto the utmost bound of the everlasting hills: they shall be on the head of Joseph, and on the crown of the head of him that was separated from his brethren."

Before his death, Moses reiterated this prophecy concerning Joseph in Deuteronomy 33:13-16, "And of Joseph he said, Blessed of the LORD be his land, for the precious things of Heaven, for the dew, and FOR THE DEEP THAT CROUCHETH BENEATH. . . . And for the precious things of the earth and fullness thereof. . . . let the blessings come upon the head of Joseph, and upon the top of the head of him that was separated from his brethren."

Moses prophesied concerning Asher, "And of Asher he said, Let Asher be blessed with children; let him be acceptable to his brethren, and LET HIM DIP HIS FOOT IN OIL" (Deut. 33:24).

Now when Joshua divided up the Promised Land to the tribes of Israel, to the sons of Joseph, who were Manasseh and Ephraim, he gave the land between the Mediterranean Sea and the Jordan River and the land between Mt. Carmel to an area just above Jerusalem. To Asher he gave the coastline of the Mediterranean Sea from Mt. Carmel to Tyre.

Based on the above Bible references, *The Wall Street Journal*, dated May 11, 2005, had an article entitled "In Israel, Oil Quest Is Based on Faith." The following is a quote from the article:

> Living in one of the few countries in the Middle East without substantial oil reserves, Israelis often joke that Moses turned left when he should have turned right.

> But Zion Oil & Gas, Inc., a small exploration company founded by an evangelical Christian from the U.S., hopes to change that and in the process transform the fortunes of a country simultaneously dependent on oil imports and at odds with the world's main exporters.

> Geopolitcally, if we have what we think we have, it's going to make Israel energy independent for a long time," said Zion Oil's founder and chairman, John Brown. "You know what that can do for Israel geopolitically – it changes everything."

Zion Oil & Gas is a private U.S. based corporation formed under Delaware corporation law, exploring for oil and gas in Israel on a licensed area of approximately 95,800 acres located onshore between Tel Aviv and Haifa. This is the area that Jacob prophesied "blessings of the deep that lieth under (beneath)" (Gen. 49:25). And "for the deep that croucheth beneath" (Deut. 33:13). It is also the area that Moses prophesied for Asher, "and let him dip his foot in oil" (Deut. 33:24).

The same article of *The Wall Street Journal* also states concerning this same area: "Independent estimates put the reserve potential of the formation at 484 million barrels, located at a depth of 16,500 feet in what is know as a Triassic reef – a structure that has yielded oil in many other regions."

Zion Oil & Gas commencement of drilling began on April 10, 2005 with the drilling contractor, Lapideth Israel Oil Prospectors Corp. The estimate for drilling time is between two to three months. Could it be that oil, agriculture and manufacturing will bring about the prosperity that the prophet Ezekiel describes in Ezekiel 38?

Currently, Israel is building walls to separate Israel from parts of the Palestinian population in order to maintain peace and safety. However, Ezekiel was describing a land of unwalled villages and people dwelling in safety and prosperity. How all this will be brought about, we can only speculate. The apostle Paul writes to the Church in 1 Thessalonians 5:3, "For when they shall say, Peace and safety; then sudden destruction comes upon them, as travail (labor pains) upon a woman with child." We will write about this later.

Israel has been without a Temple now for almost two thousand years after the Romans destroyed the Temple Jesus visited in 70 A.D. During the days that Jesus was here on earth, the Jewish High Council that administered Jewish religious life, the Temple and civil affairs, was called the Sanhedrin. For almost 1,600 years the Sanhedrin has not existed. However, on January 20, 2005, the Sanhedrin was reestablished in Tiberius, Israel.

Just a few weeks after the Sanhedrin's reestablishment, another important development took place. The religious sages began to consider the rebuilding of the Temple and reinstitution of ancient animal sacrifices as prescribed in the Law of Moses in the Old Testament.

It is reported that the Sanhedrin has determined there are only two viable theories as to where the Temple of Jesus' day stood. One teaches that the Temple stood on the same basic site on which the Muslim mosque known as the Dome of the Rock was built. The second theory is that the Temple was built north of the Dome of the Rock. Dr. Asher Kaufman developed this theory, using certain archeological evidences that he found before the Muslims destroyed them. However, the most important archeological sign is the position of the Eastern Gate. According to ancient accounts of the Temple, its east-west centerline passed through the center of the Eastern Gate. There is absolute evidence as to where the ancient Eastern Gate stood. Hal Lindsey, a well-respected student of Bible prophecy measured off the distance from this centerline to the point where the wall of the inner court of the Temple in the time of Jesus would have stood. This point was at least six meters (19 plus feet) from the nearest points of the Dome of the Rock. So what does this mean? It means that the Temple can be rebuilt and stand alongside the Dome of the Rock without requiring that the Dome of the Rock be moved.

There are two verses of the Bible that describe a third Temple. The apostle Paul writes in 2 Thessalonians 2:3-4, "Let no man deceive you by any means: for that day (second coming of Jesus) shall not come, except there come a falling away first, and that man of sin be revealed, the son of perdition; Who opposes and exalts himself above all that is called God, or that is worshipped; so that he as God sits in the Temple of God, showing himself that he is God." Jesus referred to this event in Matthew 24:15, "When you therefore shall see the abomination of desolation, spoken of by Daniel the prophet, stand in the holy place (whoso reads, let him understand)." See also Daniel 9:27.

Then the second verse that describes the third Temple is described by the apostle John in Revelation 11:1-2, "And there was given me a reed like unto a rod: and the angel stood, saying, Rise, and measure the Temple of God, and the altar, and them that worship therein. But the court which is without the Temple leave out, and measure it not, for it is given unto the Gentiles: and the holy city shall they tread under foot forty and two months."

So what does all this mean? The Temple can be rebuilt and stand alongside of the Dome of the Rock without it having to be removed. And since the outer court referred to by the apostle John, is also know as the Court of the Gentiles, is given to the Gentiles in this period just before the Messiah returns there is the inference that there could be a Gentile building there, i.e., the Dome of the Rock.

The fact that a reestablished Sanhedrin is now considering the rebuilding of the Temple after almost two thousand years is extremely important to students of Bible prophecy. Also of great importance is "The Temple Institute," which was founded in 1987, a non-profit educational and religious organization located in the Jewish quarter of Jerusalem's Old City. The Institute is dedicated to every aspect of the Biblical commandment to build the Holy Temple of God on Mount Moriah in Jerusalem. The Institute has already began to restore and construct the sacred vessels, the sacred uniforms or garments of the priests, and research is currently under way that involves the topography and makeup of the Temple mount and the structure of the Holy Temple, as well as a working architectural plan for the rebuilding of the Holy Temple on Mount Moriah, according to modern building standards and with the best materials and technology available.

The rebuilding of the third Temple should not be confused with the Temple described in Ezekiel 40-48. In the last section of this chapter, we will discuss the "Millennium" when Jesus Christ returns to this earth to reign as King of Kings and LORD of Lords for a thousand years. The prophet Zechariah describes the literal return of Jesus in Zechariah 14:4, "And His feet shall stand in that day upon the mount of Olives, which is before Jerusalem on the east, and the mount of Olives shall cleave (split in two) in the midst thereof toward the east and toward the west and there shall be a very great valley; and half of the mountain shall remove toward the north, and half of it toward the south." The whole topography of the land will be changed; a new Temple of a different size and dimensions will be built. A life-giving river will flow from this new Temple towards the Dead Sea bringing life to its waters. It will be from this fourth Temple that Jesus will reign during the Millennium.

Now we come to a very important part in Israel's prophetic future. The openly acknowledged and declared intentions of many of Israel's neighboring peoples and nations are the complete annihilation of the Jews and Israel. During the recent wars that Israel has had with the neighboring nations, the intention was to push Israel off into the Mediterranean Sea. All of these neighboring people have been Muslim and Islam has always been against other religions and especially the Jews. The Holy Qur'an, the name of the sacred book of the Muslims who believe that every word came from the lips of the holy prophet Muhammad to whom the book was revealed by divine revelation. In Chapter 9, verse 33 of the Qur'an, "He (Allah) it is Who has sent His Messenger (Muhammad) with the guidance and the Religion of Truth that He may make it prevail over all religions, though the polytheists are adverse."

The prophecy of the ultimate Triumph of Islam in the whole world is repeated three times in the Qur'an, in exactly the same words as Chapter 9, verse 33. In Chapter 48 verse 28, "He (Allah) it is Who has sent His Messenger (Muhammad) with the guidance and the Religion of Truth that He may make it prevail over all religions. And Allah is enough for a witness." The same prophecy is also given in Chapter 61 verse 9.

Israel, in her future, will have to deal directly with Islam. The Old Testament prophets Ezekiel and Joel prophesy concerning this event. In the book of Joel 2, Joel describes a great army that comes against Israel. "A day of darkness and of gloominess, a day of clouds and of thick darkness, as the morning spread upon the mountains: a great people and a strong; there has not been ever the like, neither shall be any more after it, even to the years of many generations" (Joel 2:2). Then the prophet instructs Israel in Joel 2:15-17, "Blow the trumpet in Zion, sanctify a fast, call a solemn assembly: Gather the people, sanctify the congregation, assemble the elders, gather the children. . . . Let the priests, the ministers of the LORD, weep between the porch and the altar, and let them say, Spare Your people, O LORD, and give not Your heritage to reproach, that the heathen should rule over them: wherefore should they say among the people, Where is their God?"

Then the prophet Joel gives the answer in Joel 2:18-20, "Then will the LORD be jealous (zealous) for His land, and pity His people. . . . But I will remove far off from you the northern army, and will drive him into a land barren and desolate, with his face toward the east sea (Dead Sea), and his hinder part toward the utmost sea, and his stink shall come up, and his ill savor (foul odor) shall come up, because he has done great things."

Remember that God promised Abraham when He called him to go to the Promised Land, "And I will bless them that bless you, and curse him that curses you" (Gen. 12:3). The everlasting hatred that the Muslims and Arabs have always had towards Abraham and his seed will lead to a terrible pay day coming for them.

Now let us take a close look at that PAY DAY as it is prophesied by the prophet Ezekiel in Ezekiel 38-39 in greater detail than what Joel prophesied. In order to fully understand this prophecy of Ezekiel, let us first look at four different verses of the Bible. The first one is Ephesians 6:12, "For we wrestle not against flesh and blood, but against principalities, against powers, against the rulers of the darkness of this world, against spiritual wickedness in high places." Satan, the fallen angels and demons have access to this world and are constantly endeavoring to exercise control if we allow them to do so. The apostle Paul tells us in Colossians 1:16, "For by Him were all things created, that are in heaven, and that are in earth, visible and invisible, whether they be thrones, or dominions, or principalities (rulers), or powers: all things were created by Him and for Him." All heavenly beings were created by God, however, the Bible tells us that the archangel Lucifer and one-third of the angels rebelled against God and were cast out of Heaven and have access to this world. As the apostle Peter writes, "Be sober, be vigilant; because your adversary the devil, as a roaring lion, walks about, seeking whom he may devour" (1 Pet. 5:8).

During His ministry here on earth, Jesus faced this same challenge during the time of His temptation in the wilderness, "Again, the devil takes Him up into an exceeding high mountain, and shows Him all the Kingdoms of the world, and the glory of them. And says unto Him, All these things will I give You, if You will fall down and worship me. Then said Jesus unto him, "Get you hence, Satan: for it is written, Thou shalt worship the LORD your God, and Him only shall you serve" (Matt. 4:8-10).

The fourth verse of the Bible is from the book of Daniel. The prophet had been fasting 21 days in order to understand what would happen in the last days to Israel. On the twenty first day, Daniel was visited by an angel of the LORD who said, "Fear not, Daniel: for from the first day that you did set your heart to understand, and to humble yourself before your God, your words were heard, and I am come for your words. But the prince of the kingdom of Persia withstood me one and twenty days: but, lo, Michael, one of the chief princes, came to help me; and I remained there with the kings of Persia. Now I am come to make you understand what shall befall your people in the latter days" (Dan. 10:12-14). The prince of Persia was a demon who worked in that nation to oppose God's people.

As we look at what Ezekiel prophesied in Ezekiel 38 and 39, we can begin to understand what is being said. "Son of man, set your face against Gog, the land of Magog, the chief prince of Meshech and Tubal, and prophecy against him, And say, This says the LORD God; Behold, I am against thee, O Gog, the chief prince of Meshech and Tubal" (Ezek. 38:2-3). Gog is a demon ruler. The Hebrew word "gog" means "high" or "mountain." The area of his influence is Magog or north Asia. Many students of prophecy equate it with Russia. Some students of prophecy believe that Meshech is a reference to the capital of Russia, which is Moscow, and that Tubal is a reference to Tbilisi, which is one of the oldest cities in Russia and is the capital of the former Georgian Soviet Socialist Republic, which is now an independent country.

Ezekiel prophesied that God would put hooks into his jaws and bring him forth with all the military might under his control along with Persia, Ethiopia, Libya, Gomer and the house of Togarmah of the north quarters unto the mountains of Israel in the last days. Persia would be modern day Iran. The *Westminister Dictionary of the Bible* states that the name Ethiopia was for the Hebrew name Cush and Libya was for the Hebrew name Put. Cush designates the people located in central and south Arabia. Put is mentioned in association with Egypt and other African countries, especially Libyans. *Nelson's New Illustrator Bible Dictionary* shows on its maps of the nations of Genesis 10 that Gomer and Togarmah were a part of Asia Minor.

All these areas and nations today are Muslim nations, with the exception of Russia, which has many Muslim republics. In the current news, Russia is very much tied to Iran in its development of nuclear reactors and nuclear power. There were mutual agreements between Russia and Iran that go back to the former Soviet Union.

This would explain Ezekiel 38:4 where it says, "And I will turn you around, and put hooks into your jaws, and I will bring you forth, and all your army."

Now we see the stage set for the terrible pay day coming for the Muslim and Arab nations and people that have had an everlasting hatred for the chosen people. Remember God told Abraham, "I will bless them that bless you, and curse him that curses you" (Gen. 12:3). Since the creation of man, Satan has done everything that he can do to defeat God's plan and purpose for man. Satan has had a special hatred for God's chosen people Israel.

The prophet Ezekiel says that God is going to put hooks in your jaws and bring you out with your whole army and a great horde with you against the mountains of Israel, advancing like a storm, like a cloud covering the land (Ezek. 38:9). The excuse given for this attack by Gog and Magog along with many other Muslim nations will be, "I will go up to the land of unwalled villages; I will go to them that are at rest, that dwell safely, all of them dwelling without walls, and having neither bars nor gates. To take a spoil, and to take a prey; to turn my hand upon the desolate places that are now inhabited, and upon the people that are gathered out of the nations, which have gotten cattle and goods, that dwell in the midst of the land" (Ezek. 38:11-12).

The prophet Ezekiel tells us the reason that God allows this. "You will advance against My people Israel like a cloud that covers the land. In days to come, O Gog, I will bring you against My land, so that the nations may know Me when I show Myself holy through you before their eyes" (Ezek. 38:16 NIV). Then the prophet tells us what happens when God's anger is aroused. "This is what will happen in that day: When Gog attacks the land of Israel, My hot anger will be aroused, declares the Sovereign LORD. In My zeal and fiery wrath I declare that at that time there shall be a great earthquake in the land of Israel. . . . and all the people on the face of the earth will tremble at My presence. The mountains will be overturned, the cliffs will crumble and every wall will fall to the ground. . . . Every man's sword will be against his brother. I will execute judgment upon him with plague and bloodshed; I will pour down torrents of rain, hailstones and burning sulfur on him and on his troops and on the many nations with him. And so I will show My greatness and My holiness, and I will make Myself known in the sight of many nations. Then they will know that I am the LORD" (Ezek. 38:18-23 NIV).

The prophet Ezekiel describes the results of the terrible destruction. In Ezekiel 39:2, "And I will turn you back, and leave but the sixth part of you." This means that five-sixths of the army was destroyed or over 84%. It will take Israel over seven months to bury all the dead and over seven years to burn and destroy all the weapons. Then the prophet Ezekiel describes the conclusion of this battle. "When I have brought them again from the people, and gathered them out of their enemies' lands, and am sanctified in them in the sight of many nations; Then shall they know that I am the LORD their God, which caused them to be led into captivity among the heathen (nations): but I have gathered them unto their own land, and have left none of them anymore there (in captivity)" (Ezek. 39:27-28).

The next major prophetic event to happen in Israel will be the seventieth week of Daniel's prophecy concerning Israel. Earlier in this chapter we discussed God's time clock. In Daniel 9, we read that Daniel had been inquiring of the LORD concerning the future of Israel. The angel Gabriel came to him to give Daniel skill and understanding in Israel's future. Remember the angel told Daniel there would be 490 years of special Jewish history to be fulfilled before Jesus Christ would come to earth as King of Kings and LORD of Lords. From the time the commandment would come to rebuild Jerusalem to the time the Messiah would be cut-off or crucified, it would be 483 years. The command came on March 14, 445 B.C. Using the Jewish year of 360 days with consideration for leap years would take us to April 6, 32 A.D. or Palm Sunday, the week when Jesus Christ was crucified. Then God's time clock would not start ticking again until seven years before the return of Jesus Christ to earth as King of Kings and LORD of Lords.

The signal of when God's time clock would begin ticking again would be when a last world empire would arise out of the old Roman Empire and over it the evil prince (the Antichrist) will have gained control and would make a seven year covenant with the nation of Israel for their protection. However, in the midst of that seven year covenant, the Antichrist will set himself up in the Jewish Temple (Temple number 3) as God and demand to be worshipped. During that last three-and-one-half years of the seven year covenant, Jesus said, "For then shall be great tribulation, such as was not since the beginning of the world to this time, no nor ever shall be" (Matt. 24:21).

Before going any further into Israel's prophetic future, let us look next at the prophetic future of the Church and then the prophetic future of the secular world up to this same point in time on God's Time Clock when the Antichrist sets himself up as God to be worshipped in the Jewish Temple.

4. THE CHURCH, THE PROCLAMATION OF KINGDOM OF GOD, AND THE GLORY OF THE LORD

The time point at which the Antichrist sets himself up as God in the Jewish Temple and demands to be worshipped, is the PIVOTAL point at which the prophetic future of Israel, the Church, and the Secular World merges together. From that point on into the future, the prophetic future is the Great Tribulation (the wrath of God on this world), the Second Coming, the Millennium, the Great White Throne Judgment, and the New Heavens and the New Earth.

Remember the prophet Daniel was shown by the angel Gabriel in Daniel 9 that there were 490 years of special Jewish history, that the seventieth week of years or the last seven years would begin when the Antichrist makes a covenant with Israel for the protection of Israel. As stated above, in the middle of the seven years the Antichrist sets himself up as God in their Temple. During the next three-and-one-half years, God's wrath is poured out upon this earth in a final effort of judgment to persuade man to turn to Him. This is called the GREAT TRIBULATION.

Many students of Bible prophecy call the whole seven-year period the TRIBULATION. They divide it into three-and-one-half years periods known as the "lesser tribulation" for the first half and for the last three and one-half years the "Great Tribulation". They make an effort to fit most of the events in the Book of Revelation into this seven year period of time. A good part of the Book of

Revelation gives the prophetic events that lead to the rise of the last world empire that will be known as the Kingdom of the Antichrist as well as the rise to power of the Antichrist himself.

However, remember the last seven years does not begin until the Kingdom of the Antichrist is in power and the Antichrist has become a world power. After this point, he is able to persuade the nation of Israel to enter into a covenant with him for seven years. It is apparent that Islam, after the Battle of Gog and Magog, is no longer a major threat since the Antichrist is endeavoring to establish a one world government and religion.

The question of most students of prophecy is when will the RAPTURE occur. Those that believe in a "pre-tribulation Rapture" put it at the beginning of the tribulation period or Daniel's seventieth week. Others put it at "mid-tribulation" before God pours out His wrath on this earth. The problem is that they are trying to tie the RAPTURE to Daniel's seventieth week or the last seven years of Jewish history in God's Time Clock. Later on as we look at the Bible verses concerning the RAPTURE, remember Jesus said no man knows the day or the hour. The only thing we can know is the season. Therefore, we have to understand that the Rapture is not tied to God's Time Clock but to His LOVE AND MERCY, that He has not appointed us to His wrath and judgment.

As we turn our attention to the prophetic future of the Church as we approach the final hours (days) at the end of DAY SIX on God's time clock of this world's history, we can be overwhelmed with fear and dread for those things that are yet to come. Jesus said, "Men's hearts failing them for fear, and for looking after those things which are coming on the earth: for the powers of Heaven shall be shaken" (Luke 21:26). We know there will be the rise of the Antichrist, wars, famine, disasters in nature, more than one fourth of the world's population will die in a short period of time. "And I looked, and behold a pale horse: and his name that set on him was Death, and Hell followed with him. And power was given unto them over the fourth part of the earth, to kill with sword, and with hunger, and with death, and with the beast of the earth" (Rev. 6:8). Then we know that the wrath of almighty God will be poured out on this earth over a period of three-and-one-half years. However, we as believers and as the Church are told about and encouraged with THREE great events that are to take place during this time.

(A). FIRST - THE GOSPEL OF THE KINGDOM OF GOD

Remember Jesus said, "And this Gospel of the Kingdom shall be preached in all the world for a witness unto all nations; and then shall the end come" (Matt. 24:14). Right now the Gospel is being preached in all the world to all nations. As we shared with you in chapter two, the preaching of the Kingdom of God started with Jesus Christ during His earthly ministry. Yet within 40 years after His resurrection, the apostle Peter and the apostle Paul went to the west to Rome. According to tradition, Paul went as far west as Spain. Tradition says that the apostle Thomas went to the east as far as India. Others went NORTH and others SOUTH.

By 313 A.D., less then three hundred years after the birth of Jesus, "Christians numbered about one-half the population of the Roman Empire." (See Endnote 1.) In 313 A.D., the Roman Emperor Constantine issued an Edict of Toleration granting Christians full liberty to follow their religion. In 325 A.D., Constantine issued a general exhortation to all his subjects to embrace Christianity and made Christianity the religion of his court.

Today in 2005 A.D., there are missionaries to every country of the world as the apostle John saw in a vision almost two thousand years ago, "And I saw another angel fly in the midst of Heaven, having the everlasting Gospel to preach unto them that dwell on the earth, and to every nation, and kindred, and tongue, and people" (Rev. 14:6). Today we are witnesses to the fact that many, many television stations around the world are broadcasting the Gospel 24 hours a day, seven days a week. An example is Trinity Broadcasting Network that started with one station in Santa Ana, California over 31 years ago. Now there are over 6,525 stations worldwide with broadcasts fed by over 47 satellites circling or orbiting the globe, broadcasting the Gospel in many different languages. There are many mass crusades with evangelists such as Benny Hinn, and Reinhard Bonnke, who are preaching the Gospel face to face in

Gospel crusades with more than one million to three million people. We can understand what Jesus meant when He said this Gospel of the Kingdom of God will be preached in all the world (Matt. 24:14).

In what is even more amazing, American Churches during the last century sent missionaries out to many of the nations and countries of the world. Now less than a half-century later, many of these individual countries have not only been evangelized, but have sent out missionaries to other countries and nations. Even more amazing is that the number of missionaries sent from such nations as Brazil, the Philippines and other nations are now greater than the number of missionaries sent out by America during the last century.

In 1976 I was invited to teach on the Kingdom of God at the Good News School of Evangelism in Santos, Brazil and in the seventh School of Evangelism in 1977 at Santo Andre, Sao Paulo, Brazil. At the time there were hundreds of Brazilian pastors that attended. It was a group of evangelicals under the direction of American missionaries that numbered a little more than one million adherents. For about a quarter of a century, I had no contact with these believers. Less than a year ago I was reading a world missions report that stated that according to the Brazilian Census Bureau, about 180 million people now live in Brazil and more than 19 million of them are adherents of this group of evangelicals. One of the leaders of the Good News School of Evangelism was an American missionary, Bernhard Johnson, Jr., who at the same time established Brazil Extension School of Theology in Campinas, Brazil. A few year later, he founded the Brazil Advance School of Theology. According to the World Missions report dated March 7, 2004, the two schools are self-supporting, have 20,000 extension students throughout Brazil and five other countries and have graduated more than 23,000 students. (See Endnote 2.)

In the January 1998 edition of *Charisma & Christian Life* magazine, there is an article entitled: "Miraculous Church Growth in Brazil" on page 54. The article states that Brazil has the third largest evangelical population in the world, after the United States and China. The article also states that Brazil sends more missionaries to the world than any other Latin American country. The article features the Universal Church of the Kingdom of God (UCKG).

The Church was founded by Bishop Edir Macedo in 1977 and has grown faster than any other evangelical Christian group in Brazil. In 1998 the UCKG reported adherents of eight million people in Brazil and two million in other countries. It owns over 47 TV stations and over 26 radio outlets and its programming reaches 50 countries.

If space permitted us, this same story could be repeated for other nations where the Gospel of the Kingdom of God has been proclaimed. All of this points to how near we are to the Second Coming of Jesus Christ.

(B) SECOND - THE GLORY OF GOD

Remember Jesus prayed in the Garden of Gethsemane for His Church. "And the glory which You gave Me I have given them; that they may be one, even as We are one" (John 17:22). The apostle Paul in writing to the Church states that the goal Jesus had for the Church is, "That He might present it to Himself a glorious Church, not having spot, or wrinkle, or any such thing; but that it should be holy and without blemish" (Eph. 5:27).

The LORD declared to Moses in Numbers 14:21, "But as truly as I live, all the earth shall be filled with the glory of the LORD." The prophet Isaiah prophesied, "And the glory of the LORD shall be revealed, and all flesh shall see it together: for the mouth of the LORD has spoken it" (Isa. 40:5).

The Hebrew and Greek word for "glory" has three primary meanings:
1. Something that can be seen
2. His honor, opinion, reputation
3. The manifestation of His power and works

It has been God's plan from the beginning of time to create in this world a house or body that He would fill with His "glory".
1. Heaven is filled with His glory.
2. The Tabernacle and the Temple were filled with His glory.

3. And now He is going to have a "spiritual body" or Church on this earth that He can do the very same thing with – FILL WITH HIS GLORY.

For a few moments, let us take a look at how God's GLORY appeared to man, beginning in the Old Testament. Moses probably saw more of the GLORY of God than any other man in the Old Testament. His first experience was when in the desert he saw a bush that appeared to be on fire, but when it was not consumed, he turned aside to see what was happening. That is when he first saw a manifestation of God's GLORY. God spoke to him from the bush and sent him to Pharaoh of Egypt to deliver the children of Israel from their Egyptian bondage. After leading the children of Israel out of Egypt, across the Red Sea and into the desert, Moses and the children of Israel came to Mount Sinai.

The Bible records in Exodus 24:10, "And they saw the God of Israel: and there was under His feet as it were a paved work of a sapphire stone, and as it were the body of Heaven in his clearness." (The prophet Ezekiel had a similar experience as is recorded in Ezekiel 1:26-28. In the New Testament, the apostle John also describes a similar experience in Revelation 4:1-11. In the next chapter, we will discuss this more fully.) After Moses beheld this scene, the Bible tells us, "Moses went up into the mount, and a cloud covered the mount. And the glory of the LORD abode upon mount Sinai, and the cloud covered it six days: and the seventh day He called unto Moses out of the midst of the cloud. And the sight of the glory of the LORD was like devouring fire on top of the mount in the eyes of the children of Israel" (Exod. 24:15-17).

As the above scripture says the sight of the glory of the LORD was like devouring fire or as an extremely bright light. Moses wanted to see beyond the bright light. In Exodus 33:18 Moses asks, "And he said, I beseech You, show me Your glory. And the LORD answered Moses, You cannot see My face; for there shall no man see Me, and live. And the LORD said, Behold, there is a place by Me, and you shall stand upon a rock: and it shall come to pass, while My glory passes by, that I will put you in a cleft of the rock, and will cover you with My hand while I pass by: And I will take away My hand, and you shall see My back parts: but My face shall not be seen" (Exod..33:20-23).

It is interesting to note that during the ministry of Jesus on earth that one day Jesus took Peter, James and John up to a high mountain. In Matthew 17:2-7, "And (Jesus) was transfigured before them: and His face did shine as the sun, and His raiment was white as the light. And, behold, there appeared unto them Moses and Elijah talking with Him. Then answered Peter, and said unto Jesus, LORD, it is good for us to be here: if You will, let us make here three Tabernacles, one for You, and one for Moses, and one for Elijah. While he yet spoke, behold, a bright cloud overshadowed them: and behold a voice out of the cloud, which said, This is My beloved Son, in whom I am well pleased; hear you Him. And when the disciples heard it, they fell on their face, and were sore afraid. And Jesus came and touched them, and said, Arise, and be not afraid."

Almost 1,400 years earlier Moses had asked to see God's face and God said no man shall see His face and live. Since Moses was now a part of eternity, certainly he had seen God's face. I wonder what Moses thought when he heard the request of Peter.

We read in Exodus 25:10-22 that God gave special instructions to Moses on how to make the Ark of the Covenant that was to go into the Holy of Holies in the Tabernacle and later into the Holy of Holies in the Temple that would be built by King Solomon. On the top of this Ark of the Covenant would be a lid made of pure gold that would be called the mercy seat. On either end of the mercy seat would be two cherubim (angels) facing each other with their wings spread out over the mercy seat. Then God said: "And there I will meet with you, and I will commune with you from above the mercy seat, from between the two cherubim which are upon the Ark of the Testimony, of all things which I will give you in commandment unto the children of Israel" (Exod. 25:22).

"And the LORD said unto Moses, Speak unto Aaron your brother, that he come not at all times into the holy place within the veil before the mercy seat, which is upon the Ark; that he die not; FOR I WILL APPEAR IN THE CLOUD UPON THE MERCY SEAT" (Lev. 16:2). The glory of the LORD was the cloud of light that shone between the cherubim in the Holy of Holies. The Jews referred to this "shining cloud" above the mercy seat as the SHEK-INAH GLORY. It was physical evidence of God's presence.

We read in Numbers 7:89, "And when Moses was gone into the Tabernacle of the congregation to speak with Him (God), then he heard the voice of one speaking unto him from off the mercy seat that was upon the Ark of Testimony (covenant), from between the two cherubim: and He spoke unto him." The psalmist describes this several times in the book of Psalms. "Give ear, O Shepherd of Israel, You that lead Joseph like a flock; You that dwells between the cherubim, shine forth" (Ps. 80:1). "Out of Zion, the perfection of beauty, God has shined" (Ps. 50:2).

As was stated above, in the coming days or years that remain before the Rapture of the Church, we can be overwhelmed with fear and dread for those things that are yet to come upon this earth. But remember the prayer of Jesus in the Garden of Gethsemane, "And the glory which You gave Me I have given them: that they may be one, even as We are one" (John 17:22). Remember the prophet Isaiah prophesied, "And the glory of the LORD shall be revealed, and all flesh shall see it together: for the mouth of the LORD has spoken it" (Isa. 40:5). Isaiah went on to prophesy, "For, behold, the darkness shall cover the earth, and gross darkness the people; but the LORD shall rise upon you, and His glory shall be seen upon you" (Isa. 60:2).

If you and I only look at people, world problems, circum-stances, human failures, Churches that fight each other, you soon can go into despair. But the prophet Joel prophesied of our day, "And it shall come to pass afterward, that I will pour out My Spirit upon all flesh; and your sons and your daughters shall prophesy, your old men shall dream dreams, your young men shall see visions: And also upon the servants and upon the handmaids in those days will I pour out My spirit. And I will show wonders in the Heavens and in the earth, blood, and fire, and pillars of smoke. The sun shall be turned into darkness, and the moon into blood, before the great and terrible day of the LORD come" (Joel 2:28-31). This prophecy has only partially been fulfilled. The greatest days are still ahead for the Church.

In 2 Corinthians, the apostle Paul tells us that he was caught up to the third Heaven or throne of God. "And I know such a man, whether in the body, or out of the body, I cannot tell: God knows. How that he was caught up into paradise, and heard unspeakable words, which it is not lawful for a man to utter" (2 Cor. 12:3-4). Although here Paul does not go into what he learned, in some other of his writing he does give us some details. In 1 Corinthians 2:9 he says, "Eyes has not seen, nor ear heard, neither have entered into the heart of man, the things which God has prepared for them that love Him." "That He might present it to Himself a glorious Church, not having spot, or wrinkle, or any such thing; but that it should be holy and without blemish" (Eph. 5:27).

Many only see a part of the picture. They only see the wars, famines, pollution, natural disasters, the rise of Antichrist, satanic activity and that the Rapture of the Church is a divine rescue mission to save a persecuted and defeated Church in its last gasp of breath.

But when the apostle Paul stood by the THRONE of God when he was caught up briefly to the third Heaven, Paul saw down through the corridors of time almost two thousand years to a victory celebration, a glorious wedding celebration and the CONSUMMA-TION OF GOD'S PLAN FOR THE CHURCH THROUGH THE AGES. Whoever heard of a wedding being a rescue operation? It is important that the Church and its members see that they are part of something that is tremendous in the last days. Jesus is not trying to sneak off with His raggedy bunch of saints after the Antichrist tries to take over. Jesus rules the world in the interests of His Church and when His Church reaches FULL MATURITY, He will not be one minute late in coming for the Church, or as the Bible says, "THE BRIDE OF THE LAMB." As the apostle John writes, "Let us be glad and rejoice, and give honor to Him: for the marriage of the Lamb is come, and His wife has made herself ready" (Rev. 19:7).

The apostle John also saw in Heaven the multitude from the Rapture of the Church. "After this I beheld, and lo, a great multitude, which no man could number, of all nations, and kindreds, and people, and tongues, stood before the throne, and before the Lamb, clothed with white robes, and palms in their hands. . . . These are they which came out of great tribulation, and have washed their robes, and made them white in the blood of the Lamb" (Rev. 7:9-14).

(C). THIRD - THE RAPTURE

The third great event that is to take place during the last part of DAY SIX on God's time clock is the RAPTURE OF THE CHURCH. Here we wish to cover three important areas of the Rapture of the Church, (1) The scriptural basis for the Rapture, (2) How the Rapture fits in with the Book of Revelation, and (3) How close can we define the season of the Rapture since Jesus says no man knows the day or the hour. He did say, "Behold the fig tree, and all the trees; When they now shoot forth, you see and know of your own selves that summer is now near at hand. So likewise you, when you see these things come to pass, know you that the Kingdom of God is near at hand. Verily I say unto you, This generation shall not pass away, till all be fulfilled" (Luke 21:29-32).

(1) The Scriptural Basis for the Rapture

In Genesis 18:1 the Bible declares that the LORD appeared to Abraham in the plains of Mamre with two angels. When Abraham first saw them, they appeared as three men. Abraham convinced them to let him prepare them a dinner. After eating, the LORD began to speak to Abraham that according to the time of life, he and Sarah would have a son. Now Sarah never had a child and now was 89 years old and Abraham was 99 years old. When Sarah heard this, she laughed. Then we read, "And the LORD said unto Abraham. . . . Is anything too hard for the LORD? At the time appointed I will return unto you, according to the time of life, and Sarah shall have son" (Gen. 18:13-14).

As Abraham's guest rose up to leave, the LORD told Abraham that judgment was coming to Sodom and Gomorrah. The two angels left to go to Sodom and Gomorrah, and Abraham turned to the LORD and began to intercede for his nephew Lot and his family because they lived in Sodom. In Genesis 18:23-25, we read: "And Abraham drew near, and said, Will You also destroy the righteous with the wicked? . . .That be far from You to do after this manner, to slay the righteous with the wicked: and that the righteous should be as the wicked, that be far from You: SHALL NOT THE JUDGE OF ALL THE EARTH DO RIGHT?"

Abraham understood the LORD. If there were only ten righteous in Sodom, the LORD would spare it. However, there were only Lot and his family. Yet before the angels could bring judgment, they literally had to take Lot and his family by the hand and take them out of the city for the angel said, "Haste you, escape thither; for I cannot do any thing till you arrive there" (Gen. 19:22).

The same principle applies when God's wrath is to be poured out on this earth when the coming Antichrist sets himself up as God in the Jewish Temple that will be in Jerusalem. As described earlier in this chapter, God's time clock would begin ticking again when a last world empire would arise out of the old Roman Empire and an evil prince rise over it (the Antichrist) who will gain control of this empire and would make a seven year covenant with the nation Israel for their protection. However, in the midst of that seven year covenant, the Antichrist will set himself up in the Jewish Temple (Temple number three) as God and demand to be worshipped. During that last three-and-one-half years of the seven year covenant, Jesus said, "For then shall be great tribulation, such as was not since the beginning of the world to this time, no nor ever shall be" (Matt. 24:21).

The principle is that God will not pour His wrath and judgment out upon this earth if part of His Church or the righteous are here. In the Book of Revelation the apostle John saw in a vision the harvest of the earth in two phases, one for the righteous and one of God's wrath upon the ungodly. "And I look, and behold a white cloud, and upon the cloud one sat like unto the Son of man, having on His head a golden crown, and in His hand a sharp sickle. And another angel came out of the Temple, crying with a loud voice to Him that sat on the cloud, Thrust in Your sickle, and reap: for the time is come for You to reap; for the harvest of the earth is ripe. And He that sat on the cloud thrust in His sickle on the earth; and the earth was reaped. And another angel came out of the Temple which is in Heaven, he also having a sharp sickle. And another angel came out from the altar, which had power over fire; and cried with a loud cry to him that had the sharp sickle, saying, Thrust in your sharp sickle, and gather the clusters of the vine of the earth; for her grapes are fully ripe. And the angel thrust in his sickle into the earth, and gathered the vine of the earth, and cast it into the great winepress of the wrath of God. And the winepress was trodden without the city, and blood came out of the winepress, even unto the horse bridles, by the space of a thousand and six hundred furlongs" (Rev. 14:14-20).

Here the apostle John in this vision sees that Jesus Christ personally comes to gather the righteous. Remember at the Last Supper with His disciples, Jesus said: "Let not your heart be troubled: you believe in God, believe also in Me. In My Father's house are many mansions: if it were not so, I would have told you. I go to prepare a place for you. And if I go and prepare a place for you, I will come again, and receive you unto Myself; that where I am, there you may be also" (John 14:1-3).

The apostle Paul also declares to the Church, "For this we say unto you by the word of the LORD, that we which are alive and remain unto the coming of the LORD shall not prevent (precede) them which are asleep (dead). For the LORD Himself shall descend from Heaven with a shout, with the voice of the archangel, and with the trump (trumpet) of God: and the dead in Christ shall rise first: Then we which are alive and remain shall be caught up together with them in the clouds, to meet the LORD in the air: and so shall we ever be with the LORD" (1 Thess. 4:15-17).

(2). How the Rapture Fits in With the Book of Revelation

One of the most difficult problems with the Book of Revelation is determining how all these events fit together. The main problem is that we want to believe that all of the verses of the Book of Revelation are in chronological order. When you closely study the Book of Revelation, John actually was seeing a number of visions, some are while he is on earth and some while he is in Heaven. With this in mind, I would like to show you that the apostle John was seeing the Book of Revelation in at least SEVEN DIFFERENT PHASES.

FIRST PHASE – Revelation 1-3 JOHN ON THE ISLAND OF PATMOS

Key Verse: Revelation 1:10 "I was in the Spirit on the LORD's day, and heard behind me a great voice; as of a trumpet." This is while he was still in exile on the island of Patmos.
Content: -John saw a vision of Jesus in His full glory and was to write letters to the seven Churches.

SECOND PHASE – Revelation 4-11 WHAT JOHN SAW FROM HEAVEN

Key Verse: Revelation 4:1 "After this I looked, and behold, a DOOR WAS OPENED IN HEAVEN: and the first voice which I heard was as it were of a trumpet talking with me; which said, COME UP HERE, and I will show you things which must be here after."
Content: - He saw the THRONE OF GOD
             - The elders and living creatures worshiping God
             - The book with seven seals
             - The seven seals opened
                  1st Seal – White horse (Rise of Antichrist)
                  2nd Seal – Red horse (War)
                  3rd Seal – Black horse (Famine)
                  4th Seal – Pale horse (quarter of world's
                       population killed)
                  5th Seal – Souls under altar (martyrs)
                  6th Seal – Cataclysm
                     INTERLUDE – 144,000 servants of God
                             sealed to be on earth
                             during the Wrath of God
                           - Rapture of saints
                  7th Seal – Silence in Heaven and introduc-
                        tion of seven trumpets of
                        God's Judgment given to
                        seven angels

- The seven trumpets (The wrath or judgments of God)

1st Trumpet – one-third vegetation destroyed

2nd Trumpet – one-third sea polluted

3rd Trumpet – one-third rivers and waters polluted

4th Trumpet – one-third Heavenly lights shut out

5th Trumpet – demon locust

6th Trumpet – Armageddon

-Mighty angel declares: "There should be time no longer"

-The two witnesses

7th Trumpet – Kingdom of God Established

THIRD PHASE-Revelation 12 – THE WOMAN AND THE DRAGON

Key Verse: Revelation 12:1 "And there appeared a great wonder in Heaven."

Content: - He saw a woman clothed with the sun, the moon under her feet and a crown with twelve stars. She represented Israel and the Church.

- The great red dragon with seven heads and ten horns represents Satan and the empires of this world.

- The serpent's tail that drew one-third of the stars represents the one-third of angels that rebelled with Satan.

- The man child represents Jesus who will rule all.

FOURTH PHASE – Revelation 13-16 WHAT JOHN SAW FROM
EARTH ON THE SAND
OF THE SEA

Key Verse: Revelation 13:1 "And I stood upon the sand of the sea." John was probably standing on the shores of the Mediterranean Sea around the Island of Patmos.

Content:
- Saw a beast arise from sea (represents 7 world empires)
- Rise of Anti-Christ
- Anti-Christ gains world dominion
- 144,000 servants of God to be on earth during the judgment or wrath of God.
- The first harvest – Rapture
- The second harvest – The wrath of God to be poured out on the earth
- Seven angels with the bowls of wrath

1st Bowl of Wrath – evil and grievous sores
2nd Bowl of Wrath – sea polluted
3rd Bowl of Wrath – rivers & waters polluted
4th Bowl of Wrath – Heavenly lights affected
5th Bowl of Wrath – darkness
6th Bowl of Wrath – Armageddon
7th Bowl of Wrath – A voice from the throne of God saying "IT IS DONE"

FIFTH PHASE – Revelation 17-18 – THE GREAT PROSTITUTE AND
BABYLON

Key Verse: Revelation 17:3 "So he carried me away in the spirit into the wilderness."

Content:
-He saw the mother of harlots and abominations (named Mystery Babylon) sitting on many waters and upon the beast having seven head and ten horns.
-An angel tells John the mystery of the woman (Revelation 17:7) and the judgment to come upon

her (Revelation 17:1)

SIXTH PHASE – Revelation 19-20 – THE CLIMAX (DAY SEVEN)

Key Verse: Revelation 19:1 "And after these things I heard a great voice of much people in Heaven, singing, alleluia; salvation, and glory and honor, and power unto the LORD our God."

Content: - The Hallelujah chorus in Heaven
- The Marriage of the Lamb
- The Second Coming of Jesus Christ to earth as King of Kings and LORD of Lords.
- Satan bound a thousand years
- The thousand year reign of Jesus Christ on earth (Millennium).
- The GREAT WHITE THRONE JUDGMENT
- The last enemy (DEATH) destroyed as death and hell cast into the LAKE OF FIRE.

SEVENTH PHASE – Revelation 21-22 – A NEW HEAVEN AND EARTH

Key Verse: Revelation 21:1 "And I saw a new Heaven and a new earth: for the first Heaven and earth were passed away; and there was no more sea."

Content: - The holy city, the NEW JERUSALEM coming down out of Heaven, FATHER'S HOUSE NOW TO BE FOREVER WITH MAN.
- Description of the NEW EARTH

When we read what the apostle John saw in the second, third and fourth phases, He was actually seeing the same events from different perspectives. What John saw in the second phase was from Heaven or the throne of God. If you see events from Heaven, you see the total and complete picture. In contrast, the events in the fourth phase, John was standing on the "sands of the sea" here on earth. Therefore, he would only have a localized view of these events rather than the full view as seen from Heaven.

In Revelation 6, in the Seven Seals, John was seeing the rise of the Antichrist, the events leading to his rise in power and the martyrs of the Church. When the seventh seal was opened, remember there was silence in Heaven as the angels with seven trumpets prepared to sound their trumpets, which would be the Wrath of God being poured out on earth. When John saw these judgments from Heaven, he saw the total picture.

In the fourth phase, John saw the same events from this earth as he stood on the "sands of the sea." In Revelation 13, John gives us a description of the rise of the last world empire, the rise of the Antichrist to power and the extent of his power. Then in Revelation 14, he sees the harvest or Rapture of the Church followed by God's wrath being poured out as "bowls of wrath" on the earth.

As you compare the "seven trumpets of judgment" and the "seven bowls of wrath", they are very similar in nature. From Heaven, John was able to see that one-third of the world's vegetation was destroyed, one-third of world's seas become blood, one-third of world's rivers and waters were polluted, one-third of Heavenly lights shut out, demon power released on earth, and what we call the battle of Armageddon.

However, in the fourth phase, remember John was standing on the sands of the sea. He would not be able to see how much of the earth would be affected. If the first trumpet judgment affected one-third of the world's vegetation, it would also certainly affect human beings. John describes this as grievous sores upon men under the first bowl of wrath. John describes the second and third bowls of wrath as the sea, rivers, and waters becoming blood or polluted. Being on the sands of the sea, he would not see how much of the earth would be affected. The fourth bowl of wrath affected the sun just as the fourth trumpet affected the Heavenly lights. The fifth bowl of wrath describes the great darkness poured out on the Kingdom of the Antichrist, which could also be a description of the results of the demon power being released on earth under the fifth trumpet. The sixth bowl of wrath is also a description of the battle of Armageddon as described under the sixth trumpet. The seventh bowl of wrath is the great voice out of the Temple of Heaven, from the throne saying, "IT IS DONE" (Rev. 16:17). This is the same as the seventh trumpet, "and there were great voices in Heaven, saying, "THE KINGDOMS OF THIS WORLD ARE BECOME THE KINGDOMS OF OUR LORD, AND OF HIS CHRIST; AND HE SHALL REIGN FOR EVER AND EVER" (Rev. 11:15).

Let us now take a look at the time of the "Rapture". Going back to the prophet Daniel, the angel Gabriel told Daniel in Daniel 9:21-27 that the last seven years of Israel's history before Jesus would come to earth as King of Kings and LORD of Lords, would begin when the Antichrist would make a seven year covenant with Israel for their protection and that in the midst of that seven year period, he would set himself up as God to be worshipped as God in the Jewish Temple. It would be at that point in time that God's wrath would be poured out on this earth for three-and-one-half years, which would climax with the return of Jesus Christ as King of Kings and LORD of Lords.

What about the Church? We believe that Jesus will come for His Church in Rapture before He pours out His wrath on the earth. Jesus told His disciples that no man or even angel knows the day and the hour of the Rapture. Only the Father knows. However, Jesus did say when all these things come to pass, then look up. "So likewise you, when you see these things come to pass, know you that the Kingdom of God is near at hand. Verily I say unto you, This generation shall not pass away, till all be fulfilled" (Luke 21:31-32). YOU AND I ARE LIVING IN THAT GENERATION!

(3.) How Close Can We Define the Season of the Rapture?

As was pointed out in the beginning of this chapter, in Daniel 9:22-27 the prophet Daniel was given an accurate look at God's time clock. The angel Gabriel told him that from the going forth of the command to rebuild Jerusalem and its walls until the Messiah would be cut off would be 483 years. That command came on March 14, 445 B.C. That time period would go to April 6, 32 A.D., which is Palm Sunday before Jesus was crucified. As stated previously, common sense would indicate that DAY FIVE on God's time clock would begin after the completed work of Christ or His crucifixion and resurrection. That would indicate that DAY SIX would end at 2032 A.D. which would be the beginning of DAY SEVEN or the Millennium.

It was also pointed out that in Luke 21, Jesus said Jerusalem would be trodden down until the times of the Gentiles be fulfilled. In June 1967, during the Six Day War in Israel, the nation Israel recaptured the city of Jerusalem and had political control of the city for the first time in 2,500 years. It is interesting to observe that this happened near the end of DAY SIX on God's time clock. We refer to this war as the Six Day War. As Jesus said, when you see these signs, "This generation shall not pass away, till all be fulfilled" (Luke 21:32). A generation according to Psalms 90:10 is, "The days of our lives are seventy years, and if by reason of strength they be eighty years." If you add 70 years to 1967, it takes you to 2037 A.D.

As stated above, I believe you and I are living in that last generation in which Jesus Christ shall come. Jesus could well come before the beginning of Daniel's seventieth week or the last seven years of Israel's history before the beginning of the Millennium. However, if we see Daniel's seventieth week begin and the Rapture has not taken place, then you will know that it is only a matter of months before God begins to pour out His wrath on the earth and that the Rapture would have to occur in a very, very short period of time.

The following chart is an attempt to try to illustrate all of this on one page. The time line (approximately 2032 A.D.-2037 A.D.) is an estimated time for the beginning of DAY SEVEN. It is also an estimated time for the end of a generation of 70 years from the time that Jerusalem came under the control of Israel in 1967.

TIME TABLE OF REVELATION

TIME TABLE OF REVELATION

| Adam | Crucifixion | Approximately |
| 4,000 B.C. | 32 A.D. | 2005 A.D. |

Rev. 1 — 1st PHASE - John On The Island Of Patmos

2

3

Rev. 4 — 2nd PHASE - What John Saw From Heaven

5 — Throne | 7 Seals   Rapture   7th Seal

6
1. white horse   Silence
2. red horse   in Heaven

7
3. black horse

8
4. pale horse

9
5. souls under

10
    altar-martyrs

11
6. cataclysm

Rev. 12 — 3rd PHASE - The Woman And The Dragon

Rev. 13 — 4th PHASE - What John Saw From Earth

14 — 7 World Empires   Rapture

15 — Rise of

16 — Anti-Christ

Rev. 17 — 5th PHASE - The Great Prostitute And Babylon

18

Rev. 19 — 6th PHASE - The Climax

20

Rev. 21 — 7th PHASE - ETERNITY

22

TIME TABLE OF REVELATION

Approximately
2032-2037 A.D.   3000 A.D.

(Rev. 1:10 - "I was in the Spirit on the LORD's Day")   ETERNITY

(Rev. 4:1 - "Door was opened in heaven")

7 Trumpets   Time

1. 1/3 vegetation destroyed   to be
2. 1/3 sea polluted   no more
3. 1/3 rivers & waters
   polluted
4. 1/3 heavenly light   **7th Trumpet**
   shut out   **Kingdom**
5. demon locust   **of God**
6. Armageddon   **Established**
7. 7th Trumpet

(Rev. 12:1 - "And there appeared a great wonder in heaven")

(Rev. 13:1 - "And I stood upon the sand of the sea")

7 - Bowls of Wrath
1. evil & grevious sores
2. sea polluted
3. rivers & waters polluted
4. heavenly lights affected   **7th**
                                Bowl of Wrath
5. darkness
6. Armageddon   **"IT IS DONE"**
7. 7th - Bowl of Wrath

(Rev. 17:3 - "So he carried me away in the Spirit")

(Rev. 19:1 - "and after these things")

Marriage of Lamb
Second Coming

Satan Bound 1,000 Years

Millennium

Great White Throne Judgement

(Rev. 21:1 - "And I saw a new heaven and new earth.")

New Heavens & New Earth

243

5. THE SECULAR WORLD – RISE OF LAST WORLD EMPIRE AND THE ANTI-CHRIST

Going back to the flow chart that is shown in Graphic #5, entitled: "Prophecy Update – Events Still to Come," we have discussed Israel and the Church. Now let us take a look at the SECULAR WORLD AND THE RISE OF THE LAST WORLD EMPIRE AND THE ANTICHRIST.

Two of the Biblical prophets, Daniel in the Old Testament and John in the New Testament, were given visions of what is to happen in the last days. Other prophets were also shown some of the same information. However, Daniel and John were shown especially the rise and fall of all the great empires in earth's history and future. In all there are seven great empires: Egyptian, Assyrian, Babylonian, Medes and Persians, Greece (Alexander the Great), Rome and the revived Roman Empire, which will be the empire of the Antichrist.

Back in chapter five we discussed the TRIUMPH OF THE KINGDOM and how it was revealed to the prophet Daniel in Daniel 2:31-35. Daniel told King Nebuchadnezzar of Babylon the interpretation of a dream which Nebuchadnezzar had and which Daniel had also seen in a vision. The interpretation was, "You, O king, saw and beheld a great image. This great image, whose brightness was excellent, stood before you; and the form thereof was awesome. This image's head was of fine gold, his breast and his arms of silver, his belly and his thighs of brass. His legs of iron, his feet part of iron and part of clay. You saw (the image) until a stone that was cut out without hands, smote the image upon his feet that were of iron and clay, and break them to pieces. Then was the iron, the clay, the brass, the silver, and the gold, broken (crushed) to pieces together, and became like the chaff of the summer threshing floors; and the wind carried them away, that no place (trace) was found for them and the stone that smote the image became a great mountain, and filled the whole earth" (Dan. 2:31-35).

Then Daniel gave the interpretation, "You, O king, are a king of kings: for the God of Heaven has given you a kingdom, power, and strength, and glory . . . . You are this head of gold. And after you shall arise another kingdom inferior to you, and another third kingdom of brass, which shall bear rule over all the earth. And the fourth kingdom shall be strong as iron: forasmuch as iron breaks in pieces and subdues all things: and as iron that breaks all these, shall it break in pieces and bruise (crush). And where as you saw the feet and toes, part of potter's clay, and part of iron, the kingdom shall be divided; but there shall be in it of the strength of the iron, forasmuch as you saw the iron mixed with miry clay. And as the toes of the feet were part of iron, and part of clay, so the kingdom shall be partly strong, and partly broken (brittle or fragile). And whereas you saw iron mixed with miry clay, they shall mingle themselves with the seed of men: but they shall not cleave one to another, even as iron is not mixed with clay" (Dan. 2:37-23).

Then Daniel gives the conclusion, "And in the days of these kings shall the God of Heaven set up a kingdom, which shall never be destroyed: and the kingdom shall not be left to other people, but it shall break in pieces and consume all these kingdoms, and it shall stand forever" (Dan. 2:44).

Most Bible scholars and history shows that the head of gold was the kingdom of Babylon. The shoulders and arms of silver was the kingdom of the Medes and Persians. The belly and thighs of brass were the kingdom of Alexander the Great or the Grecians. The legs of iron were the kingdom of Rome. The feet and ten toes of part iron and part clay would be the last world kingdom or empire before the Second Coming of Christ. But the STONE THAT SMOTE THE IMAGE AND BECAME A GREAT MOUNTAIN THAT SHALL FILL THE WHOLE EARTH will be Jesus Christ, who will return to this earth as KING OF KINGS AND LORD OF LORDS whose Kingdom will become as a great mountain that shall fill the whole earth.

It should be noted that at the time of this dream by King Nebuchadnezzar of Babylon, two of the seven great empires of the world had come and gone, the Egyptian and Assyrian empires.

A number of years later Daniel had another vision concerning the rise and fall of the great empires in earth's history. This time he did not see it as an "image" but as "four great beasts" that came up from the "sea", each different from the other. The sea is used to represent the multitudes of people who inhabited the earth. Daniel was shown more information about the last world kingdom. "The first was like a lion, and had eagle's wings: I beheld till the wings thereof were plucked, and it was lifted up from the earth, and made to stand upon the feet as a man, and a man's heart was given to it" (Dan. 7:4). The winged lion was the national symbol of Babylon in the days of Nebuchadnezzar.

Daniel continues, "And behold another beast, a second, like to a bear, and it raised up itself on one side, and it had three ribs in the mouth of it between the teeth of it: and they said thus unto it, Arise, devour much flesh" (Dan. 7:5). The bear is a picture of Medo-Persia, the empire that succeeded Babylon as the world power. On one side refers to Persia's dominance over Media in the Kingdom. The three ribs probably indicate three Kingdoms conquered by Medo-Persia in their ascendancy (Babylon, Lydia and Egypt).

Then Daniel describes the third beast. "After this I beheld, and lo another, like a leopard, which had upon the back of it four wings of a fowl; the beast had also four heads; and dominion was given to it" (Dan. 7:6). The leopard depicts Greece. Though naturally a swift animal, this leopard had four wings in addition to its native agility. This speaks of the lightning speed with which Alexander the Great (336-323 B.C.) conquered the ancient world. The number four represents the four generals who divided up Alexander's Kingdom after his death.

Daniel describes the fourth beast as, "Dreadful and terrible, and strong exceedingly; and it had great iron teeth: it devoured and broke in pieces, and stamped (trampled) the residue with the feet of it: and it was diverse from all the beasts that were before it; and IT HAD TEN HORNS" (Dan. 7:7). This is a good description of Rome and its armies, which conquered the whole civilized world of its time.

As Daniel considered this fourth beast he said, "I considered the horns (remember there were ten horns) and, behold, there came up among them another little horn, before whom there were three of the first horns plucked up by the roots: and behold, in THIS HORN were eyes like the eyes of man, and a mouth speaking great (pompous) things" (Dan. 7:8). The ten horns parallel the feet and ten toes of the great image that Daniel saw in the vision at the time of King Nebuchadnezzar. The legs of iron represented the Roman Empire, which was divided into the Western Empire and the Eastern Empire. The feet and ten toes were part iron and part clay that represented a last world empire that would come out of the old Roman Empire in the last days.

Daniel sees the fourth beast, which represents the Roman Empire. He pays particular attention to the ten horns on the head of the beast. This greatly troubled Daniel, so he asked one of the angels in the vision the interpretation of all this. The angel replied that the four beasts are four kings that shall arise out of the earth. (See Daniel 7:17.)

Daniel continued to ask, "Then I would know that truth of the fourth beast, which was diverse from all the others, exceeding dreadful, whose teeth were of iron, and his nails of brass; which devoured, broke in pieces, and stamped the residue with his feet; And of the ten horns that were in his head, and of the other which came up, and before whom three fell; even of that horn that had eyes, and a mouth that spoke very great things (pompous), whose look was more stout than his fellows. I beheld, and the same horn made war with the saints, and prevailed against them; Until the Ancient of days came, and judgment was given to the saints of the most High; and the time came that the saints possessed the kingdom" (Dan. 7:19-22).

The angel answered Daniel saying, "The fourth beast shall be the fourth Kingdom upon the earth, which shall be diverse from all kingdoms, and shall devour the whole earth, and shall tread it down, and break it in pieces. And the ten horns out of this kingdom are ten kings that shall arise: (the ten horns represent a last world empire that would come out of the old Roman Empire in the last days) and another shall arise after them; and he shall be diverse from the first, and he shall subdue three kings. And he shall speak great words against the most High, and shall wear (persecute) out the saints of the most High, and think (intend) to change times and laws: and they shall be given into his hand until a time and times and the dividing of time"(three and one-half years) (Dan. 7:23-25).

Daniel sees the conclusion that the Ancient of Days (Jesus Christ) comes and that the saints will possess the kingdom and His "kingdom is an everlasting kingdom, and all dominions shall serve and obey Him" (Dan. 7:22,27).

The apostle John has a similar vision as Daniel when in Revelation 13, he is standing upon the sands of the sea and sees, "a beast rise up out of the sea, having seven heads and ten horns, and upon his horns ten crowns, and upon his heads the name of blasphemy (a blasphemous name). And the beast which I saw was like unto a leopard, and his feet were as the feet of a bear, and his mouth as the mouth of a lion: and the dragon (Satan) gave him his power, and his seat, and great authority" (Rev. 13:1-2). Here the sea represents the Gentile nations. Instead of there being four beasts, as Daniel saw in his vision, the beast that John sees had resemblances to a leopard, a bear and a lion that refer to the first three beasts in the vision of Daniel 7 (representing the empires of Babylon, Medo-Persian, and Greece).

However, this time John sees the beast with seven heads and ten horns. The seven heads represent the seven great empires that are and will be in earth's history, Egyptian, Assyrian, Babylonian, Medo-Persian, Greece (Alexander the Great), Rome and the revived Roman Empire. It also appears that the ten horns were on the seventh head. The ten horns represent ten kings who will make up this seventh head or the revived Roman Empire. The apostle John further describes this seven headed beast in Revelation 17:3, "So he carried me away in the Spirit into the wilderness: and I saw a woman sit upon a scarlet-colored beast, full of names of blasphemy, having seven heads and ten horns."

The apostle John wondered at this sight. The angel that had carried him in the spirit into the wilderness asked John, "Wherefore did you marvel? I will tell you the mystery of the woman, and of the beast that carries her, which has the seven heads and the ten horns. . . . there are seven kings: five are fallen, and one is, and the other is not yet come; and when he comes, he must continue a short space (time)" (Rev. 17:7-10). The five fallen are Egypt, Assyria, Babylonia, Medo-Persian and Greece. The one that is as of the time of John's vision is Rome. The other, or number seven yet to come, will be the revived Roman Empire, which will be ruled by the Antichrist. This revived Roman Empire is represented in Daniel by the ten toes in the image of Daniel 2:41-44 and by the ten horns on the fourth beast of Daniel 7:7,20,24 and in Revelation by the ten horns on the beast of Revelation 13:1.

The angel went on to tell John, "And the ten horns which you saw are ten kings, which have received no kingdom as yet; but receive power (authority) as kings one hour with the beast" (Rev. 17:12). The one hour indicates a relatively short time. These rulers of a ten nation federation will unite and give their political authority and military power to the beast (Antichrist) to conquer the earth and make war against Jesus Christ and the Church. The purpose of Satan through the beast and fellow kings is to establish an invincible kingdom that Christ cannot overcome when He returns.

As we look at these visions and prophecies, what do we see and what can we know? There are at least a minimum of four factors.

1. There will be ten kings or nations that will arise out of the area of the old Roman Empire.
2. These ten nations will be represented as part iron and part clay. The iron represents military and economic strength. The clay represents the human side such as languages, cultures and individual goals.
3. At first they will lack real leadership.
4. A strong leader comes on the scene and gains control and a powerful empire is formed that gains control over the world.

At times I wish that I had a prophet's calling. However, I am a student of the Bible and God's Word and see the following events currently happening that appear to fit the above scenario.

Following the 1954 Paris Agreement modifying the Brussels Treaty, seven European countries organized a European security and defense organization named the Western European Union (WEU) in 1955. The member nations were Belgium, France, Germany, Great Britain, Italy, Luxemburg, and Netherlands. In 1988 two more nations joined, Portugal and Spain. Number ten, Greece, joined in 1995. All of these were nations that were at one time under the control of the old Roman Empire. In looking at this, we can see the start of a revived Roman empire.

The Western European Union (WEU)

List of 28 Delegations	
10 Member States * **(modified Brussels Treaty – 1954)** (also members of the EU and NATO)	
Belgium	Luxembourg
France	Netherlands
Germany	Portugal (1990)
Greece (1995)	Spain (1990)
Italy	United Kingdom
6 Associate Members * **(Rome – 1992)** (also members of NATO)	
Czech Republic (1999)	Norway
Hungary (1999)	Poland (1999)
Iceland	Turkey
5 Observers * **(Rome – 1992)** (also members of the EU)	
Austria (1995)	Ireland
Denmark•	Sweden (1995)
Finland (1995)	
7 Associate Partners * **(Kirchberg – 1994)** (all signatories of a Europe Agreement with the EU)	
Bulgaria	Romania
Estonia	Slovakia
Latvia	Slovenia (1996)
Lithuania	

•Denmark is also a member of NATO.

In parallel to the Western European Union is the European Union (EU). Its roots go back to the European Economic Community (informally called the Common Market) that was established by the Treaty of Rome in 1957 and implemented on January 1, 1958. Although the Treaty of Rome of 1957 is still in effect, it has been amended since then, most notably by the Maastricht treaty of 1992 which first established the current name of European Union.

On October, 29, 2004, European heads of government signed a treaty establishing a constitution for the European Union, which has been ratified by some member states and is currently awaiting ratification by the other member states. Currently there are 25 member states. This process faltered on May 29, 2005 when the people of France voted no in a referendum on the constitution. This forced a change in the prime minister of France. Three days later the Netherlands voted no against it as well. For the constitution to take effect all 25 EU members must ratify it by November 2006 or it will not take effect.

Under the Maastricht Treaty (1992), the Western European Union (WEU) was envisioned as the future military arm of the European Union (EU). In 1999 the EU voted to absorb all the functions of the WEU in preparation for the making the EU a defensive and peacekeeping military organization as well as a social and economic one. Now the European Union remains where it is and the Western European Union (WEU) remains institutionally autonomous. The military strength (the iron) remains with the WEU.

On June 21, 2005 *The Boston Globe* printed an interesting article entitled, "European Leaders Unable to Provide New Direction." The article goes on to state, "Europe is suddenly leaderless, with almost its entire political class estranged from voters on crucial questions of economic unity. . . . About two weeks ago, both France and the Netherlands defied their leaders to vote against a carefully negotiated European constitution, leaving Prime Minister Jan Peter Balkenende of the Netherlands and President Jacques Chirac of France deeply wounded. . . . Still, one thing seems clear, in the United States, Europe, and perhaps even beyond: The leaders who will emerge from the current void will either be those who can best explain the benefits of globalization or those who can most effectively argue against it."

Now let us return to the four factors that were mentioned above and do some comparisons:

1. There will be ten kings or nations that will arise out of the area of the old Roman Empire.
    Comparison:
    The European Union is composed of 25 members; the prophecies said it would be ten nations. Therefore, this would not fit what was prophesied and now appears to be defeated.
    The Western European Union is composed of ten members and the rest are only associate members, observers or associate partners.
2. These ten nations will be represented as part iron and part clay.
    Comparison:
    These ten nations in the WEU were being sought by the EU for making the EU a defensive and peacekeeping military organization which would give it the strength of iron as prophesied by the prophet Daniel.
    The differences of language, cultures and individual goals makes up the weakness in this political union which the prophet Daniel describes as clay.
    "And as the toes of the feet were part of iron and part of clay, so the Kingdom shall be partly strong and partly brittle (or fragile)" (Dan. 12:42).
3. At first they will lack real leadership.
    Comparison:
    The above article from *The Boston Globe* states Europe is suddenly leaderless.
4. A strong leader comes on the scene
    Comparison:
    This has not happened yet.

Both the prophet Daniel and the apostle John describe a leader who will come into power and leadership over these ten Kingdoms. As Daniel says in Daniel 7:20, "And of the ten horns that were in his head, and of the other which came up, and before whom three fell; even of that horn that had eyes, and a mouth that spoke very great things (pompous words), whose look was more stout than his fellows". Now with eyes we see and gather intelligence, we are able to know things and a "mouth that spoke very great things" means someone who knows how to persuade, lead and take leadership.

The "little horn" represents the Antichrist who comes in on the scene and gains control over these ten nations. In Daniel 7:8 it says, "there came up among them another little horn, before whom there were three of the first horns plucked up by the roots." Our first thought would be to think he defeats these three kings or nations in a battle or something. However, the Hebrew conveys the thought of a plant being plucked up by the roots. This may indicate that instead of these three kings (nations) being defeated in a battle that they are voted out of this political union completely.

The prophecies tell us that this new leader, or the Antichrist, gains control over the other seven kings or nations and ultimately gains control of the world. Not only is a one world government created, but the monetary system or banking system is developed into what we may term a one world monetary system that is described as the "mark of the beast" as John says in Revelation 13:17, "And that no man might buy or sell, save he that had the mark, or the name of the beast, or the number of his name."

Now as we consider this scenario, our prayers should be, "LORD Jesus is this the actual way these prophecies will unfold or should we be looking for a similar scenario?" Like the wise men at the birth of Jesus when they came to Jerusalem asking, "Where is he that is born King of the Jews? for we have seen his star in the east, and are come to see him" (Matt. 2:2).

Going back to the flow-chart that is shown in Graphic #5, we see the future histories of ISRAEL, THE CHURCH AND THE SECULAR WORLD MERGE together when this world ruler or Antichrist makes a seven year covenant with Israel supposedly for Israel's protection. Israel rebuilds the Temple (the third Temple) in Jerusalem and in the midst of the seven year covenant, the Antichrist proclaims himself God and sets himself up in the Temple as God and demands to be worshiped. In 2 Thessalonians 2:3-4 we read, "Let no man deceive you by any means: for that day shall not come, except there come a falling away first, and that man of sin be revealed, the son of perdition; Who opposes and exalts himself above all that is called God, or that is worshiped; so that he as God sits in the Temple of God, showing himself that he is God."

As has already been previously discussed, for the next three-and-one-half years, God's wrath is going to be poured out on this earth. As Jesus said, "For then shall be great tribulation, such as was not since the beginning of the world to this time, no, nor ever shall be" (Matt. 24:21).

6. THE SECOND COMING

The next great event on GOD'S TIME CLOCK is the SECOND COMING OF JESUS CHRIST. Knowing this, Satan sends out evil spirits to all the kings or rulers of nations to gather them to the battle of that great day of God Almighty called the battle of Armageddon. The apostle John saw this in his vision of God's wrath being poured out on the earth during the "seven bowls of wrath". As John writes in Revelation 16:12-16, "And the sixth angel poured out his vial (bowl) upon the great river Euphrates; and the water thereof was dried up, that the way of the kings of the east might be prepared. And I saw three unclean spirits like frogs come out of the mouth of the dragon (Satan), and out of the mouth of the beast (Antichrist), and out of the mouth of the false prophet. For they are the spirits of devils (demons), working miracles, which go forth unto the kings of the earth and of the whole world, to gather them to the battle of that great day of God Almighty . . . . And he gathered them together into a place called in the Hebrew tongue Armageddon (Mount Megiddo)."

The river Euphrates was the promised northeastern boundary of Israel. During the time of David and Solomon, it was approximately the northern boundary of the Kingdom of Israel and will be again. Here the apostle John sees the Euphrates River dried up, so that the kings of the east may come into Israel. These kings are unidentified, but many students of Bible prophecy see them as China and other Oriental nations. This same vision that John had of the "sixth bowl of wrath" also parallels with the vision John had of the seven trumpet judgments as recorded in Revelation 9:13-18, "And the sixth angel sounded, and I heard a voice from the four horns of the golden altar which is before God, Saying to the sixth angel which had the trumpet, Loose (release) the four angels which are bound in the great river Euphrates. And the four angels were loosed, which were prepared for an (the) hour, and a day, and a month, and a year, for to slay the third part of men. And the number of the army of the horseman were (200,000,000) two hundred thousand thousand: and I heard the number of them. And then I saw the horses in the vision, and them that sat on them, having breastplates of fire, and of jacinth, and brimstone (fiery red, blue and yellow): and the heads of the horses were as the heads of lions; and out of their mouths issued fire and smoke and brimstone (burning sulfur). By these three was the third part of men killed, by the fire, and by the smoke, and by the brimstone, which issued out of their mouths."

Today we know that China could field an army of up to 200,000,000 men. As John saw in the "sixth bowl of wrath", the demon spirits went unto all the kings and rulers of the earth to gather them together for this great battle to take place in Israel. THIS IS SATAN'S FINAL ATTEMPT TO PREVENT THE RETURN OF JESUS CHRIST OR HIS SECOND COMING.

The Old Testament prophet Zechariah also describes this final battle in Zechariah 12:3, "And in that day I will make Jerusalem a burdensome (very heavy) stone for all people: all that burden themselves with it shall be cut in pieces, though all the people of the earth be gathered against it." Zechariah also goes on to tell us in Zechariah 14:2-5,12, "For I will gather all nations against Jerusalem to battle: and the city shall be taken, and the houses rifled (plundered), and the women ravished; and half of the city shall go forth into captivity, and the residue of the people shall not be cut off from the city. Then shall the LORD go forth, and fight against those nations, as when He fought in the day of battle. And His feet shall stand in that day upon the mount of Olives, which is before Jerusalem on the east, and the mount of Olives shall cleave (split in two) in the midst thereof toward the east and toward the west, and there shall be a very great valley; and half of the mountain shall remove toward the north, and half if it toward the south. . . . and the LORD my God shall come, and all the saints with Him. . . . And this shall be the plague wherewith the LORD will smite all the people that have fought against Jerusalem; THEIR FLESH SHALL CONSUME AWAY WHILE THEY STAND UPON THEIR FEET, AND THEIR EYES SHALL CONSUME AWAY IN THEIR HOLES (SOCKETS), AND THEIR TONGUE SHALL CONSUME AWAY IN THEIR MOUTH."

In a neutron bomb explosion, one of the effects would be that the flesh would be consumed by the heat before the bones could drop to the ground. This may not be what actually happens, but it is believed that Israel has the neutron bomb and would exercise what is called the "Sampson Option" in a last ditch effort for survival.

The prophet Zechariah states after this: "And the LORD shall be King over all the earth: in that day shall there be one LORD, and His Name one" (Zech. 14:9).

Also it is important to note in the prophecies of Zechariah that he foretold, "And His (Jesus) feet shall stand in that day upon the mount of Olives, which is before Jerusalem on the east, and the mount of Olives shall cleave (split in two) in the midst thereof toward the east and toward the west, and there shall be a very great valley; and half of the mountain shall remove toward the north, and half if it toward the south" (Zech. 14:4). After the resurrection of Jesus following His crucifixion, He ascended back to Heaven from the Mount of Olives and the angels who stood by with the disciples told them, "this same Jesus, which is taken up from you into Heaven, shall so come in like manner as you have seen Him go into Heaven" (Acts 1:11) At the second coming of Jesus, His feet will first touch the Mount of Olives.

The prophet Joel prophesied that the LORD would "also gather all nations, and will bring them down into the valley of Jehoshaphat, and will plead (enter into judgment) with them there for My people and for My heritage Israel, whom they have scattered among the nations, and parted (divided up) My land" (Joel 3:2). The LORD went on to say, "Let the heathen (nations) be wakened, and come up to the valley of Jehoshaphat: for there will I sit to judge all the heathen (nations) around about" (Joel 3:12).

The only problem is that Biblical scholarship has never been able to accurately tell where the Valley of Jehoshaphat is. The name

Jehoshaphat means "Jehovah judges" or "God judges." From Zechariah 14:4-5, we read about a very great valley being formed when the feet of Jesus touch the Mount of Olives and it splits in two, and half of the mountain shall remove toward the north, and half of it toward the south. It will be in this newly created valley where Jesus Christ will sit in judgment of the nations.

Back in chapter five of this book where we discussed the Kingdom of God, the prophet Daniel in Daniel 2:34-35 described an image with the head of gold, the shoulders and arms of silver, the waist of brass, the legs of iron and the feet with ten toes that were part iron and clay being smashed by a stone cut out without hands and brake the image into fine pieces which were blown away as chaff of the summer threshing floors. The stone that smote the image became a great mountain, and filled the whole earth. This image represented the empires of the Babylon, Medo-Persian, Rome and the revived Roman Empire or the kingdom of the Antichrist. The stone which represents Jesus Christ, completely destroys these kingdoms and the Kingdom of God as a great mountain fills all the earth.

The apostle John tells us of this same event in the Book of Revelation. "But in the days of the voice of the seventh angel, when he shall begin to sound (the blowing of the seventh trumpet), the mystery of God should be finished, as He has declared to His servants the prophets" (Rev. 10:7). Or as John says in Revelation 16:17, "And the seventh angel poured out his vial (bowl) into the air; and there came a great voice out of the Temple of Heaven, from the throne, saying, IT IS DONE." Then John writes in Revelation 19:1,6, "And after these things. . . . I heard as it were the voice of a great multitude, and as the voice of many waters, and as the voice of mighty thunderings, saying, Alleluia: for the LORD God omnipotent reigns."

After this John said, "And I saw Heaven opened, and behold a white horse; and He that sat upon him was called Faithful and True, and in righteousness He does judge and make war. His eyes were as a flame of fire, and on His head were many crowns; and He had a name written, that no man knew, but He Himself. . . . And the armies which were in Heaven followed Him upon white horses, clothed in fine linen, white and clean. And out of His mouth goes a sharp sword, that with it He should smite the nations: and He shall rule them with a rod of iron: and He treads the winepress of the fierceness and wrath of Almighty God. And He had on his vesture (robe) and on His thigh a name written, KING OF KINGS, AND LORD OF LORDS. . . . And I saw the beast (Antichrist), and the kings of the earth, and their armies, gathered together to make war against Him that sat on the horse, and against His army. And the beast (Antichrist) was taken, and with him the false prophet that wrought miracles before him, with which he deceived them that had received the mark of the beast (Antichrist), and them that worshipped his image. These both were cast alive into a lake of fire burning with brimstone. And the remnant (rest) were slain with the sword of Him that sat upon the horse, which sword proceeded out of His mouth" (Rev. 19:11-21)

Verse 14 of the above quote says: "And the armies which were in Heaven followed Him upon white horses." We would naturally expect the angels of Heaven to follow Him. However, if it only referred to the angels, John probably would have used the word "angels." The prophet Zechariah said, "and the LORD my God shall come, and all the saints with Him" (Zech. 14:5). In the book of Jude, verse 14, it says, "And Enoch also, the seventh from Adam, prophesied of these, saying, Behold, the LORD comes with ten thousands of His saints."

After the casting of the beast (Antichrist) and his false prophet into the lake of fire and after the destruction of the Antichrist's army, the next step was Satan himself. John tells us, "And I saw an angel come down from Heaven, having the key to the bottomless pit and a great chain in his hand. And he laid hold on the dragon, that old serpent, which is the Devil, and Satan, and bound him a thousand years, And cast him into the bottomless pit, and shut him up, and set a seal upon him, that he should deceive the nations no more, till the thousand years should be fulfilled: and after that he must be loosed (released) a little season" (Rev. 20:1-3).

NOW BEGINS DAY SEVEN ON GOD'S TIME CLOCK, the day in which God will finish the plan and purpose that He has for man. When that plan and purpose has been perfected, it brings the completion. As the apostle Paul wrote in 1 Corinthians 15:24-26, "Then comes the end, when He shall have delivered up the Kingdom to God, even the Father; when He shall have put down all rule and all authority and power. For He must reign, till He has put all enemies under His feet. The last enemy that shall be destroyed is death."

7. THE MILLENNIUM

During DAY SEVEN, Jesus Christ completes His rule and reign in putting down all rule and all authority when the last enemy "death" is destroyed. As stated previously, this DAY SEVEN begins when Jesus' feet touch down on the Mount of Olives. As the prophet Zechariah describes in Zechariah 14, when all nations are gathered against the city of Jerusalem, "Then shall the LORD go forth, and fight against those nations, as when He fought in the day of battle. And His feet shall stand in that day upon the mount of Olives, which is before Jerusalem on the east, and the mount of Olives shall cleave (split in two) in the midst thereof. . . . and there shall be a very great valley, and half of the mountain shall remove toward the north, and half of it toward the south" (Zech. 14:3-4). The prophet goes on to tell us that the land shall be turned into a plain from Geba north of Jerusalem to Rimmon south of Jerusalem. This would be a plain about 35 miles long and a substantial number of miles in width. As mention previously, the prophet Joel calls this new valley the Valley of Jehosaphat (Jehovah judges). There the LORD says, "for there will I sit to judge all the nations round about" (Joel 3:12). It is here Jesus Christ sets up His Millennium Reign and throne for a thousand years.

The prophet Ezekiel tells us in Ezekiel 40:1-2 that the hand of the LORD was upon him and had brought him into the land of Israel from Babylon. In visions the LORD showed Ezekiel the land of Israel, the city of Jerusalem and a Temple he had never seen before. It is a literal Temple yet to be built because Ezekiel was told to take the measurements of the Temple and the Temple is much larger and the measurements different from any other temple or tabernacle in the Bible. It therefore awaits fulfillment which can take place only in the time of Israel's blessing and restoration during the Millennial Reign of Christ.

After taking the measurements of the Temple, Ezekiel tells us the hand of the LORD brought him to the eastern gate of the Temple. "Afterward he brought me to the gate, even the gate that looks toward the east: And behold, the glory of the God of Israel came from the way of the east: and His voice was like a noise of many waters: and the earth shined with His glory. . . . And the glory of the LORD came into the house by the way of the gate which faces toward the east. So the spirit took me up, and brought me into the inner court; and, behold, the glory of the LORD filled the house. And I heard Him speaking unto me out of the house; and the man (Jesus) stood by me. And He said unto me, Son of man, the place of My throne, and the place of the soles of My feet, where I will dwell in the midst of the children of Israel for ever, and My holy name, shall the house of Israel no more defile" (Ezek. 43:1-7).

The inner court of what Bible students call the "Millennium Temple" or "Ezekiel's Temple" will serve as the Throne of Jesus Christ during the Millennium Reign of Christ. Then Ezekiel goes on to tell us more about the inner court or Throne of Jesus in the Millennium Temple. "Then He brought me back the way of the gate of the outward sanctuary which looks toward the east; and it was shut. Then said the LORD to me; This gate shall be shut, it shall not be opened, and no man shall enter in by it; because the LORD, the God of Israel, has entered in by it, therefore it shall be shut. . . . And the LORD said unto me, Son of man, mark well, and behold with your eyes, and hear with your ears all that I say unto you concerning all ordinances of the house of the LORD, and all the laws thereof; and mark well the entering in of the house, and every going forth of the sanctuary" (Ezek. 44:1-5).

Then the LORD gives instructions concerning ministry in the outer courts of the Temple, but for the inner court He gives Ezekiel the following instructions, "But the priest the Levites, the sons of Zadok, that kept the charge of My sanctuary when the children of Israel went astray from Me, they should come near to Me to minister unto Me, and they shall stand before Me to offer unto Me the fat and the blood, says the LORD God. They shall enter into My sanctuary, and they shall come near to My table, to minister unto Me, and they shall keep My charge" (Ezek. 44:15-16).

Since the Bible indicates that much typological significance of both the Temple and its service has already been fulfilled by Christ, we might question the need for a Temple or for animal sacrifice in the Millennium. I believe the sacrifices in the Millennium will be memorial, much as observance of the LORD's Supper is memorial today.

Another very interesting observance of the prophet Zechariah and the prophet Ezekiel was, "And it shall be in that day, that living waters (fresh, wholesome water) shall go out from Jerusalem; half of them toward the former sea (Dead Sea), and half of them toward the hinder sea (Mediterranean Sea): in summer and in winter shall it be" (Zech. 14:8). The prophet Ezekiel tells us, "Afterward he brought me again unto the door of the house (Temple); and behold , waters issued out from under the threshold of the house eastward: for the forefront of the house stood toward the east, and the waters came down from under, from the right side of the house, at the south side of the altar. . . . Then said He unto me, These waters flow out toward the east country, and go down into the desert, and go into the sea (Dead Sea): which being brought forth into the sea, the waters shall be healed" (Ezek. 47:1,8). The prophet Ezekiel writes about four chapters (Ezekiel 45-48) describing how the land of Israel will be divided and used during the Millennium.

Remember the apostle John said, "And I saw thrones, and they sat upon them, and judgment was given unto them. . . and they lived and reigned with Christ a thousand years" (Rev. 20:4). Now we know from Revelation 19:16 that Jesus returns as King of Kings and LORD of Lords. Who are these other kings who will set on thrones and reigning with Christ a thousand years? The Bible tells who some of them are by name. The prophet Hosea 3:5, "Afterward shall the children of Israel return, and seek the LORD their God, and David their king; and shall fear the LORD, and His goodness in the latter days." The prophet Ezekiel describes it in more detail. "And David My servant shall be king over them; and they all shall have one shepherd. . . . and My servant David shall be their prince for ever" (Ezek. 37:24-25). The prophet tells us in Ezekiel 34:23-24, "And I will set up one shepherd over them, and he shall feed them even my servant

David; he shall feed them, and he shall be their shepherd. And I the LORD will be their God, and My servant David a prince among them; I the LORD have spoken it."

The prophet Ezekiel explains in Ezekiel 43 and 44 how the LORD will enter the Millennium Temple through the eastern gate as King of Kings and LORD of Lords. Then Ezekiel tells us, "Then said the LORD unto me; This gate shall be shut, it shall not be opened, and no man shall enter by it; because the LORD, the God of Israel, has entered in by it, therefore it shall be shut. It is for the prince; the prince, he shall sit in it to eat bread before the LORD; he shall enter by the way of the porch (vestibule) of that gate, and shall go out by way of the same" (Ezek. 44:2-3).

In Ezekiel 44-48, the prophet Ezekiel tells us the position, duties and the portion that belongs to the "prince" who the Bible describes as David for he serves as King of Israel under the King of Kings – Jesus. In Ezekiel 45:8-9, the prophet describes other "princes" who serve under David in judging and ruling Israel during the Millennium. In Matthew 19:27-28, "Then answered Peter and said unto him (Jesus), Behold, we have forsaken all, and followed You; what shall we have therefore? And Jesus said unto them, Verily I say unto you, That you which have followed Me, in the regeneration when the Son of man shall sit in the throne of His glory, you also shall sit upon twelve thrones, judging the twelve tribes of Israel."

In Luke 22:29-30, Jesus told His disciples, "And I appoint unto you a kingdom, as My Father has appointed unto Me. That you may eat and drink at My table in My Kingdom, and sit on thrones judging the twelve tribes of Israel." In Revelation 20:4, "And I saw thrones, and they sat upon them, and judgment was given unto them. . . ." The thrones represent the administration of the Millennium Kingdom and all nations will be under the rule and reign of Jesus and the saints will reign with Jesus for a thousand years here on earth. However, this will be nothing compared to what God has for us in the new Heaven and new earth coming at the close of DAY SEVEN and the beginning of eternity.

The prophets of the Old Testament had much to say about the Millennium Reign of Christ, a time when all the promises of God to

Abraham and Israel will be completely fulfilled. As Zechariah 8:3, "This says the LORD; I am returned unto Zion, and will dwell in the midst of Jerusalem: and Jerusalem shall be called a city of truth; and the mountain of the LORD of hosts the holy mountain." The prophet Zechariah goes on to proclaim, "Yes, many people and strong nations shall come to seek the LORD of hosts in Jerusalem, and to pray before the LORD" (Zech. 8:22). Then Zechariah proclaims, "And the LORD shall be king over all the earth: in that day shall there be one LORD, and His name one" (Zech. 14:9).

The prophet Isaiah prophesied, "And it shall come to pass in the last days, that the mountain of the LORD's house shall be established in the top of the mountains, and shall be exalted above the hills; and all nations shall flow unto it. And many people shall go and say, Come you, and let us go up to the mountain of the LORD, to the house of the God of Jacob, and He will teach us His ways, and we will walk in His paths, for out of Zion shall go forth the law, and the Word of the LORD from Jerusalem. And He shall judge among the nations, and shall rebuke many people: and they shall beat their swords into plowshares, and theirs spears into pruning hooks: nation shall not lift up sword against nation, neither shall they learn war any more (Isa. 2:2-4).

The prophet Micah prophesied, "But in the last days it shall come to pass, that the mountain of the house of the LORD shall be established in the top of the mountains, and it shall be exalted above the hills; and people shall flow unto it. And many nations shall come, and say, Come, and let us go up to the mountain of the LORD, and to the house of the God of Jacob; and He will teach us of His ways, and we will walk in His paths: for the law shall go forth out of Zion, and the word of the LORD from Jerusalem" (Mic. 4:1-2). Then the prophet Micah proclaims, "And the LORD shall reign over them in mount Zion from hence forth, even for ever" (Mic. 4:7).

The prophet Habakkuk proclaims, "For the earth shall be filled with the knowledge of the glory of the LORD, as waters cover the sea" (Hab. 2:14).

When the children of Israel were in the wilderness and Joshua, Caleb and the other ten spies who were sent to scout out the

Promised Land came back to report, ten of the spies gave an evil report. Joshua and Caleb reported, "Let us go up at once, and possess (take possession of) it; for we are well able to overcome it" (Num. 13:30). The people believed the evil report of the ten spies and rebelled and wanted to go back to Egypt. Moses prayed and made intercession for the people. "And the LORD said, I have pardoned according to your word: but as truly as I live, all the earth shall be filled with the glory of the LORD! (Num. 14:20-21). Or as the prophet Habakkuk prophesied, "For the earth shall be filled with the knowledge of the glory of the LORD, as the water covers the sea" (Hab. 2:14).

During these thousand years, Satan and his demons will have no influence because he will be chained and shut up in the bottomless pit (Rev. 20:1-3). However, there will be those who survive the tribulation or the wrath of God who enter the Millennium without dying and being resurrected. They will still be in their natural bodies and will have children, who will also reproduce throughout the thousand years. As Zechariah the prophet said, "And it shall come to pass, that everyone that is left of all the nations which came against Jerusalem shall even go up from year to year to worship the King, the LORD of hosts, and to keep the feast of Tabernacles" (Zech. 14:16).

Mankind during the Millennium will not have to contend with Satan or a tempter. However, those who enter the Millennium or are born during the Millennium will still have a free will and will still have to make the choice to love God and make Jesus the LORD and King of their lives. The Bible indicates that those who choose wrongly or who sin, will be dealt with immediately. As the prophet Isaiah writes, "There shall be no more thence an infant of days, nor an old man that has not filled his days; for the child shall die a hundred years old; but the sinner being a hundred years old shall be accursed" (Isa. 65:20). The Amplified Bible translates this verse, "There shall no more be in it an infant that lives but a few days, or an old man who dies prematurely, for the child shall die a hundred years old, and the sinner who dies when only a hundred years old shall be (thought only a child, cut off because he is) accursed." In other words, sin and sinners will be dealt with immediately.

When Adam was created and put on earth, the goal was that he would only choose to obey God and live a life without sin. When Jesus came as the second Adam, He lived a life without sin, a picture of what God desired for all men. In the Millennium, among those that will be born, there undoubtedly will be those who will live and fulfill the purpose that God originally planned for Adam, a life without sin and who will take dominion.

At the end of the Millennium, Satan will be released from prison for a short time to once again to try those born during the Millennium as he was allowed to try or tempt Adam and Eve. Those born during the Millennium will face a time of testing and trial just as Jesus did in the wilderness after His baptism of water and the descent of the Holy Spirit upon Him. Although there will be those who will be deceived by Satan, I also believe there will be those who will triumph over Satan just as Jesus did during His time of temptation in the wilderness.

B. THE CLOSE OF DAY SEVEN

1. THE CLIMAX

The apostle Paul declares unto us the ultimate triumph of the Kingdom of God that takes place before God brings about the NEW HEAVEN AND THE NEW EARTH. Jesus has reigned successfully and triumphantly over the Millennium Kingdom, A time on earth where and when men completely come under the rule and reign of King Jesus.

Now comes Judgment Day and the final defeat of the LAST ENEMY – DEATH. For as the apostle Paul wrote in 1 Corinthians 15:24-26, "Then comes the end, when He shall have delivered up the Kingdom to God, even the Father; when He shall have put down all rule and all authority and power. For He must reign, till He has put all enemies under His feet. The last enemy that shall be destroyed is death."

Before we enter into the NEW HEAVENS AND NEW EARTH, there are still four major events to take place: (1) The Judgment Seat of Christ, (2) The Great White Throne Judgment, (3) The defeat of the last enemy DEATH and (4) The destruction of the present earth and heavens.

2. JUDGMENT SEAT OF CHRIST

The writer of the book of Hebrews made it very clear when he wrote, "And as it is appointed unto men once to die, but after this is the judgment" (Heb. 9:27). The Bible makes it very clear that there are two judgments, one for the believer and another one for all those who did not believe or who chose to go their own way. For the believer is the Judgment Seat of Christ. For all others there is the Great White Throne Judgment.

As the apostle Paul writes for the believer in 2 Corinthians 5:10, "For we must all appear before the Judgment Seat of Christ; that every one may receive the things done in his body, according to that he has done, whether it be good or bad." Now the question is, when is the Judgment Seat of Christ?" As the apostle Paul writes in 2 Corinthians 5:6-8, "Therefore we are always confident, knowing that, while we are at home in the body, we are absent from the LORD. . . . We are confident, I say, and willing rather to be absent from the body, and to be present with the LORD." In fact this was so real to the apostle Paul that he wrote in Philippians 1:21-24, "For to me to live is Christ, and to die is gain. . . . For I am in a strait between the two, having a desire to depart, and to be with Christ; which is far better: Nevertheless to abide in the flesh is more needful for you."

For the believer, when he departs from this life, he goes to be immediately in the presence of Jesus Christ and as the believer stands before Jesus, he receives his reward. The unbeliever will be like the rich man in the parable Jesus told of Lazarus and the rich man. As the Gospel of Luke 16:22-23 tells us, "the rich man also died, and was buried; And in hell he lifted up his eyes, being in torment." The apostle John writes of his vision in Revelation 20:11-13 after the end of the Millennium reign of Jesus, "And I saw a Great White Throne, and Him that sat on it, from whose face the earth and Heaven fled away; and there was found no place for them. And I saw the dead (unbelievers), small and great, stand before God. . . . and death and hell delivered up the dead which were in them: and they were judged every man according to their works."

For the believer upon leaving this earthly life, he or she imme-diately sees Jesus and receives the reward that Jesus has for him. For the unbeliever it is hell which maybe compared to a holding place or jail until the Great White Throne Judgment at the end of the Millennium or DAY SEVEN.

When you and I enter eternity and stand before Jesus Christ at the Judgment Seat of Christ, He will examine our lives to see if we are "overcomers". The apostle Paul writes in 1 Corinthians 3:11-15 that all of us are building on the foundation of Jesus Christ, "For other foundation can no man lay than that is laid, which is Jesus Christ. Now if any man build upon this foundation gold, silver, precious stones, wood, hay, stubble; Every man's work shall be made manifest: for the day shall declare it, because it shall be revealed by fire; and the fire shall try every man's work of what sort it is. If any man's work abide which he has built thereupon, he shall receive a reward. If any man's work shall be burned, he shall suffer loss: but he himself shall be saved; yet so as by fire."

In Revelation 7:17 we read, "For the Lamb which is in the midst of the throne shall feed them, and shall lead them unto living foun-tains of waters: and God shall wipe away all tears from their eyes." If they are already in Heaven, what are they crying about? In Revelation 21:4, the apostle John is describing the new Heaven and the new earth as well as the new Jerusalem and that God Himself will be dwelling with us. Yet John goes on to say in Revelation 21:4, "And God shall wipe away all tears from their eyes; and there shall be no more death, neither sorrow, nor crying, neither shall there be any more pain: for the former things are passed away."

What do you think they are crying about? When they are in eternity, they will see what God's plan and purpose for their life was in eternity, but instead of being an "overcomer", they will see that they traded it for a position, wealth or fame or something they thought was more important in their life on earth. They will be crying "Oh, LORD I didn't." But Jesus will have to say, "Yes you did! However in My love for you , you will be with Me forever and in My final act of grace, in order for you to enjoy eternity, I am washing away all your tears (I am going to remove this memory from you and the former things will come into your mind no more)."

3. THE GREAT WHITE THRONE JUDGMENT

If a person does not appear at the Judgment Seat of Christ, it then means he will be judged at the Great White Throne Judgment. Once again going back to the apostle John's vision in Revelation 20:11-13, "And I saw a great white throne, and Him that sat on it, from whose face the earth and Heaven fled away; and there was found no place for them. And I saw the dead, small and great, stand before God; and the books were opened: and another book was opened, which is the book of life: and the dead were judged out of those things which were written in the books, according to their works. And the sea gave up the dead which were in it; and death and hell delivered up the dead which were in them: and they were judged every man according to their works."

The dead are the unbelieving dead of all ages. They are judged from two sets of books. The books contain the record of every unsaved person's life. Each unsaved person is judged in accordance with his or her works which will clearly show that each one is a guilty sinner deserving of eternal death. The Book of Life contains the name of every person who has received Jesus Christ and received eternal life through faith alone. These unsaved people are shown that they did not take advantage of the offer of eternal life through faith. Death and hell are the temporary holding places of the unsaved souls and spirits of men and women.

Then comes the TERRIBLE, TERRIBLE, TERRIBLE CONCLUSION OF THE GREAT WHITE THRONE JUDGMENT for the unbelievers and unsaved – "and death and hell were cast into the lake of fire. This is the second death. and whosoever was not found written in the Book of Life was cast into the lake of fire" (Rev. 20:14-15).

4. THE DEFEAT OF THE LAST ENEMY

Remember that the apostle Paul wrote, "Then comes the end,

when He shall have delivered up the Kingdom to God, even the Father; when He shall have put down all rule and all authority and power. For He must reign, till He has put all enemies under His feet. THE LAST ENEMY THAT SHALL BE DESTROYED IS DEATH" (1 Cor. 15:24-26).

The SECOND DEATH is the defeat of the last enemy. The "second death" is eternal punishment in the "lake of fire", experienced only by the unsaved. Once this final judgment occurs, there is no further need for either death or hell. An eternal separation is now made between those who have life and those who have death.

An interesting study that may help explain the "second death" is to take a number of Bible verses and compare them to what is being learned in astronomy today. In Revelation 20:14-15 the "second death" is being compared to a "lake of fire". Revelation 21:8 says, "But the fearful, and unbelieving, and the abominable, and murderers, and whoremongers, and sorcerers, and idolaters, and all liars, shall have their part in the lake which burns with fire and brimstone: which is the second death."

A number of times Jesus describes an eternal place of OUTER DARKNESS. "But the children of the Kingdom (children of Israel that did not believe) shall be cast out into outer darkness: there shall be weeping and gnashing of teeth" (Matt. 8:12). Or as Jesus said in the parable of the wedding feast in Matthew 22:13, "Then said the king to the servants, Bind him hand and foot, and take him away, and cast him into "outer darkness"; there shall be weeping and gnashing of teeth." Or as recorded by Jude in Jude verses 11-13, "Woe unto them! for they have gone in the way of Cain. . . . wandering stars, to whom is reserved the "blackness of darkness for ever." Here we see the place of eternity for them is a LAKE OF FIRE AND THE BLACKNESS OF DARKNESS FOREVER.

One of the most mysterious things that astronomers are finding in the universe during the last half century are areas where matter and light are continually being sucked up by devouring black holes never to be seen again. In the May 1974 issue of *The National Geographic* was an extensive article on "Black Holes." The article states that a black hole is the end product of the catastrophic collapse of a really large star. It is the ultimate concentration of matter, predicted by the Einstein theory and accepted by scientist for a number of years as a theoretical inevitability. It would be like reducing the diameter of the earth to 328 feet. The weight of a teaspoon of such material would be equivalent to the weight of two thousand million elephants. The result would be tremendous gravitation pull.

One of the world's authorities on collapsed stars, Kip Thorne of the California Institute of Technology, has theorized some of the following:

1. Its gravity is so strong that not even light can ever escape its boundaries.
2. Anything it traps can never escape.
3. The black hole can neither split nor decrease in size, it can only grow, and nothing can prevent it from growing.
4. We call it "cosmic censorship".

Imagine the intense heat that would be inside one of these black holes. If we can imagine all the above, we can begin to imagine how what the apostle Paul said could be accomplished, "THE LAST ENEMY THAT SHALL BE DESTROYED IS DEATH."

5. DESTRUCTION OF THE PRESENT EARTH AND HEAVEN

The last of DAY SEVEN will occur as the apostle Peter prophesied in 2 Peter 3:7-13, "But the heavens and the earth, which are now, by the same word are kept in store, reserved unto fire against the day of judgment and perdition of ungodly men. . . . But the day of the LORD will come as a thief in the night; in which the heavens shall pass away with a great noise, and the elements shall melt with fervent heat, the earth also and the works that are therein shall be burned up. Seeing then that all these things shall be dissolved, what manner of persons ought you to be. . . . Looking for and hastening unto the coming of the day of God, wherein the heavens being on fire shall be dissolved, and the elements shall melt with fervent heat? Nevertheless we, according to His promise, LOOK FOR A NEW HEAVENS AND A NEW EARTH, WHEREIN DWELLS

RIGHTEOUSNESS."

ENDNOTES:

[1] Henry H. Haley, *Halley's Bible Handbook*, (Zondervan Publishing House, 1965) p.759.

[2] *Today's Pentecostal Evangel*, World Missions Edition, March 7, 2004, Issue No 4687, Springfield, Mo., page 9.

CHAPTER SEVEN

FULFILLING GOD'S PLAN AND PURPOSE FOR YOUR LIFE IN ETERNITY

> "And I saw a new Heaven and a new earth: for the
> first Heaven and the first earth were passed away;
> and there was no more sea."   Revelation 21:1

In his vision, the apostle John literally sees the new Heaven and new earth. The LORD told the prophet Isaiah over seven hundred years earlier, "For, behold, I create new Heavens and a new earth: and the former shall not be remembered, nor come into mind" (Isa. 65:17). Let us take a look with the apostle John at what he and the other apostles and prophets saw under the seven following areas:

1. WE SHALL SEE GOD
2. THE NEW EARTH
3. FATHER'S HOUSE
4. WHAT WE WILL BE LIKE
5. GOD'S PLAN AND PURPOSE FOR YOU IN ETER-
   NITY – WORSHIP
6. THE THRONE – RULERHIP
7. ETERNITY – FELLOWSHIP

1. WE SHALL SEE GOD

The prophet Moses expressed the GREATEST DESIRE that all men and women of God have when he asked God to let him see God's glory or face. As we wrote in the last chapter, Moses saw the glory of the LORD on Mount Sinai as recorded in Exodus 24:17-18, "And the sight of the glory of the LORD was like a devouring fire on the top of the mount. . . . And Moses went into the midst of the cloud." However, Moses wanted to see beyond what looked like a devouring fire or as described elsewhere in the Bible as an extremely bright light. In Exodus 33:18 Moses asks, "And he said, I beseech You, show me Your glory. And the LORD answered Moses, You cannot see My face: for there shall no man see Me, and live. And the LORD said, Behold, there is a place by Me, and you shall stand upon a rock: And it shall come to pass, while My glory passes by, that I will put you in a cleft of the rock, and will cover you with My hand while I pass by: And I will take away My hand, and you shall see My back parts: but My face shall not be seen" (Exod. 33:20-23).

It is interesting to note that during the ministry of Jesus on earth that one day Jesus took Peter, James and John up to a high mountain. In Matthew 17:2-7, "And (Jesus) was transfigured before them: and His face did shine as the sun, and His raiment was white as the light. And, behold, there appeared unto them Moses and Elijah talking with Him. Then answered Peter, and said unto Jesus, LORD, it is good for us to be here: if you will, let us make here three Tabernacles; one for You, and one for Moses, and one for Elijah. While he yet spoke, behold, a bright cloud overshadowed them: and behold a voice out of the cloud, which said, This is My beloved Son, in whom I am well pleased; hear you Him. And when the disciples heard it, they fell on their faces, and were sore afraid. And Jesus came and touched them, and said, Arise, and be not afraid."

Almost 1,400 years earlier Moses had asked to see God's face and God said no man shall see My face and live. Since Moses was now a part of eternity, certainly he had seen God's face. I wonder what Moses thought when he heard Peter's request.

The apostle Paul writes in Colossians 1:15, "Who is the image of the invisible God." Or as Paul writes to Timothy, "Who only has immortality, dwelling in the light, which no man can approach unto; whom no man has seen, nor can see" (1 Tim. 6:16).

When the apostle John was caught up to Heaven in Revelation 4:2-3, "And immediately I was in the spirit: and, behold, a throne was set in Heaven, and one sat on the throne. And He that sat was to look upon like a jasper and a sardine stone: and there was a rainbow round about the throne, in sight like unto an emerald." As an unglorified human being, John was not able to see His face, only a brightness as described by Moses and Peter, James and John when they saw the presence of ALMIGHTY GOD as a "bright cloud" (Matt. 17:5). But John is able to declare in Revelation 22:3-4 in that new Heaven and that new earth, "And there shall be no more curse: but the throne of God and of the Lamb shall be in it; and His servants shall serve Him: And they SHALL SEE HIS FACE; and His name shall be in their foreheads."

The greatest blessing of eternity is that we SHALL SEE HIS FACE. As Jesus said in the Sermon on the Mount, "Blessed are the pure in heart: for they shall see God" (Matt. 5:8). Although this is now impossible for an unglorified human being, it will occur in the eternal state. Like the apostle Paul says in 1 Corinthians 13:12, "For now we see through a glass, darkly; but then face to face: now I know in part; but then shall I know even as also I am known." The prayer of King David was, "As for me, I will behold Your face in righteousness: I shall be satisfied, when I awake, with Your likeness" (Ps. 17:15).

No other earthly man had more exposure to Jesus and through many visions, exposure to God than the apostle John. Listen to the GREATEST HOPE that John had. In 1 John 3:2, John writes, "BELOVED, NOW ARE WE THE SONS OF GOD, AND IT DOES NOT YET APPEAR WHAT WE SHALL BE: BUT WE KNOW THAT, WHEN HE SHALL APPEAR, WE SHALL BE LIKE HIM; FOR WE SHALL SEE HIM AS HE IS."

When you and I kneel in prayer or raise our hands in praise, we usually close our eyes because we are unable to see Him, but we are able to talk to Him. But the time is coming when we will literally be able to see and adore the One we love and serve above all others. Not only will we sense His presence, but will see His face, His expressions and have complete communications and fellowship with Him.

It will be a time of continual discovery and receiving new revelations of God and His plans and purposes. Back in chapter three under the discussion of "How God Is Preparing You For The Plan and Purpose For Your Life", one of the most important preparations is the "Developing of Our "spirit" In Worship". Now we come to the fulfillment of that preparation. Remember that in Genesis 3:8, we are told that in the cool of the day the LORD God would walk in the Garden of Eden with Adam and Eve to talk and fellowship with them. This is a picture of our Heavenly Father, like an earthly father who looks forward to the end of the day when he can come home to his children to love, fellowship, talk and enjoy his children. Just think of the pleasure it brings an earthly father when his children come to him expressing their love and appreciation and he is able to share himself with his children along with his future plans and goals.

This is the very scene that the apostle John saw when in Revelation 4, he saw a door opened in Heaven and was told to "Come up here and I will show you things which must be hereafter." As John entered Heaven, he saw the Throne of God and all the elders, angels and saints worshipping God. And John records some of the very words that he heard them speaking, "You are worthy, O LORD, to receive glory and honor and power: for You have created all things, and for Your pleasure they are and were created" (Rev. 4:11). Notice particularly the last few words, "for Your pleasure they are and were created." Your worship and my worship give God pleasure. What is man that he has this wonderful, wonderful, wonderful privilege of being able to give "pleasure" to the Creator of the universe!

The apostle John also describes seeing four special angelic beings called seraphim. They were continually leading the elders, angels and saints in worship. It appears that each time these seraphim circled around the Throne of God, they saw or had revealed to them new dimensions of God and His glory. They would cry "Holy, holy, holy, LORD God Almighty." The rest of those before the Throne would respond in worship and praise. One of the most exciting things about God, the Throne and Heaven is that there will be a continuous discovery of new and glorious purposes, understandings, and revelations of many, many, many things beyond our understanding that have not yet even entered into our imagination.

2. THE NEW EARTH

As was shared at the end of chapter six, the last enemy that shall be destroyed is death, along with this present earth and the heavens.

The present universe will thus be cleansed from all the effects of sin. The first heaven and the first earth are replaced by a new Heaven and a new earth. As the apostle John saw in Revelation 21:1, "And I saw a new Heaven and a new earth: for the first heaven and the first earth were passed away; and there was no more sea." Since there will be no more sea, the increased land space will be fully capable of handling large numbers of redeemed people from all ages. This "new earth" will be the most beautiful creation that God has created.

3. FATHER'S HOUSE

Not only did the apostle John see a new Heaven and a new earth, he saw FATHER'S HOUSE. Remember the night before His crucifixion, Jesus had communion or the Last Supper with His disciples. As He told the disciples concerning His upcoming crucifixion, they were all filled with sorrow and their hearts very troubled. They were expecting Jesus to be made "King" of Israel and the Roman occupiers to be thrown out of power. At this time they did not understand that He had come to be "the lamb of God" to be sacrificed for their sins and all mankind on the cross.

However, Jesus revealed to them a part of what He was preparing for them in eternity. "Let not your heart be troubled: you believe in God, believe also in Me. In my Father's house are many mansions (dwelling places): if it were not so, I would have told you. I go to prepare a place for you. And if I go and prepare a place for you, I will come again, and receive you unto Myself; that where I am, there you may be also" (John 14:1-3).

The book of Genesis tells us it only took God six days to create this earth as we know it. Jesus told them, "I go to prepare a place for you." This means that He has now spent approximately two thousand years in preparing "Father's House" for you and me. Stop and imagine what a beautiful earth He created in six days. Now compare that with "Father's House" that He has been preparing for almost two thousand years.

Here in Revelation 21, not only did the apostle John see a new Heaven and new earth, he saw "Father's House". Listen to what

John says, "And I John saw the holy city, new Jerusalem, coming down from God out of Heaven, prepared as a bride adorned for her husband. And I heard a great voice out of Heaven saying, Behold, the Tabernacle of God is with men, and He will dwell with them, and they shall be His people, and God Himself shall be with them, and be their God" (Rev. 21:2-3).

This verse of Scripture is not just poetry, it is a reality. It is as true as John 3:16, "For God so loved the world, that He gave His only begotten Son, that whosoever believes in Him should not perish, but have everlasting life." Many of the cities on this earth have striven to be world capitals. Just like ancient Babylon, Nineveh, ancient Rome and modern cities such as Paris, London, New York that strive to be the cultural and economic leaders in the world.

The city that the apostle John is seeing is to be the capital of the universe. It will be absolutely new in concept and design:
1. Its location is new – The new earth
2. Its purpose is new – God will dwell with men.
3. Its style is new – It will be as tall as it is long as it is wide.
4. Its material is new – Pure, transparent gold.
5. Its utilities are new – The "glory of God"
6. Its name is new - The New Jerusalem
7. It will be everything that the old Jerusalem, where God's Temple once stood, has failed to be.

One of the seven angels that poured out one of the bowls of God's wrath during the great tribulation came to the apostle John and measured the size of "Father's House" or the New Jerusalem. "The angel held in his hand a golden measuring stick to measure the city and its gates and walls. When he measured it, he found it was a square as wide as it was long; in fact it was in the form of a cube, for its height was exactly the same as its other dimensions, 1,500 miles each way" (Rev. 21:15-16 TLB). That would be a land mass equal to the distance from the Pacific Ocean to the Mississippi River and from the Canadian border to the southern boarder of Texas with Mexico. That would be a land mass greater than two-thirds the size of the United States. It does not stop there. It is also that tall in height. One mathematician calculated that if you divided just one level into blocks, such as our America cities are divided, there would be 625,000,000 blocks. Remember John said it was also as high as it was wide. If you divided the city into levels that would be one over another with a height equal to the highest building yet erected in New York City, then there would be 937,500,000,000,000 (937 trillion, 500 billion) blocks.

Talk about having AMPLE ROOM, the same mathematician calculated that by using today's housing standards in America, there is room for 1,250,000,000,000,000,000 (one quadrillion, 250 trillion people). It is estimated that would be enough room for a thousand times more people than who have been born into this world since Adam and Eve up until now. Remember Jesus said, "In My Father's House are many mansions (or dwelling places)."

The atmosphere, radiance and charm of this city will grip you as no other city has ever done. Here on earth we have far away romantic places such as Paris, Vienna, Venice, Honolulu, and Rio de Janeiro. But nothing here will even begin to compare to the New Jerusalem. This city will be God's masterpiece as the apostle Paul writes, "Eye has not seen or ear heard, neither have entered into the heart of man, the things which God has prepared for them that love Him" (1 Cor. 2:9).

Then the apostle John makes another fascinating observation about the New Jerusalem. "And I saw no Temple therein: for the LORD God Almighty and the Lamb are the Temple of it" (Rev. 21:22). Will it not seem strange to see no spires, Churches or Temples? No more than the absence of hospitals, funeral homes, police stations and parking meters.

John saw no concrete, asphalt or clay bricks in this city. Instead, John says, "the building of the wall of it was of jasper: and the city was pure gold, like unto clear glass. And the foundations. . . of the city were garnished with all manner of precious stones. . . . And the twelve gates were twelve pearls; every several (individual) gate was of one pearl: and the street of the city was pure gold, as it were transparent glass" (Rev. 21:18-21). There is not one thing that is common about this "city".

One thing we will never have to be concerned about is the

weather or running short on electricity. For John said, "And the city had no need of the sun, neither of the moon, to shine in it: for the glory of God did lighten it, and the Lamb is the light thereof" (Rev. 21:23). John also talks about the beautiful waters and vegetation. "And he showed me a pure river of water of life, clear as crystal, proceeding out of the throne of God and of the Lamb. In the midst of the street of it, and on either side of the river, was there the tree of life, which bare twelve manner of fruits, and yielded her fruit every month: and the leaves of the tree were for the healing of the nations" (Rev. 22:1-2).

4. WHAT WILL WE BE LIKE?

As a pastor comforting the bereaved at the graveside of a loved one so many times, I have been asked, "Pastor, is my loved one still conscious? Will he or she know other people in Heaven? When I die, will I still be myself?" The primary truth that all of us must remember is that we are not bodies with spirits. INSTEAD, WE ARE SPIRITS LIVING IN A BODY.

When this body dies, the REAL YOU is still living. The REAL YOU is your "spirit", your "soul", your personality. The real you is like a hand and the body is like a glove. However, when the hand slips out of the glove, the glove or body is still here, but the hand is gone. As we look at life, we see this subtly implied in many and varied ways. When the body is inactive in sleep, the mind still continues to function. Science tells us that even in our deepest sleep our mind still functions. It works independently. We still think, we still dream. This body is only a house for the REAL YOU.

This is why Jesus said, "Whosoever lives and believes in Me shall never die" (John 11:26). Or as the apostle Paul said, "For to me to live is Christ, and to die is gain" (Phil. 1:21). Then Paul goes on to talk about his struggle. "For I am in a strait between the two, having a desire to depart, and to be with Christ; which is far better: Nevertheless to abide in the flesh (body) is more needful for you" (Phil. 1:23-24).

To the apostle Paul, DEATH WAS FANTASTIC. He looked forward to it. However, he was not the only one. Many other great men of God looked forward to that time. The writer of the book of Hebrews tells us, "By faith he (Abraham) sojourned in the land of promise, as in a strange (foreign) country, dwelling in tents with Isaac and Jacob, the heirs with him of the same promise: For he looked for a city which has foundations, whose builder and maker is God. . . . These all died in faith, not having received the promises, but having seen them afar off, and were persuaded of them, and embraced them, and confessed that they were strangers and pilgrims on the earth. . . . But now they desire a better country, that is, a Heavenly: wherefore God is not ashamed to be called their God: for He has prepared for them a city" (Heb. 11:9-16).

Then there was Moses. "By faith Moses, when he was come to years, refused to be called the son of Pharaoh's daughter; Choosing rather to suffer affliction with the people of God, than to enjoy the pleasures of sin for a season; Esteeming the reproach of Christ greater riches than the treasures in Egypt: for he had respect unto the recompense of the reward" (Heb. 11:24-26). WHY? WHY? WHY DID THESE MEN LOOK FORWARD TO DEATH? Because they caught a glimpse of what God had in mind for them. They began to understand God's plan and purpose for their lives and that this earthly time was just a time of being schooled for God's ultimate plan and purpose for their lives. That is why the apostle Paul said, "For I reckon that the sufferings of this present time are not worthy to be compared with the glory which shall be revealed in us" (Rom. 8:18).

So in answer to the many questions such as, "Will I still be myself? Will I be conscious? Will I know other people and will they know me? What will Heaven (eternity) be like?" What will we be doing?" The popular "myth" that Satan has caused people to believe is that in Heaven we will be sitting on a cloud playing a harp.

A man once said, "I would give a fortune to know what happens to a man five minutes after he dies." In the Bible, Jesus gives us a number of graphic illustrations. To begin with, we learn that our life does not cease and start over again. The very moment we leave this body, we are living in the next realm. Some think we will sleep in the grave until the trumpet of God sounds, then we will rise for the JUDGMENT.

When Jesus was hanging on the cross, He was crucified between two thieves. As all three of them were dying, one thief said, "LORD, remember me when You come into Your Kingdom. And Jesus said unto him, Verily I say unto you, Today shall you be with Me in paradise" (Luke 23:42-43). Notice Jesus said, "TODAY," not in some distant future, but TODAY. Not at some general resurrection, but TODAY. Not when Gabriel blows his horn, but TODAY.

After death, the Bible teaches us that we immediately enter the next realm. Those who believed on Jesus, will be with Jesus. For those who have not believed and accepted Jesus, it will be HELL. Jesus told the story of a rich man that lived in luxury every day. There was a certain beggar named Lazarus which laid at his gate, full of sores begging for bread. The dogs came and licked his sores. The rich man had no regard for God, while the beggar Lazarus loved God. One day both men died. The beggar Lazarus was carried by the angels to Paradise. The rich man died and the next moment, "And in hell he lifted up his eyes, being in torments, and sees Abraham afar off, and Lazarus in his bosom" (Luke 16:23).

In this story, Jesus tells us of six different things that all will be able to do when they enter into the next realm, whether it be Hell or Heaven.

1. RECOGNIZE – "And in hell he (the rich man) lift up his eyes. . . and sees Abraham afar off, and Lazarus in his bosom" (Luke 16:23).
2. COMMUNICATE – "And he cried and said, Father Abraham, have mercy on me" (Luke 16:24).
3. FEEL – "being in torments. . . send Lazarus, that he may dip the tip of his finger in water, and cool my tongue; for I am tormented in this flame" (Luke 16:23-24).
4. REMEMBER – "But Abraham said, Son, remember that you in your lifetime received your good things, and likewise Lazarus evil things: but now he is comforted, and you are tormented" (Luke 16:25).
5. LOVE – Even though the rich man was in hell, he was concerned for his brothers. "Then he (rich man) said, "I pray you therefore, father (Abraham), that you would

send him (Lazarus) to my father's house: For I have five brothers; that he may testify unto them, lest they also come into this place of torment" (Luke 16:27-28).

6. <u>REASON</u> – Although Abraham told the rich man that his brothers had Moses and the prophets to warn them, the rich man reasoned that, "No, father Abraham: but if one went unto them from the dead, they will repent" (Luke 16:30).

The moment we depart from this world, we will be very much alive in the "spirit realm" even though we are absent from our bodies. All of us will be consciously alive after we leave these bodies at death. Death makes a lot of changes in the life of a person. But it does not change the person. If you are saved here, you will be saved there. If you are without God here, you will be without God there. The only difference death makes is it separates people. Some will go to Heaven, some will go to Hell. "And these shall go away into everlasting punishment: but the righteous into eternal life" (Matt. 25:46).

The next big question many people have is, WILL I HAVE A BODY OR BE JUST A SPIRIT FLOATING AROUND? WHAT KIND OF BODY WILL I HAVE? WILL I HAVE A BODY RIGHT AWAY?

As mentioned earlier, while Jesus was nailed to the cross between the two thieves, the thief that asked Jesus to remember him when He came into His Kingdom, Jesus replied, "Today shall you be with Me in paradise" (Luke 23:43). The evening of that same day, the body of Jesus was placed in a garden tomb with a large stone rolled in front of it and a guard was posted to guard the tomb. At that time His "spirit" entered into Paradise while His body remained in the tomb.

On the third day, which was the first day of the week or Sunday, several of the women followers of Jesus went to the tomb to complete the burial process. When they arrived, the stone was rolled away and two angels stood by the tomb. One of the angels said, "Do not fear, for I know that you seek Jesus, which was crucified. He is not here: for He is risen, as He said. Come, see the place where the LORD lay" (Matt. 28:5-6).

As the "SPIRIT" of Jesus was reunited with His body that had been changed into a "glorified" body, it is a picture of what will happen for all believers at the RAPTURE in the SECOND COMING OF JESUS. As the apostle Paul writes, "But now is Christ risen from the dead, and become the first fruits of them that slept" (1 Cor. 15:20). When our present physical body dies, our "spirit" goes to be with the LORD. However, in the RAPTURE, just as the physical body of Jesus in that tomb was changed into a glorified body as His SPIRIT returned to it, so will our physical bodies be changed into a "glorified body" and reunited with our "spirit".

"But I would not have you to be ignorant, brethren, concerning them which are asleep, that you sorrow not, even as others which have no hope. For if we believe that Jesus died and rose again, even so them also which sleep in Jesus will God bring with him. For this we say unto you by the word of the LORD, that we which are alive and remain unto the coming of the LORD shall not prevent them which are asleep. (Those who are described as "asleep" are with the LORD, but their natural bodies are still in the grave awaiting the coming of the LORD and being united again with their spirit) For the LORD Himself shall descend from Heaven with a shout, with the voice of the archangel, and with the trump of God: and the dead in Christ shall rise first: Then we which are alive and remain shall be caught up together with them in the clouds, to meet the LORD in the air: and so shall we ever be with the LORD" (1 Thess. 4:13-17).

The apostle Paul further explains this resurrection in 1 Corinthians 15:51-54, "Behold, I show you a mystery; We shall not all sleep, but we shall all be changed, In a moment, in the twinkling of an eye, at the last trump: for the trumpet shall sound, and the dead shall be raised incorruptible, and we shall be changed. For this corruptible must put on incorruption, and this mortal must put on immortality. So when this corruptible shall have put on incorruption, and this mortal shall have put on immortality, then shall be brought to pass the saying that is written, DEATH IS SWALLOWED UP IN VICTORY."

The apostle Paul shrinks from the thought of life without a body as he writes the Church in Corinth, "For we shall not be merely spirits without bodies. These earthly bodies make us groan and sigh, but we wouldn't like to think of dying and having no bodies at all. We want to slip into our new bodies so that these dying bodies will, as it were, be swallowed up by everlasting life" (2 Cor. 5:3-4 TLB).

What will our resurrection bodies be like? The apostle John wrote, "Beloved, now are we the sons of God, and it does not yet appear what we shall be: but we know that, when he shall appear, we shall be like Him" (1 John 3:2). The apostle Paul wrote, "Who shall change our vile body, that it may be fashioned like unto His glorious body, according to the working whereby He is able even to subdue all things unto Himself" (Phil. 3:21).

Let us take a look at what the disciples observed at the resurrection of Jesus. As Peter and John heard the report that the tomb was empty, they ran there to investigate. Upon entering the tomb, they were astonished to see the grave clothes there, but there was no body in them. The grave clothes were undisturbed and it looked like the body just passed through them. Remember, when Jesus called Lazarus from the dead with a loud voice, "Lazarus, come forth. And he that was dead came forth, bound hand and foot with grave clothes: and his face was bound (wrapped with a cloth) about with a napkin. Jesus said unto them, Loose him, and let him go" (John 11:43-44).

That same evening of the resurrection, the disciples had gathered together in a room with the doors and windows shut and locked for fear of the Jews. When suddenly there was Jesus standing in front of them and said, "Peace be unto you. But they were terrified and frightened, and supposed that they had seen a spirit" (Luke 24:36-37). Then Jesus allays their fears, deals with their doubts, and makes His bodily presence unmistakable. He said, "Behold My hands and My feet, that it is I Myself: handle Me, and see (i.e. touch my scars); for a spirit has not flesh and bones, as you see Me have" (Luke 24:39). As further proof, He asked them for food and ate some fish and honey before them as a person with a normal body would.

Although the glorified body of Jesus was capable of physical functions, it was not subject to human limitations. Today you and I grow tired and weary. Often times we are unable to complete our tasks, or to do the work we long to do. We have to rest and sleep is necessary. But with our resurrected bodies we will never know fatigue. Never again will we say, "I am tired." When Peter, James and John were with Jesus on a high mountain, Jesus was transfigured before them: "and His face did shine as the sun, and His raiment was white as the light" (Matt. 17:2). Years later when the apostle John was on the island of Patmos, Jesus appeared to him again in bodily form. And John said, "and His countenance was as the sun shinning in his strength. And when I saw Him, I fell at His feet as dead." (Revelation 1:16-17). The prophet Daniel prophesied that in the end time, "And many of them that sleep in the dust of the earth shall awake. . . to everlasting life. . . And they that be wise shall shine as the brightness of the firmament; and they that turn many to righteousness as the stars for ever and ever" (Dan. 12:2-3).

As previously quoted from Philippians 3:21, "Who shall change our vile body, that it may be fashioned like unto His glorious body, according to the working whereby He is able even to subdue all things unto Himself." The above give us a foretaste of what our glorified bodies will be like.

Some may ask what happens when the body is completely destroyed in a fire. In the atomic age we live in, science knows that matter cannot be completely destroyed. All matter is made up of atomic particles and matter can be changed from one form into another such as water into steam. However, matter cannot be destroyed.

A great physicist by the name of Michael Faraday lived more than a century ago. He was also a Christian. One day in class he spoke of the resurrection. Some of the students scoffed at the idea. A few days later Faraday brought a silver cup and a jar of sulfuric acid to class with him. The entire class watched as he placed the silver cup in the acid and as he did so, the silver cup entirely disappeared. Then he put a particular salt into the acid, which acted as a catalyst. The catalyst brought those particles and molecules of silver together again into a mass of silver that fell to the bottom of the jar. He took the mass of silver to a silver smith who refashioned the mass of silver into a beautiful silver cup again. He brought the silver cup back to class and said, "If God can bring back a silver cup, then cannot God bring back a body and then fashion it like unto His own?"

Though the worms may destroy this body, even though it returns to dust, Jesus can and will bring body, soul and spirit together again, and will refashion the body in His likeness. As the apostle Paul said, "Who shall change our vile body, that it may be fashioned like unto His glorious body, according to the working whereby He is able even to subdue all things unto Himself" (Phil. 3:21).

During the earthly ministry of Jesus, some of the Jewish religious leaders came to Jesus with a question. A woman married and then her husband died. Later on she remarried and then that husband died. This happened seven times. Their question to Jesus was, "In the resurrection therefore, when they shall rise, whose wife shall she be of them? For the seven had her to wife" (Mark 12:23). Jesus answered, "For when they shall rise from the dead, they neither marry, nor are given in marriage; but are as the angels which are in Heaven" (Mark 12:25).

These religious leaders thought that the resurrection would be the same kind of life as we experience here on earth. However, this earthly life is a time of preparing us for the eternal life that we will live with the LORD forever. The fellowship of marriage, as high an ideal as this is in the Bible, will be superseded by the depth and diversity of new life in the eternal presence of God. Death will be a thing of the past. Like the angels, we will be incapable of ever again experiencing death. Life will certainly not be reduced to some level beneath that of marriage. Rather, all will be taken up into the fuller life of God's eternal family and Kingdom. It will not be a physical or sexual level, but the emotional intimacy and affection of heart, now experienced and restricted only to one's spouse, is only a hint or glimpse of what THE FELLOWSHIP will be with God and all the family of Heaven or Kingdom of God in eternity.

5. GOD'S PLAN AND PURPOSE FOR YOU IN ETERNITY – WORSHIP

Now we come to the conclusion of what is the plan and purpose that God has for your life. It can be summed up in three words: WORSHIP, RULERSHIP and FELLOWSHIP. In the introduction to this book, we started with this verse of Scripture, "God has made everything beautiful in its time. He has also set ETERNITY in the hearts of men; yet they cannot fathom what God had done from beginning to end" (Eccles. 3:11 NIV).

Most scholarship believes that King Solomon of Israel wrote this book of the Bible. He writes, "So I hated life, because the work that is done UNDER THE SUN was grievous to me. All of it is meaningless, a chasing after the wind" (Eccles. 2:17 NIV). Here one of the richest men that ever lived who tried to do most everything concludes, "Vanity of vanities, said the Preacher, vanity of vanities; all is vanity" (Eccles. 1:2). The New International version translates this verse as follows, "Meaningless! Meaningless! says the Teacher. Utterly meaningless! Everything is meaningless."

To understand our earthly life from only the observation of our earthly life, a wise man like Solomon would conclude that earthly life is, in itself is "meaningless". He goes on to write, "For the living know that they will die. . . . never again will they have a part in anything that happens UNDER THE SUN" (Eccles. 9:5-6 NIV). When we look beyond THE SUN or to ETERNITY, we are able to see what God's eternal plan and purpose is for our lives. We learn from these verses that our life on earth is the arena of opportunity for us to prepare for the plan and purpose God has for us in eternity.

King Solomon concluded the book of Ecclesiastes by writing, "Let us hear the conclusion of the whole matter: Fear God, and keep His commandments: for this is the whole duty of man" (Eccles. 12:13). The word "duty" does not appear in the Hebrew Bible. A literal translation would be, "for this is the whole of man." Our earthly life is not a duty. Instead it is a purpose, goal, a plan that God has for you in eternity. As we read in Ecclesiastes 3:11, "He has also set eternity in the hearts of men." This life is our preparation for eternity. Only in eternity will we fully understand the meaning of our earthly life.

Our first and primary purpose is to be a priest for all eternity. As the apostle Peter writes, "You also, as living stones, are being built up a spiritual house, a holy priesthood, to offer up spiritual sacrifices, acceptable to God by Jesus Christ" (1 Peter 2:5). Or as the apostle John writes, "And has made us kings and priests unto God and His Father" (Rev. 1:6). John goes on to write, "Blessed and holy is he that has part in the first resurrection. . . they shall be priests of God and of Christ" (Rev. 20:6). The prophet Ezekiel was told, "But the priests. . . shall come near to Me to minister unto Me, and they shall stand before Me to offer unto Me the fat and the blood, say the LORD God: They shall enter unto My sanctuary, and they shall come near to My table, to minister unto Me" (Ezek. 44:15-16). In Revelation 4 and 5, John beheld the THRONE OF GOD and the continual worship of the LORD.

WHY ALL THE WORSHIP? DOES GOD NEED ALL THAT ATTENTION AND ADULATION? God does not need it for He is already complete. The PURPOSE is that you and I need to worship God. Why? If our focus is on God, then it will not be on ourselves. Let us look for a moment at the most colossal failure (Satan) in the universe who was the archangel of God by the name of Lucifer, the son of the morning. He was in charge of all the angels, but instead of his focus being on God, it was on himself. For he said to himself:

- "I will ascend into Heaven"
- "I will exalt my throne above the stars of God"
- "I will sit also upon the mount of the congregation, in the sides of the north"
- "I will ascend above the heights of the clouds"
- "I will be like the most High" (Isaiah 14:13-14).

The prophet Ezekiel describes this colossal failure (Satan) as follows, "You were the model of perfection, full of wisdom and perfect in beauty. You were in Eden, the garden of God. . . . You were anointed as guardian cherub, for so I ordained you. You were on the holy mount of God; you walked among the fiery stones. You were blameless in your ways from the day you were created till wickedness was found in you. . . . Your heart became proud on account of your beauty, and you corrupted your wisdom because of your splendor. So I threw you to the earth" (Ezek. 28:12-17 NIV).

Instead of Lucifer or Satan's focus being on God, it was on himself, "I, I, I." Just think if his focus had been only on God, WHAT A DIFFERENCE IN THE UNIVERSE THAT WOULD HAVE MADE!. Had he continually worshipped God, he would not have worshipped himself.

When Jesus was tempted in the wilderness after His baptism in water, it was Satan who endeavored to entice Jesus to worship him instead of God only. Yet Jesus said unto him, "Get you hence, Satan: for it is written, YOU SHALL WORSHIP THE LORD YOUR GOD, AND HIM ONLY SHALL YOU SERVE" (Matt. 4:10). As you and I continuously worship the LORD, it keeps our focus on Him and away from ourselves and others. It was Satan's downfall when he changed his focus to himself and he tried to convince Jesus to do the same thing.

Another example of Satan trying to get man to take his focus off worshipping the LORD and to focus upon himself is found in the book of Zechariah 3. In a vision, the prophet Zechariah was shown a vision of the high priest Joshua standing before the LORD and Satan standing at his right hand to oppose him. Once again Satan was endeavoring to get Joshua the high priest to take his focus off the LORD and focus on himself. Then the LORD gave Joshua this charge, "If you will walk in My ways, and if you will keep My charge (command), then you shall also keep My courts, and I will give you places to walk among these that stand by (standing here at the THRONE)" (Zech. 3:7).

Our ministry of worship as priests before the LORD, keeps our focus on the LORD and away from our selves. When our focus is on the LORD, then and only then can we safely rule and reign with the LORD Jesus Christ and fellowship with Him for eternity.

One of the greatest examples of this is John the Baptist. He had a tremendous ministry preparing the people for the earthly ministry of Jesus with his proclaiming the coming of the Kingdom of God and baptizing people in water for the repentance of their sins. Jesus told His disciples, "For I say unto you, Among those that are born of women there is not a greater prophet than John the Baptist" (Luke 7:28). The religious leaders of John's time came to him and asked him if he was the Messiah. John replied, "I am not the Christ" (John 1:20). Then came even John's disciples with the religious leaders and asked about Jesus who was now baptizing people. John reminded them that he had said, "I am not the Christ, but that I am sent before him. He that has the bride is the bridegroom: but the friend of the bridegroom, which stands and hears him, rejoices greatly because of the bridegroom's voice: this my joy therefore is fulfilled" (John 3:28-29).

Then John the Baptist tells very pointedly where his focus was. "He must increase, but I must decrease" (John 3:30). The Bible tells us that John was arrested by King Herod and languished in prison for a time until he was beheaded. However, in his worship of the LORD, he had arrived at that place of total focus on the LORD. It will be our ministry as priests of the LORD to come to the place of total focus on the LORD through worship. Then and only then will we be ready for the ultimate plan and purpose that the LORD has for our lives, THAT OF RULERSHIP AND FELLOWSHIP.

6. THE THRONE – RULERSHIP

Going back to Genesis 1:26 when God said, "Let us make man in our image, after our likeness: and let them have dominion," the first two goals were accomplished. Man was made a "spirit" in God's image, for God is SPIRIT, and in God's likeness man was made a triune being of spirit, soul and body as God is Father, Son and Holy Spirit. It is during our earthly sojourn that we would be prepared for the ultimate dominion that God had purposed for you and me. As Jesus said, "To him that overcomes will I grant to sit with Me in My throne, even as I also overcame, and am set down with My Father in His throne" (Rev. 3:21).

As the apostle Paul writes to the Church at Ephesus, "God, who is rich in mercy, for His great love wherewith He loved us, Even when we were dead in sins, has quickened (made us alive) us together with Christ, And has raised us up together, and made us sit together in Heavenly places in Christ Jesus: That in the ages to come (eternity) He might show the exceeding riches of His grace in His kindness toward us through Christ Jesus" (Eph. 2:4-7).

As was pointed out in chapter one of this book, one of the great saints of the Old Testament was King David, who realized that God's plan and purpose for his life was far above and greater than being the king of Israel with all of its wealth, power and prestige. Listen to what King David declares in Psalms 8:3-8, "When I consider Your Heavens, the works of Your fingers, the moon and the stars, which You have ordained: What is man, that You are mindful of him? and the son of man, that You visited him? For You have made him a little lower than the angels." (The word "angels" does not appear in the original language of the Hebrew Bible. Instead it is the Hebrew word "Elohim" which we translate as God. What David is actually saying: "For You have made him a little lower than God"). David goes on to say, "For You have made him a little lower than God, and have crowned him with glory and honor. You have made him to have dominion over the works of Your hands; You have put all things under his feet."

When Moses had led the children of Israel to Mount Sinai, the LORD called Moses up to the top of the mount and gave him this word for Israel, "This shall you say to the house of Jacob, and tell the children of Israel; You have seen what I did unto the Egyptians, and how I bare you on eagles' wings, and brought you unto Myself. Now, therefore, if you will obey My voice indeed, and keep My covenant, then you shall be a peculiar (special) treasure unto Me above all people. . . . and you shall be unto Me a Kingdom of priests, and a holy nation" (Exod. 19:3-6).

The apostle Peter declares these same words to the New Testament Church, "But you are a chosen generation, a royal priesthood, a holy nation, a peculiar (special) people; that you should show forth (proclaim) the praises of Him who has called you out of darkness into His marvelous light" (1 Peter 2:9). It is God's plan and purpose for you and I to be a part of a ROYAL PRIESTHOOD. Not only will we worship and minister unto the LORD, but as a part of "divine royalty", He will share with us what He is doing and where He is going. As Moses prayed to the LORD as he was leading the children of Israel in the wilderness, "I pray You, if I have found grace in Your sight, SHOW ME NOW YOUR WAY, THAT I MAY KNOW YOU, that I may find grace in Your sight" (Exod. 33:13).

As the apostle Paul says, "But God. . . has quickened (made us alive) us together with Christ, And has raised us up together, and made us sit together in Heavenly places in Christ Jesus" (Eph. 2:4-6). And why is God doing this? GOD WILL INVOLVE US IN ALL THAT HE IS DOING THROUGHOUT ETERNITY AS CO-RULERS. "That in the ages to come He might show the exceeding riches of His grace in His kindness toward us through Christ Jesus" (Eph. 2:7).

We see a number of examples of this throughout the Bible. They are pictures of how the LORD is going to share the THRONE AND RULERSHIP with us in eternity. In Genesis 18, the LORD visited Abraham with two angels prior to the destruction of Sodom and Gomorrah. The LORD told Abraham that he and Sarah would have a son according to the time of life or in nine months. Then the Bible tells us that they rose up and looked toward Sodom. Abraham went with them to bring them on the way. "And the LORD said, Shall I hide from Abraham that thing which I do, Seeing that Abraham shall surely become a great and mighty nation, and all the nations of the earth shall be blessed in him?" (Gen. 18:17-18). Then the LORD shared with Abraham what He was going to do.

The psalmist David wrote, "He made known His ways unto Moses, His acts unto the children of Israel" (Ps. 103:7). Men such as Abraham, Moses, Isaiah, Daniel, the apostle John, to name just a few, were given tremendous visions and visitations with the LORD and to whom the LORD revealed His plans, purposes and future events. On the mount of transfiguration, Jesus was transfigured back to His former glory and there appeared with Him Moses and Elijah. "Who appeared in glory, and spake of His decease (departure) which He should (was about to) accomplish at Jerusalem" (Luke 9:31). Here is the picture of the King of Kings taking counsel with those who are reigning and ruling with Him. All of these are a picture of how we will rule and reign with the LORD.

Remember that Jesus said, "To him that overcomes will I grant to sit with Me in My throne, even as I also overcame, and am set down with My Father in His throne" (Rev. 3:21). One of my daily prayers is, "LORD Jesus, by Your grace and the power of the Holy Spirit, help me to be an "overcomer" and to be a part of that "royal priesthood" that will sit with You on Your throne. Let me be with You and a part of what You are doing, for the rest of time and for eternity. IT IS HIS PLAN AND PURPOSE FOR YOU TO BE A PART OF HIS THRONE AND TO RULE AND REIGN WITH HIM FOR ETERNITY. Remember the LORD said to Joshua the high priest, "If you will walk in My ways, and if you will keep My charge (command), then you shall also judge My house, and shall also keep My courts, and I will give you places to walk among these that stand by (here)" (Zech. 3:7).

All that happens to us in our earthly sojourn is an endeavor by the LORD to prepare us for this "HIGH CALLING" to rule and reign with Him. As the apostle Paul writes, "And we know that all things work together for good to them that love God, to them who are the called according to His purpose" (Rom. 8:28).

As we endeavored in chapter one of this book to get you to imagine the size and extent of the universe that God has created, the LORD has a divine plan for all of this creation. As the apostle Paul writes, "But as it is written, EYE HAS NOT SEEN, NOR EAR HEARD, NEITHER HAVE ENTERED INTO THE HEART OF MAN, THE THINGS WHICH GOD HAS PREPARED FOR THEM THAT LOVE HIM" (1 Cor. 2:9). This is also a quote from the prophet Isaiah, "For since the beginning of the world men have not heard, nor perceived by the ear, neither has the eye seen, O God, beside You, what He has prepared for him that waits for Him" (Isa. 64:4).

One thing we know with all certainty is that the Kingdom of God will be complete throughout the entire universe and that we have been called to rule and reign with Him. I can imagine that various ones of us will be given various assignments in rulership.

In His teachings to the disciples and the people, Jesus illustrated this by a number of parables. In the parable of the talents, Jesus said that the Kingdom of God is as a man traveling into a far country, who called his own servants, and delivered unto them his goods. Unto one he gave five talents, to another two, and to another one. Each servant was to make use of his talents and when the master returned, each man would give an account of how he handled that which was committed to his care.

The one that received five talent went and traded with the five talents and gained another five talents. And the one who had received two talents went and traded with the two talents and gained another two talents. The one who received one talent, did nothing. When the master returned, each man gave a report of his use of the talents that had been given to him The two men who had taken their talents and used them to gain other talents, the master said, "Well done, you good and faithful servant: you have been faithful over a few things, I will make you ruler over many things:

enter you into the joy of your lord." (Mathew 25:21).

To the man who did nothing with the talent given unto him, the master said, "You wicked and lazy servant....Take therefore the talent from him....And cast the unprofitable servant into outer darkness: there shall be weeping and gnashing of teeth." (Matthew 25:26-30).

To those who will allow or receive the preparation that the LORD brings them through in preparing them for the "plan and purpose for their life", the LORD will say, "Come, you blessed of My Father, inherit the kingdom prepared for you from the foundation of the world." (Matthew 25:34).

In Luke 12:41-44, Peter asked Jesus the question: "LORD, do You speak this parable unto us, or even to all (the people)? And the LORD said, Who then is that faithful and wise steward, whom his LORD shall make ruler over His household, to give them their portion of food in due season? Blessed is that servant, whom his LORD when He comes shall find so doing. Of a truth I say unto you, THAT HE WILL MAKE HIM RULER OVER ALL THAT HE HAS."

The apostle John in his vision of the new heaven and new earth writes in Revelation 21:5-7, "And He that sat upon the throne said, Behold, I make all things new. And He said unto me, Write: for these words are true and faithful . . . . He that overcomes shall inherit all things; and I will be his God, and he shall be My son."

Another aspect of the LORD's rulership is that He enjoys creating and doing many things in extreme detail. Just think of this earth and all the details of His creation, the creation of all the various forms of life, such as animals, birds, fish, insects and planet life. As science is continuously discovering new forms of life in all the intricate details, there will be an eternity of eternal discoveries to be made by each one of us.

7. ETERNITY – FELLOWSHIP

God purposed and planned to have a FAMILY of beings who would be a higher order than the angels, who would be His sons or children to share, FELLOWSHIP WITH HIM and participate with Him in His vast KINGDOM (the universe). As the apostle John wrote, "Beloved, now are we the sons of God, and it does not yet appear what we shall be: but we know that, when He shall appear, we shall be like Him; for we shall see Him as He is" (1 John 3:2). However, there was one truth that the apostle John definitely knew – WE ARE FAMILY AND FAMILY MEANS THE CLOSEST TYPE OF FELLOWSHIP THAT IS POSSIBLE.

The apostle Paul also recognized this truth. For he writes, "For now we see through a glass darkly; but then face to face: now I know in part; but then shall I know even as also I am known" (1 Cor. 13:12). There are many relationships between people, but the closest relationship between people is the family and marriage relationship. Usually no one knows you better than your family or your spouse, if married. In Heaven, there will be no strangers. We will all be family and we will all know one another.

The one plan and purpose of God for your life that should come through loud and clear is that God's destiny for you and me is to become the FAMILY AND COMPANION OF GOD THROUGH THE AGES OR ETERNITY.

As we wrote earlier, the fellowship of marriage, as high an ideal as this is in the Bible, will be superseded by the depth and diversity of new life in the eternal presence of God. Life will not be reduced to some level beneath that of marriage, but will be taken up into the fuller life of God's eternal family and Kingdom. The emotional intimacy and affection of heart, now experienced and restricted only to one's spouse, is only a hint or glimpse of what the FELLOWSHIP will be with God and all the FAMILY OF GOD.

When Jesus was with His twelve disciples here on earth, there was a real fellowship and bond between them. However, this will not even begin to compare to the fellowship, love, and bond that all the redeemed family of God will have in eternity.

The fellowship, love and bond that we have with the LORD began when God entered into a "Blood Covenant" with Abraham. As was described in chapter two of this book, God made a "Blood Covenant" relationship with Abraham that foreshadowed the EVERLASTING BLOOD COVENANT that Jesus made on the cross for all mankind. As you remember, the Bible is divided into two sections: the Old Testament and the New Testament. In the original language of the Bible, Hebrew and Greek, the word actually was "covenant". At the LAST SUPPER Jesus took the cup and gave it to His disciples saying, "Drink you all of it; For this is My blood of the new testament (covenant), which is shed for many for the remission of sins" (Matt. 26:27-28). As we described in chapter two of this book, a "blood covenant" is where two parties come together and through the cutting of blood, an eternal covenant is entered into. In the first Blood Covenant, an animal sacrifice was used for God and circumcision was used for Abraham. In the second Blood Covenant, Jesus, who represented both God and man, was crucified on the cross. With His own blood and life He paid the price for our sins and gave us the gift of eternal life to be with Him forever as members of a "blood covenant" and members of His eternal family. "For God so loved the world, that He gave His only begotten Son, that whosoever believes in Him should not perish, but have everlasting life" (John 3:16). For a full description of the "blood covenant", please go back to chapter two of the book.

Here on earth, in order to have strong family ties, the father, the mother and the children have a family home where they live, eat, sleep and above all have fellowship. As we discussed earlier in this chapter, Jesus is currently preparing FATHER'S HOUSE for us which is also called the "New Jerusalem", a place where the Father, the Son and the Holy Spirit along with all the redeemed will abide. Fellowship not only involves a place to be together, but a most enjoyable part of family life is the fellowship that we have around the dinner table. As Jesus told His disciples, "And I appoint unto you a Kingdom, as My Father has appointed unto Me; That you may eat and drink at My table in My Kingdom" (Luke 22:29-30).

Remember the apostle Paul tells us, "And has raised us up together, and made us sit together in Heavenly places in Christ Jesus. That in the ages to come He might show the exceeding riches of His grace in His kindness towards us through Jesus Christ" (Eph. 2:6-7).

Jesus in His high priestly prayer before His crucifixion prayed, "That they all may be one; as You, Father, are in Me, and I in You, that they also may be one in Us. . . . And the glory which You gave Me I have given them: that they may be one, even as We are one: I in them, and You in Me, that they may be made perfect in one; . . . Father, I will that they also, whom You have given Me, be with Me where I am; that they may behold My glory, which You have given Me: for You loved Me before the foundation of the world" (John 17:21-24).

One of the greatest benedictions to a study on "God has a plan and purpose for your life" is the declaration of King David who said in Psalm 23:6, "SURELY GOODNESS AND MERCY SHALL FOLLOW ME. . . AND I WILL DWELL IN THE HOUSE OF THE LORD FOREVER."

Printed in the United States
54713LVS00003BD/103-510

9 781597 816984